THE ANVIL OF WAR

THE ANVIL OF WAR

German Generalship in Defense of the Eastern Front during World War II

Erhard Rauss

and

Oldwig von Natzmer

Edited by Peter G. Tsouras

Skyhorse Publishing

Skyhorse Publishing books may be purchased in bulk at special discounts for sales promotion, corporate gifts, fund-raising, or educational purposes. Special editions can also be created to specifications. For details, contact the Special Sales Department, Skyhorse Publishing, 307 West 36th Street, 11th Floor, New York, NY 10018 or info@skyhorsepublishing.com.

Skyhorse® and Skyhorse Publishing® are registered trademarks of Skyhorse Publishing, Inc.®, a Delaware corporation.

Visit our website at www.skyhorsepublishing.com.

10 9 8 7 6 5 4 3 2 1

Library of Congress Cataloging-in-Publication Data is available on file.

Cover design by Qualcom

Print ISBN: 978-1-63450-531-4
Ebook ISBN: 978-1-63450-835-3

Printed in the United States of America

The Anvil of War comprises three U.S. Department of the Army publications that have been adjusted for this edition, with a new introduction: *Military Improvisations During the Russian Campaign*, Department of the Army pamphlet no. 20–201, Washington, DC, August 1951; *German Defense Tactics Against Russian Breakthroughs*, Department of the Army pamphlet no. 20–233, Washington, DC, October 1951; and *Operations of Encircled Forces: German Experiences in Russia*, Department of the Army pamphlet no. 20–234, Washington, DC, January 1952.

Contents

Maps

Introduction

Greenhill Books has gathered three of the most brilliant distillations of the German experience on the Russian Front into this single volume, *The Anvil of War*. These three monographs: *Military Improvisations During the Russian Campaign, German Defense Tactics against Russian Breakthroughs*, and *Operations of Encircled Forces*, written by experienced German general officers, under the aegis of the U.S. Army after World War II, represent the German attempt to deal with the increasingly effective use of massive numerical superiority by the Soviets when the tide of war had turned. The Soviets had become the hammer and the Germans the anvil in the last half of the war. This then is the story of the German Army in adversity. Although ultimately doomed to defeat, the German retreat from Russia was conducted with skill and heroism against incredible odds. Upon his return to Moscow by car after the Potsdam Conference, a senior American diplomat noted that his route followed the retreat of one of the main German armies and was littered with the debris of war. But repeatedly he would see the same scene: one or two burnt-out German tanks in defensive positions with arcs of twenty to thirty destroyed Soviet tanks arrayed around them. The authors of *The Anvil of War*, Erhard Rauss and Oldwig von Natzmer, fought through this very ground. Only in 1990, in the full glare of *glasnost*, did the Soviet General Staff announce its true military losses of the war, an incredible 8,668,400 dead and eighteen million wounded, grim testimony to the achievements of the German soldier in both the offense and defense.[1]

I first came across the three monographs gathered in this new edition as *The Anvil of War* in early 1971 while serving as a young armor officer in the First Battalion, 64th Armor Regiment (3rd Infantry Division), stationed at the old Hindenburg Kaserne (Harvey Barracks), in Kitzingen am Main, West Germany. Published as Department of the Army pamphlets, they had lain untouched in my company commander's office for ages, it seemed, from all the dust I disturbed when I pulled them out of the bookcase. Being something of a Germanophile at the time, I was fascinated by these little gems of history. As I read on, it was obvious that the distilled experiences of German generals on the Russian Front were of such immediacy to our present mission (the victors of Stalingrad, the 8th Guards Army, were just forty kilometers east of us) that I wondered why they were so little known. After all, the Soviet Armed Forces were in the full flood of expansion, preparing for the great Theater Strategic Operation (TSO) meant to carry them to the Channel and the Pyrenees.

9

About the Authors

The first two monographs, *Military Improvisations During the Russian Campaign* and *German Defense Tactics against Russian Breakthroughs*, were written chiefly by Generaloberst Erhard Rauss, originally an Austrian Army officer, transferred to the Wehrmacht along with so many others after the Anschluss in 1938. Rauss served on the Russian Front and the subsequent retreat into northern Germany.

Rauss' record in command, especially after the middle of 1943, is a remarkable saga of a skilful fighting retreat against an enemy flood tide which he repeatedly delayed, halted, or drove back with a variety of deadly ripostes and improvisations. Rauss was a man who could 'quickly grasp' a situation and then act decisively, employing 'speed' and 'shock', the troika of qualities of the great commander, as defined by Suvorov. He was also an extremely cool-headed officer, a characteristic much-remarked by subordinates and superiors alike. The variety and mix of means he employed to frustrate repeatedly the Soviet steamroller showed also a mind open to new ideas.

Rauss initially commanded the 4th Panzergrenadier Regiment of 6th Panzer Division in XLI Panzer Corps' Drive on Leningrad in the late summer of 1941. His command, assisted by elements of the Brandenburger (special operations) Regiment seized the twin bridges over the Luga River at Porechye on 14 July, one of the last remaining obstacles in front of Leningrad. By the end of August, he was commanding the 6th Rifle Brigade as the Germans reached the outer defenses of the city. He was subsequently given command of 6th Panzer Division. In early December 1942, 6th Panzer was resting in France when it was hurriedly returned to Russia to take part in the attempted relief of the 6th Army at Stalingrad. Although the relief failed, the 6th Panzer Division under Rauss acquitted itself with skill and style, an impressive achievement for a division that had been pulled suddenly from the cozy plenty of France to the frozen hell of Stalingrad.[2]

After the Soviets frustrated the relief of 6th Army, they launched a major attack westwards to drive the Germans further from the beleaguered Germans in Stalingrad. The spearhead of 1st Tank Army overran the great supply and communications centre at Tatsinskaya, a bare 130 kilometers to Rostov. If it should lunge that much further the whole German position in the southern Soviet Union would collapse. Rauss and 6th Panzer rode to the rescue and snapped the spearhead of the 1st Tank Army, destroying its lead corps and recovering Tatsinskaya. Paul Carrell describes Rauss' night attack:

And now General Rauss opened the nocturnal tank battle between Maryevka and Romanov. The enemy, held up frontally, was attacked from both flanks and in the rear. The Russians were taken by surprise and reacted confusedly and nervously. Rauss, on the other hand, calmly conducted the battle like a game of chess.[3]

The Army Group Commander, Field Marshal Erich von Manstein, was later to write:

> The very versatility of our armour and the superiority of our tank crews were brilliantly demonstrated in this period, as were the bravery of the panzer grenadiers and the skill of our anti-tank units. At the same time it was seen what an experienced old armoured division like 6 Panzer could achieve under its admirable commander General Rauss ... when it went into action with its full complement of armoured vehicles and assault guns.[4]

After Stalingrad, the much-decorated Rauss (he was eventually to win the oak leaves to the Knights Cross of the Iron Cross)[5] was promoted to the rank of General der Panzertruppen and given command successively of the XI Army Corps (March through October 1943) in the fighting around Belgorod and in the 4th Battle of Kharkov and the XLVII Panzer Corps (5–25 November 1943). In the grim fighting around Belgorod in August 1943, during which he successfully employed the technique of delay on successive positions, he offered a self-portrait, during the crisis of the battle when Soviet penetrations had begun to panic XI Corps:

> Every experienced commander is familiar with this sort of panic which, in a critical situation, may seize an entire body of troops. Mass hysteria of this type can be overcome only by energetic actions and a display of perfect composure. The example set by a true leader can have miraculous effects. He must stay with his troops, remain cool, issue precise orders, and inspire confidence by his behavior. Good soldiers never desert such a leader. News of the presence of high ranking commanders up front travels like wildfire along the entire front line, bolstering everyone's morale. It means a sudden change from gloom to hope, from imminent defeat to victory.... This is exactly what happened.[6]

Shortly after Belgorod, Rauss found himself in another desperate defensive operation in the 4th Battle of Kharkov. With five divisions spread in an arc around that unhappy city, XI Corps was attacked by the 5th Tank Army fresh from its triumphs at Kursk. For eight days Rauss slowly fell back to the outer defenses of Kharkov, in a dogged delaying action in the scorching late Russian summer. Now, instead of attacking all along the arc of the German defense, the Soviets struck at the bottleneck of the German salient around Kharkov. But Rauss was quicker, and luckier.[7] He concentrated his armor just at that point. Repeated hammer blows of the 5th Tank Army eventually shattered on the anvil of XI Corps' defense. Fifth Tank Army lost 420 tanks in three days' fighting. Rauss had left it a burnt-out husk.[8]

With his brilliant defensive operations at Belgorod and Kharkov, Rauss had saved the Army Group South from one disaster after another. The Army Group South commander, General Erich von Manstein, showed his regard for Rauss by bringing him on his own initiative to a conference called by Hitler at Vinnitsa in late August. He had proven himself the right man in a crisis. And suddenly a great new crisis fell upon the Germans. The Soviets had torn open the front west of Kiev in November and were preparing to exploit the opening and conduct a major envelopment of major parts of the army group. The disaster was the result of Hitler's decisions, but he needed a scapegoat and relieved Generaloberst Hoth, commander of 4th Panzer Army. Rauss seemed the ideal man to take over 4th Panzer Army. It was just in time. He assumed command on 1 December 1943 near Ternopol. Within three days of his assumption of command, Rauss seized the initiative and launched a major spoiling attack against 1st Ukrainian Front which

> . . . achieved the dual purpose of relieving an encircled corps and enabling the Germans to build up a continuous front where previously there had been a wide gap. The annihilation of strong enemy forces was an incidental, though important result of this operation.[9]

Shortly thereafter Rauss employed a different technique, delaying and blocking actions, to blunt the Soviet Christmas offensive west of Kiev. The Soviet armies thrust and hammered at 4th Panzer Army to break through but succeeded only in shoving it about 100 kilometers west in five weeks of sustained operations despite a superiority in tanks of 1200 to 200. Generalleutnant F.W. von Mellenthin, XLVIII Corps Chief of Staff in these battles was to write:

> The calm and able leadership of Colonel General Rauss, the commander of Fourth Panzer Army, had succeeded in overcoming a dangerous crisis. It is true that the Russians captured Zhitomir on 31 December, and on 3 January had the satisfaction of crossing the 1939 frontier of Poland. But in fact their offensive power had been worn down, the German front in Western Ukraine was still relatively intact, and the fighting spirit of our troops remained unbroken.[10]

Rauss continued to command 4th Panzer Army through the fighting retreat of Army Group North Ukraine to the Carpathian Mountains. In the summer of 1944, he conducted a masterful zone defense against a major Soviet break-through attempt in the area of Lvov, in Western Ukraine.[11] On 16 August 1944 he was transferred to Army Group Center and command of the 3rd Panzer Army, badly mauled in the catastrophe of the destruction of Army Group Center in June. He commanded this army in the long nightmarish retreat through Lithuania, East Prussia, and Pomerania. In East Prussia in December 1944, he was able to repeat the success of the zone defense against a

Russian breakthrough for an entire month. In this operation, 3rd Panzer Army consisted of 9 weak divisions with 50 tanks, 400 guns, and insignificant air support. The Soviet front opposed to it consisted of 44 divisions with 800 tanks, 3000 guns, and strong air support.[12]

In March 1945 3rd Panzer Army, now under Army Group Vistula, occupied a pocket east of Stettin on the Baltic and was engaged in a furious battle when Hitler called Rauss to come to Berlin to report on the situation. Generaloberst Heinz Guderian, Chief of OKH (Oberkommando des Heeres – Army High Command), was present at the meeting and recorded Hitler's surreal conduct:

> Rauss began by outlining the general situation. Hitler interrupted him: 'I'm already in the picture so far as the general situation goes. What I want from you is a detailed exposition of the combat ability of your divisions.' Rauss now gave an exact description which showed that he knew every yard of his front and was capable of judging the value of every unit under his command. I was present while he spoke and found his exposition outstandingly lucid.[13]

Hitler's treatment of Rauss was typical of his wildly erratic and bizarre behavior in the last weeks of the war. He was to turn on the general when he could not achieve miracles, just as, in his last hours, he would condemn the German people as unworthy. Guderian went on:

> When he had finished, Hitler dismissed him without comment. Rauss had scarcely left the Chancellery shelter, where the conference had taken place, before Hitler turned to Keitel, Jodl, and myself and shouted: 'What a miserable speech! The man talked of nothing but details. Judging by the way he speaks, he must be a Berliner or an East Prussian. He must be relieved of his appointment at once!' I replied: 'Colonel-General Rauss is one of our most capable panzer generals. You, my Führer, interrupted him yourself when he was trying to tell you about the general situation, and you ordered him to give you a detailed exposition of the state of his divisions. And as for his origin, Rauss is an Austrian and therefore a compatriot of yours, my Führer.'[14]

Then Jodl and Hitler argued whether Rauss was really an Austrian. Guderian resumed his pleading for Rauss:

> ... Please let me urge you, before you make any decisions, to remember that Colonel-General Rauss showed an exact knowledge of all his front, that he was able to give a personal evaluation of every division under his command, that throughout a long war he has consistently fought with great distinction, and that finally – as I already said – he is one of our best panzer generals.[15]

Guderian had argued in vain. As usual, Hitler clung tightly to his worst decisions. Rauss was relieved and replaced by General der Panzertruppen Hasso-Eccard von Manteuffel.

The third monograph, *Operations of Encircled Forces*, was written by Generalleutnant Oldwig von Natzmer. Originally a cavalry officer, von Natzmer saw considerable action before Leningrad, near Voronezh, and Stalingrad. He served as the 1.a (operations officer) of the Panzergrenadier Division Grossdeutschland in the rank of lieutenant colonel in 1943–44 under the beloved General 'Papa' Hoernlein and in the last year under Generalleutnant Hasso-Eccard von Manteuffel. Von Natzmer was awarded the Knights Cross of the Iron Cross while with Grossdeutschland.[16] Thereafter von Natzmer received rapid promotion and jumped two levels to be the chief of staff successively of Army Groups North and Center in the German retreat out of the Soviet Union. Von Natzmer does not appear in the memoirs and histories of the great battles on the Russian front as does Erhard Rauss. Instead, his retention in the demanding position of army group chief of staff for such a long and arduous period is a silent testimony to his abilities. His absence in the popular literature is, in a sense, a testament to his ability, for he lived up to the German motto of a staff officer – to be more than he appears.

There was one exception to the staff officer's anonymity in von Natzmer's career and that was at its end. Von Natzmer had the misfortune to serve in Army Group Center under General Schöner in the last phase of the war in Silesia and Czechoslovakia. Schöner was one of Hitler's stalwarts, a man of incredible brutality who hanged thousands of his own troops at the slightest provocation, to insure that every man would rather fight to the last. On 7 May 1945, Schöner's headquarters received orders from OKW that fighting would cease on 9 May. Schöner decided that Army Group Center would fight on until von Natzmer pointed out that such a course would remove all protection of international law from the troops under his command. Von Natzmer suggested that Schöner simply allow his forces to flee west and into American captivity rather than succumb to the horrors of surrender to the Red Army. Schöner's fury soon abated when he realized that von Natzmer had showed him a personal escape. He ordered a small plane put at his disposal and then filled a briefcase full of money. He told von Natzmer that he was going to fly to a hideaway in the Bavarian Alps and that von Natzmer was free to come along and share the loot.

Von Natzmer's face turned red, then white. Next day, he said, the Army Group would be marching for its life. The commander could not desert at such a time. Never before had a central command been more essential. And even in the dealing with the Americans, Schöner's high rank was of the utmost weight.[17]

Von Natzmer defied Schöner and seized his plane, but Schöner browbeat the elderly militia guards and flew off. He later turned himself in to the Americans who promptly turned him over to the Soviets. Von Natzmer did his best to shepherd the million men of the army group to the west, but it was too late. Those that reached the American zone were turned back to the Soviets. Only those who infiltrated west survived.[18]

S.L.A. Marshall Gets the Ball Rolling

At the end of World War II, the U.S. Army embarked on an unprecedented effort to find out what had actually happened on the European battlefields, and more importantly, why events played out as they did. Most modern armies write postmortems from their own records, but this one was dramatically unique. It sought to include for the first time 'the other side of the hill'. In other wars, the enemy's side of the story had never been systematically exploited. Memoirs and official accounts had come out over time and been used, but the passage of time and the defense of reputations had dulled their usefulness.

The American effort was based on the unprecedented opportunity that lay in total victory. Most of the enemy's senior officers who had opposed the American armed forces were in captivity. As with most unorthodox ideas, the concept was not an institutional product. In this case, the need was matched to the resource by the then Colonel S.L.A. Marshall of the Army Historical Division, one of the senior Army historians in the European Theater of Operations (ETO). Marshall had become famous for an innovative and effective form of immediate post-combat interview with the troops that would capture their experiences before they became lost to memory.

> . . . my official duties required me to get a full and final accounting of what had happened on that field.
>
> It was done by assembling the survivors of every unit that had fought, interviewing them as a group, and recording their experiences personal and in common from the beginning of movement till the end of fighting.
>
> The method of reconstructing what develops in combat, relating cause to effect, and eliminating the fog, is my own . . . It works because it is simple and because what one man remembers will stir recall in another. The one inviolable rule, if each group interviewing is to get valid results, is that the question-and-answer routine must be in sequence step-by-step from first to last.[19]

Now that the war had just ended in Europe, this same energetic and innovative mind was again working outside the normal, approved groove.

> For months my head had buzzed with the idea that I had to find a way to enfold the German high commanders and their main staff officers in our operation, or else we would never know more than half of what had happened to our forces

from Normandy on. The Germans would never do their history. We had captured most of the records, but the records were not enough. We needed to know
the reasons for decisions, and we could only get them from live witnesses. Failing
that, our story would show only one side of the hill.[20]

Marshall's efforts to prod the Army into doing the obviously right thing then
took on the aspects of a conspiracy produced by Machiavelli and Puck. Marshall
had several things going for him that the similarly perceptive Fuller and Liddell
Hart did not a generation before. For one, Marshall had the knack of being 'one
of the boys' with officers far senior to himself. Already at this date, he had many
friends in high places disposed to be helpful. For another, he was skilful at
navigating the military bureaucracy and had a fine touch at knowing exactly
how much audacity the system would bear and a sense of timing to maximize
its effect. He also knew that the approval of a few key individuals would smooth
the way for him.

His first step was to do his homework. No amount of approval from on high
would help if the German generals were not disposed to cooperate. He flew to
London to interview the grand old man of the German Army, Field Marshal
Gerd von Rundstedt, then a British POW. Von Rundstedt was cordial but
admitted the subject was out of his field. He did recommend that Marshall ask
General Walter Warlimont, former deputy chief of operations of OKW
(Oberkommando der Wehrmacht – High Command of the Armed Forces). If
Warlimont agreed, the rest would follow. Marshall flew back to Germany and
immediately interviewed Warlimont who was so excited he said, 'Oberst
Marshall, I am so certain it will work that I would volunteer right now for your
operation if you would have me.'

Marshall's first test of the waters was not encouraging. At the next regular
staff meeting of the higher headquarters responsible for the German officers,
Marshall raised the subject and was met by gales of laughter from everyone else.
He would have to bide his time.

Then Marshall attached one of his key officers, Major Kenneth Hechler, to
the staff of a visiting American historian interviewing captured Nazi officials on
wartime economics. Hechler was to sound out a broader range of German
officers on the idea. At the same time Marshall sent a team on his own authority
into the German POW camps to explore in detail the 'conditions we had fixed
upon the enemy high commanders'. Upon Hechler's return with a positive
report of the willingness of many German officers to cooperate, Marshall
ordered him to sign four German officers out of the Oberursel POW camp and
bring them to the I.G. Farben Building in Frankfurt for a one day interrogation. They were Generals Fritz Bayerlein, Heinrich von Lüttwitz, and Heinz
Kokott, and Colonel Meinhard von Lauchert, the main German commanders in
the Battle of Bastogne. In Frankfurt, Marshall ordered Hechler to spirit all four

Germans to the Historical Division's new facility in the Château Hennemont in France. When Hechler's orderly mind gasped out the word, 'kidnapping', Marshall was not perturbed. He knew that the military bureaucracy would not miss the Germans for at least three weeks, and by then he would have his pilot project hammered out and the results ready to display. One never thinks that military historians can work by the SAS motto, 'Who dares wins'.

Immediately upon arriving at Hennemont, Marshall found himself breaking more new ground. He directed that the Germans would be escorted to the officers' mess and brazened out the objections from a few of the American officers. As he expected, human nature quickly reversed opinions. There were no leaks to *Stars and Stripes* or official complaints up the chain of command. Marshall's request among the officers for tobacco, candy, and small luxuries for the Germans were cheerfully filled. Unknowingly, Marshall had extended the first hand of friendship and respect to the German officer corps, a gesture that would later repeat itself and create a close relationship with the German Army when it was reborn in 1956.

Marshall immediately began with his four German officers on the Bastogne pilot project. It had the advantage of being a fairly small operation and one with which he was quite familiar. Marshall quickly had his eyes opened to the world of German military politics as old animosities came to the surface.

Bayerlein, who had served under Rommel before commanding Panzer Lehr Division, was the spark plug of the group. A terrierlike individual, then age fifty, he fairly vibrated when he spoke. His contempt for von Luttwitz, who as corps commander in the attack on Bastogne had been his superior, was my first tipoff that in a POW situation, rank, even among Germans, no longer had the privilege of imposing its view. Thus, by getting staff officers grouped with their commanders as we went along, we would elicit corrective and more dependable information.[21]

Marshall also quickly discovered that among his German charges captivity stripped rank of its deference.

When von Luttwitz rambled in his conversation, Bayerlein would wave a hand in his face and snarl, 'Not important! Not important!' And when the somewhat paunchy Junker tried to strike a pompous pose (he still wore a monocle), Bayerlein would turn him livid by howling, 'Nuts! Nuts!' It was Luttwitz who at Bastogne had received Tony McAuliffe's four-letter reply heard around the world. Bayerlein believed that von Luttwitz had made the worst fumbles at Bastogne, though the record showed that Bayerlein's individual actions and estimates had cost the corps some of its finest opportunities. About those mistakes, and the mistakes of others, he was brutally frank. They became almost a mania with him. When confronted with his own gross blunders, he would put his head back and laugh with abandon. At times he seemed more than a little bit unhinged, but still thoroughly likeable.[22]

The pilot project was a success. At the next staff meeting, Marshall raised the subject again.

There followed the longest wait of the day. The chief of staff turned about to speak softly with General Lee. With that exception, there wasn't a whisper in the room during the prolonged two-way conversation.

Then quick as a wink the tension lifted as the chief looked up to say to me; 'I agree with you completely. I take it that you already have your formula. Bring it to me tomorrow morning and I will act.'[23]

With that, Marshall and the Germans were in business. By the next week, thirty German generals were transferred from the Oberursel POW camp to Château Hennemont. Another twenty generals were transferred to a separate historical shop within the Oberursel camp itself. At Hennemont, Marshall dismissed the guards on the Germans' compound and gave them the freedom of the estate. When the change of policy sank in, the Germans bolted for the door, poured out through the compound gate and disappeared, into the estate's surrounding forest. They were all back for the evening meal. Not one, then or later, was to violate the parole and leave the grounds.

After working with the Germans, Marshall categorized them into three groups: (1) the professionals who were keen to work because it interested them; (2) the 'apple-polishers'; and (3) the Nazi diehards. The first group was no problem; the second was a fact of life; but the third, even the most intractable, after a while began to come around and cooperate, even Hitler's personal adjutant, Major Buchs.[24] The subsequent Chief Historian for Headquarters, U.S. Army, Europe, Colonel W.S. Nye, would have a slightly different and perhaps more official perspective.

In the initial phases of the program all of the contributors were prisoners of war or internees; participation, however, was always voluntary. While participants were reimbursed for their work, they have been motivated mainly by professional interest and by the desire to promote western solidarity and mutual defense.[25]

Marshall's Brainchild Becomes an Institution

The program continued and expanded after Marshall's departure from Europe in 1946. As Colonel Wye observed:

Originally the mission of the program was only to obtain information on enemy operations in the European Theater for use in the preparation of an official history of the U.S. Army in World War II. In 1946 the program was broadened to include the Mediterranean and Russian war theaters. Beginning in 1947 emphasis was placed on the preparation of operational studies for use by U.S. Army planning and training agencies and service schools.[26]

Eventually over 200 German general officers and senior staff officers were gathered together at a new facility at Allendorf (later Neustadt) in Germany in early 1946 to begin the thorough exploitation of their experiences, a process that continued well into the 1960s, employing none other than the former Chief of OKH, Generaloberst Franz Halder, as the head of the program for fifteen years. The three monographs included in *The Anvil of War* were only a small part of the number that grew into the hundreds. By mid-August 1946, the German group had been thoroughly organized and was fully engaged in writing narrative histories of German operations units which opposed American troops under the command of SHAEF (Supreme Headquarters Allied Expeditionary Force).

When the Americans concentrated so many German general officers and staff officers, they were, perhaps, not quite prepared for the replay of wartime rivalries and animosities among their guests. In addition to the direction of the overall research effort, they hoped that Generalobersts Franz Halder and Heinz Guderian would jointly lead a special project on an organizational history of OKH (Oberkommando des Heeres – Germany Army High Command) to facilitate an understanding of the problems involved in the proposed merger of the United States Armed Forces. Halder and Guderian, as former chiefs of OKH (1940–42 and 1944–45 respectively) were the two officers most qualified to lead this unprecedented historical research effort. Unfortunately, the Americans were to be disappointed.

> Of the two, Halder had more experience in OKH, and any idea of placing Guderian in charge of the OKH project was rendered completely academic by his angry refusal to begin work unless officially assured that he would not be tried for war crimes.[27]

He also feared the more chilling prospect of being turned over to the Poles or Soviets. Furthermore, Guderian and Halder had become so alienated that they were not on speaking terms. The leadership of this great coordination effort then fell naturally into the hands of the more scholarly and less flamboyant Halder. At the highpoint of the work, his staff included twelve lieutenant generals, four major generals, nine brigadier generals, nine colonels, and four lieutenant colonels.[28]

By the middle of 1947 Guderian had emerged from his cocoon. He had been told on 18 June, his birthday, that he would not be prosecuted, and it now seemed in his best interest to cooperate. By then, the work of the historical research group was firmly in Halder's hands, and Guderian contented himself with commenting and writing on projects only in which he had a special expertise. However, Guderian did contribute to the OKH project which had become Halder's special effort. Halder had conceived of the OKH project as a trilogy: OKH 'as it was', OKH 'as it should have been', and OKH 'as it should be'. Halder essentially completed the first two parts. Guderian, who had just agreed to cooperate at last, and Kurt Zeitzler (Chief, OKH, 1942–44) were asked to write commentaries on Halder's first two parts. The third part was taken out of Halder's hands and specifically given to Guderian.[29] Guderian's authoritative biographer, Kenneth Macksey, observed:

> As much for the insight they gave into his way of thinking as in the nature of their contribution to the matters with which he dealt, his commentaries are valuable reading: prejudices and pride are intermingled with caustic shafts which won him a special recognition among the Americans.[30]

The cost of Guderian's talent for invective to the overall effort was high. Cliques formed around the two great men. As might be expected, the conservatives championed Halder and the progressives rallied around Guderian. So bitter did the factionalism become that certain officers, such as Field Marshals von Blomberg and Milch (the real builder of the Luftwaffe) who associated openly with Guderian became guilty by association in the mind of Halder. Such was the feeling that Halder refused even to shake hands with Milch, and even Guderian's attempts to resolve the issue were rebuffed. Those who find such behavior unlikely among men who have held such enormous responsibilities should remember the hammer and tongs recriminations and animosities among the defeated Confederate generals after the American Civil War. The venomous feud between Generals Longstreet and Early come easily to mind. Macksey recounts one such incident in which Guderian's overbearing attitude convulsed the research effort:

> In this military university the members of rival academic factions, in the process of relieving the tedium of captivity, hurled verbal darts at each other while they refought – on paper – the battles of the past. A passage at arms with General der Infantrie Edgar Roehricht provides a good example of Guderian's invective when roused. Roehricht, in a paper describing, somewhat inaccurately from memory, the training organization of OKH, had seen fit to criticize the methods employed by the Panzer Command, and to resurrect the infantry's fundamental distastes for the tank men. As an opening retort Guderian wrote: 'This study shows that the author had just as little peacetime training experience as wartime

combat experience' – a tart piece of defamation since Roehricht had much experience in many capacities, as Guderian should have known. Guderian went on to object to remarks such as, 'The arbitrary manners of the armoured forces from the very beginning ...' and summarized his views (to the satisfaction of the American editors who deleted Roehricht's offending passages) with 'The contributor ... also knows nothing about the Inspector General of the Panzer Troops. Who was "disturbed" by the Inspector General? The work of the Inspector General did not lead to any "duplication of effort" nor did it cause any lack of uniformity in tactical views. It certainly had no "fatal consequences".'[31]

Halder and Guderian continued to openly hammer each other. It did not help that some of Halder's comments on Guderian's work on unified command were on the mark and constructive; the scathing nature of those comments set the two men figuratively at daggers' points. Halder intimated that Guderian was shallow while Guderian stated that Halder was a man of little substance. It was an unworthy spectacle which did no credit to either man, as Macksey again noted: 'Halder the cool intellectual with a schoolmasterly manner, and Guderian, the dynamic man of ideas and action were worthy of better things.' In the end, the problem departed with Guderian who was released from captivity on his 60th birthday in 1948.[32] The Army Historical Division must have been secretly relieved to see such a forceful personality depart. The short biography written by the Historical Division Staff in the preface of his favorite monograph, *Unification or Coordination – The Armed Forces Problem*, betrayed an enormous respect liberally laced with exasperation:

> The military career of Heinz Guderian is in itself enough to establish his ability as an organizer, a theorist, and an aggressive field commander. Even in an American prisoner-of-war enclosure he retained his exceptional intellectual integrity, his firm and uncompromising attitude, his untactfulness under stress, and his alloy of courtliness and acid humor. He is a man who writes what he thinks and who does not alter his opinions to suit his audience.[33]

After Guderian's departure, Halder's position was secure. He continued to serve as leader of the Military History Program and a civilian employee of the U.S. Army until 1961. At his retirement he was awarded, in recognition for his work, the highest decoration offered to civilian employees by the U.S. Government: the Meritorious Civilian Service Award.[34]

History Marches On

More characteristic of the senior German officers was Field Marshal Albert Kesselring:

> I was taken away with Field Marshals List and von Weichs and a junior officer in

a magnificent car to the American Historical Division's camp Allendorf. Our escort was an officer and a gentleman, his kindness making us feel that we were among people of our own kind. The officers of the Historical Division, under their excellent Colonel Potter, went to great trouble to alleviate the customary hardships of camp life. At Allendorf I began to persuade a number of generals and General Staff officers to participate in the compilation of a history of the war. As my main argument I pointed out that this was our only chance of paying a tribute to our soldiers and at the same time influencing Allied historians in the interests of the truth – recording of our experiences being a secondary purpose. Our chief difficulties lay in the lack of documentary material. All the same, our work, in my opinion, has been useful evidence for any final account of the period. I cannot name all the officers of the Historical Division who deserve my thanks for their understanding of our situation and that of our families – there were too many. Almost without exception they were, and are still, the ambassadors of good will and 'fraternisation'.[35]

Kesselring was as good as his word. He proved to be one of the most prolific authors, writing thirty-five separate monographs. Other major contributors were Generals Fritz Bayerlein, Günther Blumentritt, Rudolf von Gersdorff, Franz Halder, Friedrich Koechling, Fritz Kraemer, Heinrich von Lüttwitz, Burkhart Müller-Hildebrand, Lothar Rendulic, Alfred Toppe, Walter Warlimont, Carl Gustav Wagener, and Siegfried Westphal.[36]

Generaloberst Rauss was a major contributor to the German Report Series. Of the first fourteen manuscripts published by the Army, he was the author of four, including the two in this volume. The others included *Russian Combat Methods* (DA Pam 20–230, 1950) and *The Effects of Climate on Combat in European Russia* (DA Pam 20–291, 1952). Other monographs included *The Pomeranian Battle and the Command in the East* (D-189, 1947) and *Small Unit Tactics – Unusual Situations* (P-060g, Parts I–IV).[37]

In addition to his contribution to the German Report Series reproduced in this volume, Generalleutnant von Natzmer also wrote a number of other monographs: *Commitment of German Armor, 1943–45* (C-033, 1948), *High Command in Future – Military Top Level Organization*, with Generaloberst Halder (P-013a, 1949), *Engineer Project – River Crossings by the Red Army in World War II* (P-020a, 1949), *The Field Transportation Branch and its Functions* (P-041s, 1948), and *Theoretical Foundations of the Army High Command* (P-041kk, 1952).[38]

By 1948 most of the German contributors had returned to civilian life which allowed a change in the tempo and administrative organization of the research program. Contributors could now work on their projects in their own homes, supervised by a small control group of selected former high-ranking officers, headed by Halder. As the number of manuscripts grew into the hundreds, the creation of a thorough index became necessary to make the program's contents accessible. This project was assumed in September 1951 by General der Artillerie Friedrich von Boetticher, German military attaché in Washington (1933–41), and completed by the following spring. At that time another index was undertaken to evaluate all the manuscripts in the collection according to historical, operational, and technical interest.[39]

Other German officers, such as General der Artillerie Walter Warlimont, Deputy Chief of the Operations Staff of OKW, continued to work on the project from prison cells where they were serving sentences for war crimes. Warlimont's superior at OKW, Generaloberst Alfred Jodl, consented to work on manuscripts during his trial, as did a number of other men tried as war criminals such as Hermann Goering, Albert Speer, Wilhelm Keitel, Sepp Dietrich, and Joachim Peiper. The contributions of Goering, Jodl, and Keitel, however, were cut short by their subsequent convictions, and in the case of Goering, suicide, and of the others, hangings. Warlimont was serving a life sentence in Landsberg Prison in Bavaria (Hitler's prison where he wrote *Mein Kampf* after the 1921 Putsch) when he was asked to review the study of the organization and functioning of the German Armed Forces High Command, prepared by his successor at OKW. His summary of an armed forces high command 'as it should be', *The Unification Problem: Some Lessons from the German Experience*, was published in 1950 as part of the German Report Series, only one of twenty-four studies he prepared.[40] No doubt the research done by a number of the officers in the program advanced the cause of the German military memoir. S.L.A. Marshall discovered years later with some amusement that one of his 'guests' at Hennemont, Generalleutnant Friedrich von Mellenthin, had used his time there to research his own well-received memoirs, *Panzer Battles*.[41]

As the advent of the Cold War made the enmity of the Soviet Union towards the Western Allies unmistakable, the accounts of the German officers assumed more than a purely historical value. Many of these officers had recent and exhaustive experience in fighting the armed forces of the Soviet Union. That knowledge would be of great help to the U.S. Army, if properly analyzed and disseminated. In June of 1950 with the invasion of South Korea, the value of these works increased greatly. The United States believed that Korea was only a diversion and that the main blow would soon fall in Europe. For that reason, the build-up of forces in Europe was greater than that in Korea itself. The three monographs collected in this volume were published separately as part of the German Report Series at the height of the Korean War. These three titles, *Military Improvisations During the Russian Campaign* (DA Pam 20–201, Aug 51), *German Defense Tactics against Russian Breakthroughs* (DA Pam 20–233, Oct 51) and *Operations of Encircled Forces* (DA Pam 20–234, Jan 52) were among the first published in the series and clearly addressed situations that already had been experienced in Korea and were anticipated in fighting in Europe.

By 1954 the number of Germans who had been involved in the project numbered 730, of whom 642 were officers. The latter figure broke down by rank as follows:

Reichsmarschall (no British/American equivalent)   1
Generalfeldmarschall (Field Marshal/General of the Army).   5
Generaloberst (General) 21
General der Panzertruppen, etc. (Lieutenant General) 134
Generalleutnant (Major General). 160
Generalmajor (Brigadier General) 180
Oberst (Colonel) 78
Oberstleutnant (Lieutenant Colonel) 34
Major. 23
Hauptmann/Rittmeister (Captain).   7

In the end, 501 Army, Waffen-SS, and Luftwaffe generals and another eleven Navy admirals were drawn into the program in addition to hundreds of other specialists. The more prominent officers were practically a Who's Who of the German Armed Forces in World War II.

Arnim, Generaloberst Hans-Jürgen
Bayerlein, Generalleutnant Fritz
Bittrich, General der W-SS, Wilhelm
Blaskowitz, Generaloberst Johannes
Blumentritt, General der Infantrie Günther
Choltitz, General der Infantrie Dietrich von
Dietrich, Generaloberst (W-SS), Joseph ('Sepp')
Doenitz, Grossadmiral Karl
Erfurth, General der Infantrie Dr. Waldemar
Goering, Reichsmarschall Hermann
Guderian, Generaloberst Heinz
Halder, Generaloberst Franz
Hausser, Generaloberst (W-SS) Paul
Heinrich, Generaloberst Gotthard
Heydte, Oberst Friedrich Frhr. von der
Hollidt, Generaloberst Karl
Hube, General der Panzertruppen Hans
Jodl, Generaloberst Alfred
Keitel, Generalfeldmarschall Wilhelm
Kesselring, Generalfeldmarschall Albert
Leeb, Generalfeldmarschall Wilhelm Ritter von
List, Generalfeldmarschall Wilhelm

Lüttwitz, General der Panzertruppen Heinrich Frhr. von
Lüttwitz, General der Panzertruppen Smilo Frhr. von
Mackensen, Generaloberst Eberhard von
Manteuffel, General der Panzertruppen Hasso-Eccard von
Meindl, General der Fallschirmtruppen Eugen
Mellenthin, Generalmajor Friedrich von
Nehring, General der Panzertruppen Walter
Peiper, Oberst (W-SS) Joachim
Rauss, Generaloberst Erhard
Rendulic, Generaloberst Dr. Lothar
Ruge, Vizeadmiral Friedrich
Rundstedt, Generalfeldmarschall Gerd von
Salmuth, Generaloberst Hans von
Seidemann, General der Flieger Hans
Senger und Etterlin, General der Panzertruppen Fridolin von
Skorzeny, Oberstleutnant (W-SS) Otto
Speer, Reichsminister Dr. Albert
Speidel, Generalleutnant Dr. Hans
Student, Generaloberst Kurt
Vietinghoff, Generaloberst Heinrich von
Warlimont, General der Artillerie Walter
Westphal, General der Kavallerie Siegfried
Zeitzler, Generaloberst Kurt

With these figures in mind, it was perhaps an understatement by Colonel Nye when he wrote in 1954 that 'The program represents an unusual degree of collaboration between officers of nations recently at war.'[42] But it was much more than that. Strangely, it was an American officer who spent his life documenting the exploits of his own American troops, S.L.A. Marshall, who helped the Germans remember their own fallen comrades. It was, as Field Marshal Kesselring said, the German general officer corps' 'only chance of paying a tribute to our soldiers . . .' In the end, it was simply a matter of keeping faith.

Peter G. Tsouras
Alexandria, Virginia
1994

Notes

1. General M.A. Moiseyev, Chief of the General Staff, *Voyenno-istoricheskiy zhurnal*, No. 3, March 1990.
2. Paul Carrell, *Hitler Moves East 1941–1943* (London and Boston, 1963) pp. 226, 248, 604.
3. Carrell, *Scorched Earth: The Russian-German War, 1943–1945* (Boston, 1966) pp. 118–123; UK title, *Hitler's War on Russia* (London, 1966).

26　The Anvil of War

4. Erich von Manstein, *Lost Victories* (London and New York, 1958); (London and Novato, CA, 1982) p. 330.

5. French L. MacLean, *The Unknown Generals – German Corps Commanders in World War II* (Fort Leavenworth, KS: A Thesis presented to the Faculty of the U.S. Army Command and General Staff College, 1988) pp. 127, 146. U.S. Army, *Order of Battle of the German Army* (Fort Riley, KS: Army General School, 1 March 1945) p. 609. Earl F. Ziemke, *Stalingrad to Berlin: The German Defeat in the East* (Washington, DC: Office of the Chief of Military History, U.S. Army, 1968) pp. 343, 460.

6. Erhard Rauss, *Defense Tactics against Russian Breakthroughs.*

7. Carrell, *Scorched Earth*, op cit, pp. 305–306. Rauss was also lucky. The 5th Tank Army ran into the German Army Group South supply dump at Feski northwest of Kharkov crammed with two months' supply of everything necessary to support two armies for three months. That included booze. At Feski was an entire year's production of the French spirits industry as well as alcohol looted from all of conquered Europe. There was so much vodka that it was stored in carboys. The German quartermaster threw open the dumps to any German unit that had transportation. Within two days it had been cleaned out except for the vodka. None was touched. With French cognac, Spanish port, and Italian Chianti to choose from, who would want vodka? It was then that 5th Guards Army overran Feski – and did not move for three days. When the Russians had drunk the last carboy dry and recovered from their hangovers, they discovered that SS Panzer Division Wiking had reinforced Rauss' defense and occupied the high ground in front of them.

8. Rauss, *Russian Combat Methods*, DA Pam 20–230 (Washington, DC: Department of the Army, 1950), pp. 53–56.

9. Rauss, *Defense Tactics against Russian Breakthroughs.*

10. F.W. von Mellenthin, *Panzer Battles* (Norman, OK: Oklahoma University Press, 1971) pp. 269–270.

11. Rauss, *Military Improvisations During the Russian Campaign.*

12. Rauss, *Defense Tactics against Russian Breakthroughs.*

13. Heinz Guderian, *Panzer Leader* (London and New York, 1952); (London and New York, 1987) pp. 348–349.

14. Guderian, ibid., pp. 348–349.

15. Guderian, ibid., p. 349.

16. U.S. Army, *Order of Battle of the German Army*, op cit, p. 599. Horst Scheibert, *Panzer-Grenadier-Division Grossdeutschland und ihre Schwesterverbände* (Dorheim: Podzun-Verlag, 1970) p. 147.

17. Jürgen Thorwald, *Defeat in the East* (New York, 1967) pp. 243–46.

18. Thorwald, ibid.

19. S.L.A. Marshall, *The Fields of Bamboo* (New York, 1971) p. 1.

20. Marshall, *Bringing Up the Rear* (San Rafael, CA, 1979) p. 153.

21. Marshall, ibid., pp. 156–157.

22. Marshall, ibid., pp. 156–157.

23. Marshall, ibid., p. 157.

24. Marshall, ibid., p. 159.

25. Historical Division, Headquarters, U.S. Army, Europe, *Guide to Foreign Military Studies*, 1954, p. iii.

26. Historical Division, ibid., pp. iii–iv.

27. Heinz Guderian, *Unification or Coordination – the Armed Forces Problem* (Historical Division, Special Staff, U.S. Army, February 1949) p. v.

28. Guderian, ibid.

29. Guderian, ibid.

30. Kenneth Macksey, *Guderian: Creator of the Blitzkrieg* (London and New York, 1975) p. 240; (London and Novato, CA, 1992).

31. Macksey, ibid., pp. 240–241.

32. Macksey, ibid., p. 241.

33. Guderian, *Unification or Coordination*, op cit.

34. Franz Halder, *The Halder War Diary*, ed. Charles Burdick and Hans-Adolf Jacobson (London and Novato, CA, 1988) p. 10.

35. Albert Kesselring, *The Memoirs of Field Marshal Kesselring* (London and New York, 1953); (London and Novato, CA, 1988) p. 296.

36. Historical Division, op cit, pp. 242–251.

37. Historical Division, ibid., p. 248.

38. Historical Division, ibid., p. 247.

39. Historical Division, ibid., pp. iii–iv.

40. Walter Warlimont, *The Unification Problem: Some Lessons From the German Experience*, Department of the Army, Office of the Chief of Military History, April 1950, p. ii.

41. Marshall, *Bringing Up the Rear*, op cit, p. 159.

42. Historical Division, op cit, p. iv.

Part One

Military Improvisations during the Russian Campaign

BY GENERALOBERST ERHARD RAUSS

Commander, 4th and 3rd Panzer Armies

Introduction

The art of war involves the correct estimation and careful weighing of one's own as well as the enemy's capabilities and is marked by the conduct of military operations in a manner promising the highest degree of success. Success in war can be achieved only if the military commander employs his resources with correct timing in suitable terrain and in a way that guarantees maximum effect.

The conduct of war is subject to the same imperfections and frailties as any other field of human endeavor; for this reason emergencies which, of necessity, lead to improvisations arise from time to time in every war and in every army. Faulty planning, unsatisfactory performance of matériel, and violations of basic principles of warfare cause deficiencies which can be alleviated through improvisation but can only be overcome by sacrificing time, space, and strength. Blunders are made in every military sphere, in all places, and on the highest as well as on the lowest level. No wonder that such blunders, oversights, and frictions entail improvisations of all types, from the simplest to the most elaborate, from the strictly temporary to the chronic.

By dint of its long duration and ever-widening scope, World War II created a persistent state of deficiencies in the German Army which forced the military agencies to introduce a multitude of improvisations of all types. Insufficiently prepared for the campaign in the East, for example, the Army was faced with a great calamity as early as the muddy period and winter of 1941–42. Top-level staffs and field forces alike were forced to improvise extensively. As the campaign wore on and the German military potential continued to decline, improvisations of the widest variety became increasingly prevalent. Toward the end of the war the ratio of strength between the German and Russian Armies became so disproportionate that improvisations, especially in combat operations, were rampant. Finally, the entire conduct of war was one great improvisation.

The present study lays no claim to comprehensiveness, but even this fragmentary account may show the main characteristics of German improvisations and the part they played in military operations. The many separate examples are presented along functional lines, and the material is subdivided into tactical, logistical, technical and organizational improvisations. Other bases could have been adopted. Some readers may be interested in analyzing the German improvisations in terms of their causes, or of their inevitability, or even chronologically as indicators of the extremes to which an army fighting Soviet Russia was put.

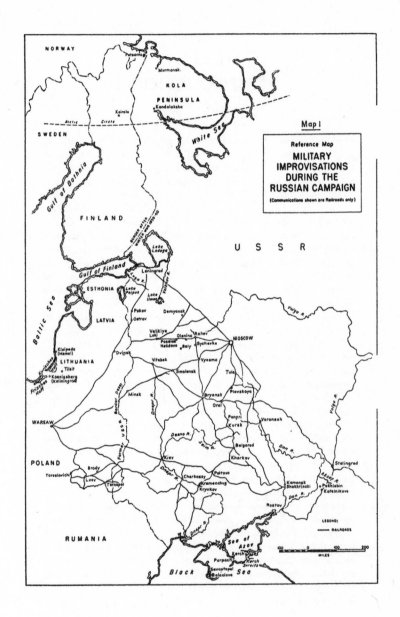

NORWAY

Petsamo

Murmansk

KOLA
PENINSULA

Kairela
Kandalaksha

SWEDEN

Arctic Circle

White Sea

Map I

Reference Map

MILITARY
IMPROVISATIONS
DURING THE
RUSSIAN CAMPAIGN

(Communications shown are Railroads only)

Gulf of Bothnia

FINLAND

U S S R

Lake Ladoga

Gulf of Finland

Leningrad

ESTONIA

Lake Peipus

Lake Ilmen

Baltic Sea

Pskov

Demyansk

LATVIA

Ostrov

Volga R.

Velikiye
Luki

Olenino
Rzhev

Klaipeda
(Memel)

Poselok
Nelidovo
Bely
Sychevka

MOSCOW

LITHUANIA

Tilsit

Dvinsk

Vitebsk

Vyazma

Koenigsberg
(Kaliningrad)

Smolensk

Tula

Frisches Haff

Minsk

Dnepr R.

Bryansk
Plavskaya

Volga R.

WARSAW

Desna R.

Orel

Panyri
Kursk

Voronezh

Seim R.

POLAND

Kiev

Belgorod

Don R.

Yaroslavichi

Brody

Kharkov

Stalingrad

Lvov
Tarnopol

Dnepr R.

Charkassy

Poltava

Kremenchug
Krykov

Kamensk
Shakhtinski
Pokhlebin
Kotelnikovo

Don R.

Rostov

LEGEND:

RAILROADS

Dnepr R.

*Sea of
Azov*

RUMANIA

100   0   100   200

MILES

Kerch
*Kerch
Straits*

Parpach

Savastopol
Balaclava

Black Sea

CHAPTER 1

The Offensive

As the pillar of Germany's military might, the Army had to bear the brunt of the fighting during World War II. The heartbeat of the Army was at the front, where deficiencies and shortages of any kind were immediately felt. Improvisations and expedients introduced at the front had to show quick results because, in the face of the enemy, time was of the essence. With the territorial expansion of the war, tactical commanders frequently became responsible for areas that they were unable to control with the troops and matériel at their disposal. Resources were particularly taxed whenever the forces suffered heavy casualties for which replacements could not be expected to arrive for a long time. High and low echelons alike were therefore very often forced to introduce improvisations to solve their problems as well as possible. Their efforts were concentrated on three types of tactical improvisations – the formation and commitment of combat staffs and units in sudden critical situations, the employment of units for missions outside their normal scope, and the adaptation of tactics to unexpected situations. A combination of two or more tactical improvisations had to be introduced in many cases.

The Elimination of Russian Forces in a German Rear Area

THE BLITZKRIEG BOGGED DOWN IN MUD (MAP 2)

On 22 June 1941 the 6th Panzer Division moved out of the Tilsit area as part of a provisional panzer army. In true blitzkrieg manner it rolled across Lithuania and Latvia within a few days, overran every enemy position in its way, broke through the Stalin Line, crossed the Dvina River, and opened the gateway to Leningrad on the Luga River – all within three weeks from its day of departure. This 500-mile trip led through dust and sand, woods and swamps, and across rivers and antitank ditches. Leningrad was within sight.

At this very time the division was called upon to assume the leading part in the German attack on the central front. Once again the division moved with lightning speed and covered 600 miles to join Army Group Center. On 10 October 1941, the first day of the offensive, its 260 tanks made a deep penetration into the enemy lines near Vyazma. Ten days later the Russians were encircled and the mission was accomplished.

The 6th Panzer Division was then to lead the attack on Moscow and take the city. Its spearheads were approaching the objective when nature suddenly put a protective wall around the Russian capital. The autumn mud brought the blitzkrieg to a sudden end. It swallowed the most valuable equipment. The cold winter continued the terrible destruction. Then came the German withdrawal during which every tank, every antitank gun, and almost every artillery piece of the division had to be sacrificed. Enemy attacks and cold weather caused innumerable casualties during rear guard actions. When the once-proud 6th Panzer Division finally assembled its forces in January 1942, all that remained were 57 riflemen, 20 engineers, and 3 guns.

After this terrible hemorrhage the remaining staffs and the supply and rear elements were assembled forty miles behind the front line for the purpose of reorganizing the division. Every day a few tankers, artillery men, and others who had escaped the carnage trickled back to the divisional area. As soon as they arrived they had to help guard the highway and railroad between Smolensk and Vyazma, the life lines of Fourth and Ninth Armies, against attacks by Russian cavalry, parachute troops, and partisans who had penetrated deep into the rear areas. The enemy first advanced southward and then turned east toward the railroad and highway connecting Vyazma with Rzhev in order to cut off the supply of Ninth Army. The field hospitals and motor pools of several divisions were under attack, and two airfields were in immediate danger. Far and wide no combat troops were available. The over-all situation did not permit the release of even the few remnants of 6th Panzer Division to serve as cadre for an alert unit which was to be improvised in the rear. By the end of January 1942 the situation was so tense that Marshal Stalin felt justified in announcing the impending annihilation of two German armies in the biggest battle of encirclement in history. But events were to develop differently.

DESPERATE IMPROVISATIONS

Emergency alert units had to be improvised and committed immediately even though no combat cadres were available. Actually the 6th Panzer Division had not the necessary service personnel to organize even one such unit. Ninth Army therefore issued orders that the division assemble immediately all the service and supply units, as well as construction and roadbuilding battalions in the army rear area, and intercept all stragglers. Between Sychevka and Vyazma a defensive front was to be built up in the most expeditious manner (map 3). Even the Luftwaffe units at the Novo-Dugino airfield were subordinated to the division commander for use in ground combat.

Within twenty-four hours the staffs of all units now subordinate to 6th Panzer Division were busy intercepting every available officer and man in their respective areas and forming emergency alert units of varied strength and composition. Special care was taken that men from the same unit remained together. Depending on their number, they formed squads, platoons, or companies under the command of their former officers. Whenever possible emergency alert units of similar composition were organized into battalions and two or more battalions were placed under the command of one of the previously mentioned staffs. Each unit was to keep the weapons and supplies it had salvaged from its parent unit. This procedure was a guarantee against unnecessary splitting up of available manpower and resources. It seemed a better policy to commit units of differing strength and composition rather than to destroy unit integrity by equalizing numbers. The strength and composition of individual units was taken into account in the assignment of defense sectors.

Most men were armed with rifles. Each company had one or two machine guns, and some of the battalions had a few mortars and small antitank guns which had been procured from ordnance shops in the vicinity. Initially only one recently repaired artillery piece was available, but the flow of weapons and equipment improved daily because the maintenance and repair shops made a maximum effort to send matériel to the front. Numerous convalescents and men returning from furlough were employed along the rapidly forming front facing west.

The newly formed units had to be committed without delay wherever the danger was greatest. Frequently this baptism occurred on the very day of their initial organization. If possible, the alert units were committed in a sector where they could protect their own service and rear installations, a task with which they were only too glad to comply. For the same reason Luftwaffe units were assigned to the defense sectors that covered their own airfields. The remaining gaps were closed by alert units which had their assembly area farther away from the new front.

The most important sectors of the forty-mile front were occupied on the first day, gaps were filled in on the following day, and by the third a continuous though thinly-occupied line was formed. By the end of the first week it was held by 35,000 men. Small general reserve units were improvised by that time, including one platoon of five damaged tanks with limited mobility.

By the tenth day the division had improvised a full-strength, completely equipped motorcycle company utilizing men returning from furlough and convalescents. Several armored reconnaissance cars were turned over to this mobile reserve which could be moved to any danger spot along the *Rollbahn* {road designated as a main axis of motorized transportation} that ran parallel to and closely behind the front. This force was also versed in skiing and carried skis on the motorcycles in order to have cross-country mobility even though the snow was three feet deep in some places. This was a crack unit especially suited for local attacks and commanded by battle-tested officers.

The Luftwaffe signal battalion of VIII Air Corps at Novo-Dugino laid the necessary telephone lines and connected them with the airfield switchboard. During the organization of the new front enemy attacks on the airfield and the adjacent sector to the north were repelled by alert units. In the central sector the enemy occupied several villages before the arrival of alert units. On the southern wing he occupied other villages and stood only a half to one mile from the highway which he interdicted with his mortars. At night enemy ski units infiltrated through the German lines, which initially were not continuous, and disrupted the supply of Ninth Army at several points between Vyazma and Rzhev. In view of the extreme cold and deep snow, the front line was almost exclusively a line of strong points based on villages. Although repeatedly under attack, the center of this line held from the outset.

Thus, the improvised front facing west served its initial purpose. Within a few days the whole sector threatened from the west was protected by alert units. Moreover, contact was established with the forces that fought in an arc around Rzhev to the north and with similarly improvised Fourth Army units in the south. However, the *Rollbahn* and the railroad were so close behind the front line that the continuous disruptions became unbearable. Furthermore, the slightest setback of the improvised units could result in the complete blocking of the traffic arteries by the enemy. This handicap could only be remedied by advancing the German outposts farther to the west. This involved a winter offensive in extreme cold and deep snow with improvised units which were without training in offensive operations. Yet, it had to be done. The operation could not be an offensive in the usual sense, let alone a blitzkrieg. The tactics to be used necessarily deviated from the conventional pattern and had to be especially suited to the peculiarities of the prevailing situation and the forces available.

THE SNAIL OFFENSIVE (MAP 3)

At the beginning of February 1942, on the eighth day after the initial formation of the new front, the sector commanders were called to a meeting, informed of the necessity of an offensive, and indoctrinated in the combat methods to be used. The mere thought of starting an offensive with their motley units caused all commanders to raise serious objections which could be fully expressed by one single word: impossible. Only a detailed explanation of the tactics to be employed, for which the division commander coined the term 'snail offensive', gradually dispelled the numerous objections which were perfectly valid from the conventional military standpoint.

First of all, it was pointed out to the commanders that time was not an important factor in this offensive. The speed of a snail would be sufficient. In selecting the place of attack they were to proceed like a snail which would move only to a place where it could find a worthwhile objective without incurring any danger. The method of advance was to resemble that of a snail slowly groping its way and immediately retracting its feelers or changing its direction whenever faced by an obstacle. Any setback must be avoided because it would discourage the weak German forces and tie them up for a long time just as a snail withdraws into its shell in a dangerous situation and does not dare continue on its way for quite a while. Nor were the commanders to forget the shell of the snail which affords safety and shelter in case of danger. Despite all precautions, however, the sector commanders had to keep in mind the rewarding objective at all times, exactly as a snail would do in the same situation.

This comparison served to illustrate the basic idea of the combat methods to be employed in the snail offensive. The practical application of this doctrine was subsequently explained at the site where the first offensive actions were to be launched. The objective of the snail offensive was to push back the Russians far enough to place the supply lines of Ninth Army beyond their reach. This meant that a line favorable for defense was to be reached which followed the edge of the vast wooded marshes. All villages in the fertile region to the east of it therefore had to be taken from the enemy. A secondary but important intention was to deprive the enemy of valuable shelter and sources of supply and to make these villages available to the German troops. This would be a hard blow to the enemy since there were only a few small, poor villages in the marshy forests, and the entire enemy force in the rear of Ninth Army was beginning to suffer from supply difficulties. After the Germans launched a successful panzer attack on Bely, the Russian force was practically surrounded by German units except for a narrow pathless strip across the front.

The final objective of the 6th Panzer Division was to roll back the enemy to a distance of ten to twenty miles from the *Rollbahn*, but this plan was at first not revealed to the commanders of the various sectors. The success of the initial operations was of paramount importance.

First of all, the central forces were ordered to eliminate the deep enemy wedge in the German lines. The enemy salient included three villages held by Russian security detachments (see map 3). There an initial victory should be easy to obtain. The attack was not to start until everything had been so well prepared that success could be expected with certainty. The three villages could be observed from the high German positions and dominated by cross fire from two sides. The enemy dispositions were under constant observation. The foremost village was held by the strongest enemy detachment, the two farther to the rear by smaller ones. A platoon of volunteers led by an experienced officer was to sneak up at night on each of the small villages, effect a penetration from the rear, make a surprise raid at dawn, and annihilate the enemy. Surprise was achieved, two villages were taken and the large one in front was cut off. Enemy attempts to break out during daytime were stopped by fire. At dusk the German forces in both villages were reinforced, the large village was surrounded and the enemy force which attempted to break out under cover of darkness was captured. When all three villages were in German hands, they were immediately prepared for defense. Farther to the south another Russian strong point was taken by similar tactics. A strong covering force with heavy weapons remained in the old main line of resistance to stop any possible reverses. The main line of resistance was moved forward only after positions had been constructed in the frozen ground and supply and communication routes cleared of snow. As long as the enemy showed intentions of counterattacking, strong reserves were positioned behind the danger points and no further moves were initiated.

Similarly the initial operations in other sectors were adapted to local conditions and carried out at irregular intervals. The first week of the snail offensive resulted in the occupation of fourteen villages and the capture of numerous prisoners. Losses on the German side were negligible. Most important was the confidence the German units gained in this combat method.

Gradually more complicated missions could be undertaken. However, it remained essential to attack in the most effective manner and to reach the objective without becoming involved in a heavy engagement. Although the Russian forces in this sector were better trained and equipped, their supply of ammunition was limited and they were numerically too weak to organize a continuous line of defense. Their strong points were secured by outpost lines. The best method of overcoming these obstacles was to capture the villages where the outposts were located in order to isolate each main strong point until its encirclement was almost completed. Then the enemy troops usually abandoned their strong points voluntarily.

Bogdanovo, a village situated in dominating terrain on the southern wing, was one of the most important enemy strong points. From here the Russians frequently made thrusts into the adjacent sector to the south, penetrated to the *Rollbahn*, and stopped all traffic. In order to eliminate these inconvenient disruptions, the Fuehrer Escort Battalion, a crack SS unit which normally served as Hitler's personal bodyguard, was reinforced with heavy weapons and artillery and moved into the adjacent sector to take this enemy defense anchor by assault. After a short briefing and hasty preparations the battalion launched a frontal attack in the orthodox manner, forced the weak outposts to withdraw, and advanced almost to the edge of the main strong point. There the enemy, counterattacking from all sides and inflicting considerable losses, pushed back the battalion and encircled one company. The company was finally liberated under great difficulties, but the attack was not repeated because of the heavy casualties.

After this failure Ninth Army shifted the boundaries to include Bogdanovo in the 6th Panzer Division sector and ordered the division to capture it. Within a few days the snail offensive procedure scored another success by almost completely isolating the enemy strong point. When the divisional reserves attempted to close the ring, the Russians, though raked by heavy German fire, hastily evacuated the strong point in a daylight withdrawal. The village was immediately occupied and held against all later counterattacks.

In one month the snail offensive achieved the capture of eighty villages, and advanced the front line from five to eight miles. The principal effect, however, was to put the enemy on the defensive along the entire front, making thrusts in the direction of the *Rollbahn* and railroad out of the question. More and more battle-tested soldiers and reconditioned weapons had meanwhile been made available and supplied to the front. The number of tanks increased to eight, the artillery pieces to twelve. By then the operations of all units were well co-ordinated and the commanders had full confidence in the new combat tactics; thorough preparations and careful implementation of all instructions had prevented the slightest failure.

The subordinate commanders could now be granted much greater freedom for the continuation of the offensive. Division headquarters no longer interfered with details. Each sector was assigned a weekly phase line that was to be reached under optimum conditions. This line was not to be crossed without approval from division because safety considerations outweighed those of speed. Whenever the alert units ran into particular difficulties, they called upon divisional reserves which by now included a few tanks and dive bombers. All enemy attempts failed to halt the slow but steady advance of the improvised front. The snail offensive only paused in places where the enemy committed strong reserves; it started to move again immediately after these were trans-ferred to another danger point. Since the enemy did not have sufficient forces and matériel to appear in strength in several places at the same time, he lost ground slowly but steadily. By the end of March 1942, two months after the start of the snail offensive, the Russians had been pushed back into the marshy forests and forced to relinquish more than two hundred villages.

This tactical, organizational, and logistical improvisation, a product of extreme emergency, had reached its intended objective. To go farther would have been impossible at this time because the two adjacent units had not joined the division in the offensive. The 6th Panzer Division units on the extreme ends of the sector had remained in their initial positions in order to prevent the opening of gaps in the flanks which would have permitted the enemy to infiltrate into the rear of the snail-offensive front. Ninth Army then widened the sector of 6th Panzer Division with orders to eliminate enemy interference in the adjacent areas by similar offensive action.

THE SCORPION OFFENSIVE

Despite the successes obtained by the use of snail-offensive tactics in the central zone, the Germans holding the entire front facing west were still inferior to the opposing Russian forces which included some first-rate Guards units around Rzhev. It was the mission of the 6th Panzer Division to launch another offensive to push back the enemy from the only German highway and railroad line leading from Sychevka to Rzhev (map 4). The Russian outposts were located one to three miles from these essential supply routes and disrupted the traffic on many occasions.

The available forces and matériel were still inadequate for an offensive in the conventional manner. Once again it became necessary to improvise tactics. Only successive surprise attacks with limited objectives plus close co-ordination of all arms had any chance of success. Free choice of time and place for each intended thrust was another prerequisite since the issue would be in doubt if the enemy recognized the German intentions and took countermeasures. Whenever the element of surprise was lost, the objective had to be changed and the blow delivered at some distant vulnerable point. All this had to be achieved with a relatively weak striking force which was to be shifted to a different sector of the front immediately after each thrust. The tactics to be employed thus consisted of a well co-ordinated but flexible system of limited objective attacks. They could best be compared to a series of paralyzing stings a scorpion would inflict in a life-and-death struggle against a physically superior opponent.

Taken individually, the various lunges were not novel. A frontal breakthrough thrust in the center was followed by a double envelopment farther to the south. Only a few days later the same combat forces attacked through a deep forest to the north, accomplished their mission, and were immediately replaced by reserve units. Before the enemy had caught his breath, he was surprised by a deceptive thrust into his flank. Diagonal jabs at the northern and southern ends of the front consolidated the territorial gains achieved by the preceding operations. While the German forces suffered only slight losses, the enemy was prevented from seizing the initiative during the spring of 1942. He was dislodged from the favorable terrain he held and was forced to withdraw his forces approximately 12 miles along a 75-mile front. The German supply lines from Vyazma to Rzhev were finally secure, and a base of operations was acquired for the summer offensive which led to the annihilation of all Russian units holding out in the rear of Ninth Army.

CAVALRY BRIGADE MODEL IN OPERATION SEYDLITZ (MAP 4)

The Russian elements that had broken through the German lines during the winter of 1941–42 and threatened the German supply lines during the spring, succeeded in gaining a foothold in the extensive, impassable, primeval forest swamps between Rzhev and Bely. Constantly receiving reinforcements of infantry, cavalry, and armored units, the Russians assembled a force of 60,000 men in the rear of Ninth Army and forced the Germans to fight on two fronts. They tied down strong forces and increasingly menaced the army rear. Russian supply arrived by a road leading via Poselok Nelidovo toward Bely.

In order to eliminate this danger and regain full freedom of action, General Model, commanding the Ninth Army, planned Operation SEYDLITZ, a concentric counterattack which started on 2 July 1942. During the first stage of the operation the Germans, in difficult forest fighting, dislodged the Soviet forces from their deeply echeloned positions and hemmed them into a narrow area. A quick German thrust into the Obsha valley anticipated the apparent enemy intention of breaking through the newly formed German switch position northeast of Bely. The Russians attacked simultaneously from the inside and the outside and attempted to escape through the breach thus made. The enemy units were split along the Obsha River and encircled in two pockets. All Russian attempts to break out were frustrated. Russian forces northeast of Bely directed relief attacks from the outside toward the pockets. These attacks were also repulsed. Strong tactical reserves which the enemy brought in by forced marches via Poselok Nelidovo arrived too late. After a battle lasting eleven days Operation SEYDLITZ ended with a complete German victory.

An improvised cavalry brigade, the formation of which General Model had ordered when operation SEYDLITZ was still in the planning stage, played a major role in this success. Its organization was unique in many ways. Since most of the terrain was very swampy or covered with extensive marshy forests, the brigade was to be organized in such a manner that it would be able to fight in any terrain and under any weather conditions. It was even to be mobile in mud.

The first organizational problem was the procurement of men and equipment. Obviously only officers and enlisted men with combat experience in the East could be selected for such a specialized unit. Moreover they had to be trained cavalrymen. None but tough, healthy, brave men who were in no way pampered and who felt a close kinship with nature could be used. Replacements from the western theater or the zone of the interior were therefore out of the question because the troops from the West were softened by the easy ways of occupation life, and the recruits from the training camps at home lacked combat experience. Even though the latter had received a certain amount of specialized training for the eastern front, these recently inducted soldiers were incapable of enduring the physical hardships which the Russian theater imposed on the individual. There was not a commander in the field who was not aware that the difference between war in the East and war in the West was the difference between day and night.

General Model therefore decided to pull out the reconnaissance battalion from each of the eight divisions under his command and place them at the disposal of the newly appointed brigade commander. This was a very favorable solution for the brigade but hard on the infantry divisions, for the reconnaissance battalions were valuable combat units and were greatly missed by their parent divisions.

Organization and equipment of the brigade

The organization and equipment of the brigade was as follows:

(1) A headquarters staff with one signal communication troop.
(2) Three cavalry regiments, each consisting of one or two mounted troops

and three to four bicycle troops, with a total of five troops per regiment. Within a few hours all mounted troops of the regiments could be assembled and a complete cavalry regiment formed for an emergency. Each troop had twelve sections and each section was equipped with two light machine guns. Thus each troop had twenty-four light machine guns and two heavies. In addition, officers and enlisted men were equipped with submachine guns when possible.

(3) Each bicycle troop was issued two horse-drawn wagons which carried ammunition, baggage, and rations. Of course, these wagons were drawn by small native *Panje* horses because only they could master the terrain. The mounted troops had German military mounts. Mobility in mud was achieved because the *Panje* horses and wagons could pull through practically anywhere.

(4) In addition, the brigade included an engineer company, a medical company, and one motorized and one horse-drawn supply column.

(5) Tanks and antitank units were to assist the brigade whenever terrain conditions permitted. Each regiment had only six organic light infantry howitzers. Additional artillery support was also to be provided when necessary. The assistance of infantry and additional artillery units for flank protection was promised in case of a deep penetration or a breakthrough.

Training and commitment of the brigade

After about four to six weeks of combined arms training, the brigade was committed south of Olenino along the Luchesa River. A so-called *Rollbahn* led from Olenino southward which, although it was supposed to be a fairly good highway, was really no more than an unimproved country road. Short stretches of corduroy road covered particularly wet, swampy sections. Only the Luchesa valley was clear of woods to approximately one to three miles in width. Large, swampy forests extended on both sides of the valley with but a few clearings of varying sizes. Small, swampy creeks flowed through the woods. Maps and interrogation of local inhabitants provided the Germans with exact information on the terrain behind the enemy lines. Once the brigade had broken through the Russian positions at the edge of the woods, it would have to contend with swampy forests ten miles in depth where scarcely a path was to be found.

A panzer division was committed to the right of the brigade with the mission of attacking along the *Rollbahn* to the south. Since the Russians rightly expected the main effort of the attack along this axis of advance, the division was faced by a very difficult task. From aerial photographs and the interrogation of deserters it was known that strong enemy fortifications such as road blocks and fortified antitank positions were situated along the *Rollbahn*. The positions farther east and west from this road were not as strongly fortified but were secured by mine fields in which there were only a few gaps. The Russians thought it most improbable that a major attack could be launched east of the Luchesa River because the Germans would be unable to move tanks up to the line of departure through the swampy forests. They also felt certain that a tank attack across the open terrain, the Luchesa River, and through the mine fields would hardly be hazarded.

Approximately ten days before the attack the brigade moved up to the line of departure. Intensive reconnaissance of the intermediate terrain began immediately with the assistance of veteran tankers. Within a short time a complete picture of the enemy positions and the intervening terrain was available. From this picture it was obvious that, after the necessary preparations, an attack with armored support was definitely feasible.

For Operation SEYDLITZ the cavalry brigade was attached to its right neighbor, the panzer division which was to advance along the *Rollbahn*. The brigade was to thrust through the ten-mile-deep forest in one sweep and, if possible, cut the Russian supply line on the north–south highway if the main body of the panzer division was unable to make any progress. Six artillery batteries and one tank company with fourteen tanks were attached to the brigade for the execution of this mission.

The unit adjacent to the left, an infantry division, was not to jump off until the next day after the initial attack had been successful. For the first day the left flank would therefore be exposed. In the marshy forest terrain this was not a matter of particular concern because a small covering force would surely prove sufficient.

The first difficulties arose when the fourteen tanks had to be moved up to the line of departure through the swampy forests. Forty-eight hours before the beginning of the attack a company of engineers with power saws started to cut trees at intervals of about one yard along the edge of the forest so that the trees fell on open ground along a stretch leading through the assembly area. In a very short time and with relatively little effort a tank path was built which in effect was a corduroy road with about one-yard-wide gaps. Few branches had to be cut off the trees. For obvious reasons this road could only be used by a limited number of tanks and tracked vehicles.

A few hours after the engineers had gone to work the tanks started to move into their assembly area in daylight. This was possible because the wooded terrain afforded sufficient cover. The noise of the tanks was drowned by harassing fire and low-flying reconnaissance planes. All tanks arrived at their destination without incident. Experienced mine-clearing squads were assigned to each tank and ordered to ride on the tanks.

The attack started at 0300. During the artillery preparation the tanks started out together with the cavalry troops. Their movements were favored by a heavy fog which covered the river valley. They crossed most of the intervening terrain without encountering resistance. A ford across the Luchesa River which had been reconnoitered in advance was found to be adequate for the fourteen tanks. Enemy mine fields were immediately recognized by the experienced tankers and engineers and the lanes through the fields were found and widened. Suffering no losses, the tanks and cavalry suddenly rose in front of a completely surprised enemy. In one sweep the first and second lines were overrun and great confusion seized the Russians. The tanks had accomplished their mission. They could not penetrate any farther into the enemy-held forest without sufficient reconnaissance and additional preparation, and were therefore ordered to halt and stay in reserve. By then the cavalry had penetrated the enemy lines three to four miles.

The situation on the right was entirely different. Here the panzer division was to advance along the *Rollbahn*. The Russians were prepared for an attack. The German tanks ran into deeply echeloned antitank positions which were camouflaged with the usual Russian skill. The infantry also could not make headway and suffered heavy casualties in the forest fighting. The entire operation seemed in danger of bogging down.

At noon the brigade received orders to pivot toward the west with all available forces and to attack the *Rollbahn* from the east. One regiment turned to the right and thrust toward the *Rollbahn* through primeval forest swamps. At times the men sank in up to their knees. Direction had to be maintained by compass. The troops performed seemingly impossible feats and the surprise attack was a full success. By nightfall the regiment controlled a stretch of the *Rollbahn*, the pressure on the panzer division subsided, and the enemy was in an untenable position. The *Panje* supply wagons were able to move through the swamps and bring rations and ammunition to the completely exhausted troops.

On the following morning the continuation of the attack met hardly any resistance. On the other hand the physical requirements were extraordinarily high since the men had to traverse six miles of wooded swamps. Before noon the brigade emerged from the forest and a few hours later the first heavy equipment arrived. The terrain ahead extended over a wide area and Russian columns, single vehicles, and individuals could be seen moving about in wild disorder. It was obvious that the enemy command had lost control over its troops. The Russian defense lines had collapsed and the German divisions were advancing everywhere.

Conclusions

Even though Operation SEYDLITZ would probably have been successful without the cavalry brigade, it would have involved a much greater loss of men and equipment. During the eleven days of the operation 50,000 prisoners, 230 tanks, 760 artillery pieces, and thousands of small arms were captured. The situation of Ninth Army had been improved by the elimination of these Russian forces in its rear. The army rear area was safe except for partisan activities.

The composition of the brigade proved to be effective. The proper training for such a special mission requires from six to eight weeks with troops already experienced in Russian warfare. Before the attack the units must be in their jump-off positions for at least two weeks in order to become well-acquainted with terrain conditions through intensive reconnaissance. All intelligence and reconnaissance information must be carefully rechecked because the slightest inaccuracy can result in failure in that type of terrain.

Preliminary training in teamwork between armor and cavalry is of definite advantage. In an attack over this kind of terrain it may occasionally happen that the cavalry advances too fast. In that case the tanks must radio the cavalry to slow down because terrain difficulties prevent them from keeping up. Portable radio sets are not always reliable because of the density of the forest, and telephone communications therefore have to be used extensively. For that reason each regiment must carry more than the customary quantity of wire.

If possible every officer and enlisted man should be equipped with a sub-machine gun.

Rations should be concentrated; the lighter they are, the better. The American combat ration (K ration) would be well suited, particularly since it is also protected against moisture.

It would be advantageous to equip troops with rubber boots and impregnated raincoats, camouflage jackets and windbreakers, because dew causes a high degree of moisture in the underbrush. Camouflage covers for steel helmets are essential and camouflage in general is of utmost importance.

The commissioned and noncommissioned officers must be versatile and able to make quick decisions and improvise. Every officer must be able to act independently and ready to assume responsibility. Detailed inquiries addressed to higher echelons cause delays and unfavorable developments which can usually be avoided. Leaders with good common sense and a portion of recklessness are best suited for such special assignments. The scholarly type of officer who relies chiefly on maps is completely out of place.

In general, it may be said that the composition and equipment of the cavalry brigade proved effective for the special mission of advancing and attacking through marshy forests and along muddy paths.

Some Improvisations Used During Operation ZITADELLE

THE CROSSING OF RUSSIAN MINE FIELDS

In preparation for Operation ZITADELLE, the German pincer attack on Kursk during the summer of 1943, XI Infantry Corps made a thorough study of the problem of crossing the extensive mine fields on the east side of the Donets. The usual procedure of sending engineer detachments to clear narrow lanes for the advance of the infantry spearheads was not considered satisfactory since the terrain offered no cover and the enemy could inflict heavy casualties upon engineers and infantry by concentrating his fire on these lanes. Several improvised methods for overcoming this obstacle were therefore under consideration.

The identification of the mined area was the first prerequisite since the infantry had to know its exact location prior to the crossings. This was possible because the German-held west bank commanded the Russian positions on the other side of the river. Another prerequisite was that the infantry should be able to spot the location of individual mines at close range with the naked eye. In many places small mounds or depressions, dry grass, differences in the coloring of the ground, or some other external marks facilitated the spotting. The engineers had made a number of experiments in mine detecting. In the early days of the war, the infantry sometimes crossed narrow mine fields after individual engineers lay down beside the mines as human markers, taking great care not to set them off by pressure. Although neither engineers nor infantry troops suffered losses during these early experiments, the procedure was risky and could only be applied on a small scale. It was therefore of little consequence during the later stages of the war.

A second, more promising method that fulfilled expectations consisted of marking individual mines by placing small flags or other simple markers next to the mines. This was done by engineers or infantrymen who were trained in the recognition of mines. This procedure was applied repeatedly and showed better results than the first but its large-scale use presented difficulties. The third and best method was to thoroughly instruct all infantrymen in enemy mine-laying techniques and in spotting mines by using captured enemy mine fields as training grounds. This procedure required that all infantrymen be sent to rear areas in rotation and was therefore rather time-consuming.

These requirements could be met in the case of Operation ZITADELLE since the time of the attack had been twice postponed with an ensuing delay of several weeks. The divisions committed in the narrow attack zone had moved two thirds of their combat forces to the rear where the daily training schedule featured tanks passing over foxholes and the crossing of Russian-type mine fields. This training paid off since it helped the soldiers to overcome their fear of tanks and mines.

The beginning of the attack was so timed that the infantry would be able to detect the enemy mines without difficulty. All the mine fields were quickly crossed by spearheads which suffered practically no casualties. Only one battalion acted contrary to orders and attacked before daybreak, its commander being afraid that he might otherwise suffer heavy casualties from enemy fire while his men were crossing the extended open terrain in his zone. In the dark, this battalion ran into the previously uncovered mine fields and the two advance companies suffered approximately twenty casualties from mine explosions. When the battalion continued its advance by daylight it had no further losses.

After the first wave had passed through, the engineers rapidly cleared a number of lanes and marked them with colored tape so that the reserves and heavy weapons could follow. Again there were no mine casualties. Only when the supply units followed the infantry through the mine fields were some of the men and horses blown up by the mines because they were careless or tried to bypass obstacles.

How safely anyone experienced in the detection of mines could move around in these mine fields was demonstrated during a conference on a completely mined hill, attended by about twenty unit commanders and specialists. No one had previously set foot on this hill but it was the only place which afforded a good view of the terrain. During the ascent of the hill each mine was clearly marked and no accidents occurred even though the mine field was crossed in various directions.

This improvised procedure of crossing mine fields became common practice because it avoided many casualties, resulted in quick capture of enemy positions, and was therefore very effective in the Russian theater.

A FLAK DIVISION SERVES AS CORPS ARTILLERY

In the plan for Operation ZITADELLE XI Infantry Corps was to cover the southern wing of the panzer corps that was to spearhead the attack. For this purpose corps was reinforced by two light motorized artillery battalions and by the fully reorganized 7th Flak Division. This Luftwaffe division, composed of three regiments with seventy-two 88-mm. and approximately 900 smaller antiaircraft guns, was to serve as a substitute for missing medium artillery.

According to Luftwaffe policy the subordination of Flak officers to Army unit commanders was prohibited. The corps artillery commander therefore depended on the voluntary co-operation of the Flak division commander. This led to repeated minor frictions but worked out quite well in general.

The division's first mission was to take part in the artillery preparation under the direction of the corps artillery commander. For this purpose the division was echeloned in depth and committed in three waves of one regiment each. The first echelon was in position in the main line of resistance and closely behind it; its mission was to place direct fire on enemy heavy weapons and pillboxes. In addition it had to form Flak assault detachments for antitank combat to give close support to the advancing infantry. Together with the corps artillery, the two other regiments were to shatter the first enemy line of defense and paralyze his infantry by delivering sustained concentrations. After that, elements of the first echelon, with the exception of the assault detachments, as well as the entire second echelon, were to support the advancing infantry. The third echelon was to take over the antiaircraft protection of the entire artillery area and was also to participate in counterbattery missions.

Enemy intelligence found out that the attack was to start on 5 July at dawn. The Russians laid down intensive harassing fire on the jump-off positions but this interference ceased as soon as the German artillery concentrations started. These were placed so well and the initial shock was so great that the first assault wave was able to cross the enemy mine fields, penetrate his main line of resistance without delay, and thrust a few hundred yards beyond it. Thousands of tracers fired by the numerous small Flak guns proved particularly effective. The Russians abandoned the trenches immediately and fled into their deep dugouts where the advancing infantry surprised them and had no difficulty in ferreting them out. But when the infantry reached the two- to three-mile-deep zone of battle positions prepared during the preceding months, they had to make extensive use of hand grenades in order to mop up the maze of deeply dug-in trenches and bunkers, some of which were a dozen or more feet deep. At the same time artillery and Flak fired counterbattery on enemy heavy weapons which resumed fire from rear positions, on reserves infiltrating through trenches, and on medium artillery. The third echelon of the antiaircraft division was fully occupied with defense against enemy bombers which attacked the corps area incessantly. During the first two hours they downed more than twenty enemy planes.

Within eight hours the German infantry penetrated the enemy fortification system in its entire depth and reached the railroad embankment parallel to the Donets. Suddenly a Russian counterattack supported by forty tanks threw back the German covering force from the woods on the south flank and hit the right wing division which was echeloned in depth. But the defensive fire of the divisional artillery and a concentration of all medium antiaircraft batteries stopped the enemy counterattack at the edge of the forest. Then the medium Flak was directed against tank concentrations, which had been recognized in the underbrush, and dispersed them. Repeated enemy attempts to resume the attack from this area failed without exception. Flank protection was soon restored and the threat eliminated.

On the second day of the operation, the high ground ahead was captured under the protection of Flak artillery fire; all counterthrusts were repelled. On the morning of the third day the enemy attempted to recover lost ground and counterattacked with two heavy tank brigades and motorized infantry units. The tanks overran the battle line of the German infantry and penetrated deeply, but the motorized infantry which followed was repelled. The enemy tank break-through hit the corps center behind which, however, several Flak assault detachments and numerous medium antitank guns were sited in a mutually-supporting formation. The enemy ran into this dense network of antitank defenses as well as a flank attack by thirty-two assault guns and was completely annihilated. The last enemy tank which had penetrated to a divisional command post was surprised by an assault detachment carrying gasoline cans and was set on fire. Sixty-four enemy tanks had begun the counterattack and two hours later sixty-four black columns of smoke gave proof of their destruction. Discouraged by his failure, the enemy made no further attempts at an armored break-through at any point of the corps sector even though he had plenty of additional armored units available. The improvised commitment of the anti-aircraft division contributed decisively to this defensive success and the formation of Flak assault detachments proved highly effective in the destruction of Russian armor.

CHAPTER 2

The Defensive

Improvised Hedgehog Defenses

From the very first days of the campaign, the vastness of European Russia and the peculiarities of Russian warfare led to the repeated isolation of individual units and combat teams. All-around defenses and security measures were the only possible remedy. Far from being stressed, these defense tactics were frequently not even mentioned in the field service regulations. The field forces improvised them and designated them very appropriately as 'hedgehog defenses'. As time went on these tactics were applied more and more frequently and adopted by larger units. Their use was not confined to defense. During offensive actions advance detachments had to build hedgehog defenses as protection against enemy surprise attacks by night. For instance, during their advance through a swampy forest region in Lithuania where strong, dispersed enemy forces were reassembling, combat teams of 6th Panzer Division formed the first hedgehog positions during the initial week of the Russian campaign. Several hay barns in a major clearing were selected as the location for the divisional command post. Covered by thick underbrush, the tanks were placed in a wide circle around the barns with their guns ready to fire at the edge of the woods. In front of the tanks was an outer ring of infantry in foxholes and ditches and behind embankments which enabled the tanks to fire over their heads. Security patrols and outposts formed an outer cordon. The Russians recognized the strength of these protective measures and did not dare carry out the surprise attack they had planned. They resigned themselves to harassing the hedgehog area with tank and machine gun fire and a few rounds of artillery shells.

The hedgehog defense provided the troops with security and rest and thus passed its first major test. Before long these precautions became a routine security and defense measure for armored spearheads. The first large-scale employment of this measure occurred during the thrust toward Vyazma in October 1941 when an entire panzer division with 260 tanks spent the first night of the attack in an elaborate system of hedgehog positions in the woods (map 2). Forming the spearhead of a powerful wedge, the division had penetrated the enemy lines to a depth of twenty miles. In its rear and on its flanks defeated enemy divisions were withdrawing under cover of darkness. A retreating enemy corps staff sought refuge in a small isolated village in the forest which was occupied by the German divisional staff. Enemy troop units were around the entire system of tank hedgehogs. As long as the German tanks were on their own, the intermittent firing of flares and machine guns indicated their great uneasiness. This changed with the arrival of the armored infantry which followed the tanks. When the divisional artillery and engineers arrived and were also integrated into the hedgehog defense system, a restful night was had by all. Early next morning the Russians departed very quietly because they were unable to find any rest in the immediate vicinity of the German division.

DEFENSIVE IMPROVISATIONS IN EXTREME COLD

During the last days of 1941, the 6th Panzer Division was outmaneuvered by superior Russian forces and dislodged from a chain of villages which surrounded a large forest region. The division was faced with two alternatives: it could either withdraw a certain distance to another group of communities and be enveloped and split up, or it could establish defense positions in front of or between these indefensible villages in a temperature of $-49°F$ without adequate shelter which would mean certain death from exposure. During the engagements of the last few days, most of which had of necessity taken place in open terrain, the daily casualties from frostbite had increased at an alarming rate. By 3 January 1942 the number of moderate and severe frostbite casualties had risen to 800 per day. At that rate the division would soon have ceased to exist. The immediate construction of shelters and bunkers, with whatever heating facilities could be installed, was mandatory. But these defensive positions could not be built because only one corps and two divisional engineer battalions with 40 to 60 men each and very little equipment were available. On the other hand a large quantity of explosives had recently arrived at division. In view of the critical situation, the engineer battalion commanders were ordered to disregard the frost and to blast enough craters into the solidly frozen ground along the tentative defense line to provide shelter for all combat units including the reserves. These craters were to be echeloned in width and depth and were to hold three to five men each. The engineers were also to mine certain areas and build tank obstacles in three places. The reserves and service troops were ordered to pack down paths between the craters and to the rear. They were to use readily available lumber to cover the craters.

The blasting along the entire line started early next morning. The noise of the 10,000-pound explosive charges somehow gave the impression of a heavy barrage. Fountains of earth rose all around and dense smoke filled the air. The enemy watched with surprise, could not understand what was happening, and remained quiet. The blasting was over by noon and by nightfall the craters were covered and occupied by the combat elements. Soon afterward smoke rose from the craters where the crews kept warm at open fires. The craters formed an uninterrupted line of positions in front of which outposts were established. A maze of abatis lay in front of these, guns were emplaced along the thorough-fares behind the tank obstacles, and the entire front line was ready for defense within twelve hours after the first detonation. This position withstood all enemy attacks and was not abandoned until ten days later, in milder weather, when the adjacent units on both wings were forced to withdraw after enemy tanks had penetrated their lines.

The engineers who prepared the positions in the fiercest cold and suffered 40 percent frostbite casualties saved the combat units and restored the situation by their sacrifice. The very next day the casualties from frostbite dropped from 800 to 4 cases and thus practically ceased.

This improvisation was introduced at a time when 6th Panzer Division had lost all its tanks during the preceding withdrawal. Before blasting the positions, fighting had centered upon the possession of villages which alone could offer shelter from the extreme cold. Groups of villages had formed natural phase lines for both the attacker and the defender who had been forced to ignore all other tactical considerations. Whenever the Russians failed to capture a village by day, they withdrew to the last friendly village for the night. Not even the best-equipped Siberian troops attempted to continue an attack on a village after dusk. Blasting positions in open terrain was therefore an innovation that served the double purpose of stabilizing the front and maintaining the combat efficiency of the remnants of the division.

On another occasion the blasting of ice proved much less effective. In order to prevent the enemy from making an enveloping thrust across Lake Pskov on the Russian-Estonian border during the winter of 1943–44, Army Group North blasted a ten-foot-wide, several-mile-long canal into the ice north of the isle of Salita. At that time the ice was so thick that it could carry medium guns and prime movers. But here, as in other instances, it became apparent that the blasting of ice created no permanent obstacle because the water froze immediately in the extreme cold and shortly afterward the ice was again capable of carrying heavy loads. In extremely low temperatures all attempts to stop enemy advances by blasting frozen bodies of water were doomed to fail.

Almost a year later, toward the end of 1944, the Germans devised another improvisation to prevent the Russians from crossing a frozen body of water. By late autumn the Russians had driven a wedge into the German front near Memel [now Klaipeda] and had reached the Kurisches Haff (map 5). The Germans intended to prevent the landing of enemy forces on the west side of the Haff. A large-scale landing was not expected because the prerequisites for such an undertaking did not exist, but it seemed quite likely that the enemy would attempt to land sabotage or raiding parties, spies, agents, or commandos along the coast under cover of darkness. The coastal defenses composed of service units, volunteer organizations, and Volkssturm [peoples' militia assembled during the last years of the war] supported by weak reserve elements from Koenigsberg [now Kaliningrad] were thought to be sufficient to thwart any such operation.

It was a known fact that the Haff froze over in winter and that the ice cover would carry men and vehicles. This might encourage enemy attempts to envelop the exposed German wing, cut off the only supply route to Memel, or undertake some other major operation. For that reason plans were drawn up to block the Kurisches Haff in its entire width of ten miles.

In the late fall of 1944 a number of wooden bunkers with heating facilities were constructed for this purpose. They were approximately five feet high and could hold a crew of three to five men and their weapons. The bunkers were placed on rafts with sled runners in order to give them mobility on ice and simultaneously to protect them from sinking into the water in case the ice suddenly broke. This possibility had to be taken into account because of the sudden changes in temperature which occur in this area. By the end of December 1944 the first groups of bunkers were moved onto the freezing Haff, the edges of which were by then sufficiently strong to carry them. The bunker positions were spread over the ice as the freezing process progressed. Approximately 150 bunkers were laid out in two parallel lines in checkerboard formation, giving each other fire support. The bunkers were reinforced with blocks of ice on the outside and camouflaged with snow. A continuous line of entanglements with alarm signals was to prevent the enemy from infiltrating between the bunkers. Reserves were held in readiness behind both lines of bunkers. Ice boats and motor sleighs needed by the reserves to give them mobility did not arrive in time and the plans for organizing a combined ice-boat and motor-sleigh brigade had to be abandoned. Artillery support was provided from both shores.

Since the Russians lacked fast means of transportation on ice, they could only have advanced on foot over the long distances of the Haff. This was probably the reason why they failed to attack during the winter and this improvised position was therefore never put to the test.

A Moving Pocket Regains the German Lines

In some instances German divisions were left behind the Russian advance and were forced to fight their way back to the west. For example during the large-scale Russian offensive in the winter of 1942, the 320th Infantry Division, which had held a sector on the Don front with two Italian divisions at its sides, suddenly found itself behind the enemy lines because of the rapid disintegration of the allied units. The division commander decided to fight his way back to the German lines. On the way all the divisional motor vehicles ran out of gasoline and had to be destroyed. The horse-drawn batteries and trains also lost a great number of horses in battle and from exhaustion. Altogether, the fighting power and mobility of the division was greatly impaired. If it was not to resign itself to its fate, it had to resort to improvisations. What was needed either had to be wrested from the enemy or taken from the land. In this manner the division procured hundreds of small draft horses for the light vehicles. The medium artillery was drawn by oxen. Cows and oxen were used as draft animals for the transportation of radio and signal equipment. Even the division commander decided to use such a team as a sure means of transportation. The loss of many weapons such as machine guns, anti-tank guns, and artillery pieces could only be offset by weapons captured from weak enemy detachments on occasional raids. The ammunition needed for the use of captured weapons was also taken from the enemy and the same methods were applied in obtaining rations. Small radio sets and other sensitive equipment had to be carried on litters. Infantrymen mounted on *Panje* horses were charged with reconnaissance and security. The difficult retreat of the division took several weeks and was an uninterrupted series of marches, combat actions, and improvisations. As the division approached Kharkov, it suddenly made radio contact and asked the German units in the city for assistance in its attempt to break through to the German lines. A strong armored thrust from inside the city was co-ordinated with a simultaneous attack by the division. The enemy lines were pierced at the point designated by the division and it was able to rejoin the German lines. Its appearance hardly resembled that of a German unit. A strange conglomeration of weapons, equipment, vehicles, and litters, small and large shaggy horses, oxen and cows, accompanied by soldiers in a variety of winter clothing created the impression of a travelling circus on parade. And yet it was a battle-tested unit with excellent morale that had courageously fought its way through enemy territory, had returned to its own lines, and was to be considered a precious addition to the corps strength. By the following day the division once again stood shoulder to shoulder with the other corps units and held a sector facing east. Its strong will to survive and skillful improvisations enabled the division to regain its freedom.

Zone Defense Tactics

During the last years of the war, Russian break-throughs were accomplished by the same methods that had been employed so successfully by the same enemy in World War I. These methods had little in common with customary tactical doctrines but were based on great superiority of manpower and matériel. After weeks of logistical build-up and moving up the enormous quantities of ammunition needed, the German front was breached after several hours of concentrated fire. This was followed by the break-through of massed infantry forces and deep thrusts of armored units in order to gain freedom of maneuver. The system was absolutely foolproof so long as the opponent did not interfere with the sequence of events. An essential prerequisite was that the defender would rigidly hold that sector of the front, which was to be attacked, until he received the deadly blow. In the East the Germans complied with this pre-requisite since their forces had strict orders not to relinquish one inch of ground voluntarily. These defense tactics were enforced almost without exception until the end of the war. Being aware of the army's numerical inferiority and its loss of combat efficiency caused by heavy casualties, Hitler perhaps doubted its capability of conducting a flexible active defense and therefore ordered all army units to cling rigidly to prepared positions. But such tactics could never prevent an enemy break-through, let alone lead to victory. Despite the fact that Russian casualties were relatively heavier than those suffered by the Germans and the fighting qualities of the Russian soldiers vastly inferior to those of their opponents, the always-present crucial problem was to make up for the Russian superiority in men and matériel. Aside from their greater fighting capabilities the Germans had no other means of offsetting their inferiority than by employing more flexible and superior tactics. If the military leaders lost their faith in the superiority of the German armed forces in these two fields, or if shortages of matériel became so acute that these advantages could not be exploited, then a favorable outcome of this war was no more to be expected than in World War I. It was the responsibility of the Supreme Commander, Adolf Hitler, to recognize this fact and draw the necessary conclusions. Until that time it was the duty of the commanders in the field to do their utmost to prevent a collapse of the front lines. The greatest imminent threats to the fighting front were the Russian massed attacks with subsequent break-throughs. Since adequate reserves for successful defense were rarely available, it became all the more necessary to prevent the annihilation of the front-line units by Russian fire concentrations, bombing attacks, and massed armored thrusts in order to preserve their combat efficiency.

An improvisation devised for this purpose was the zone defense tactics introduced toward the end of the war. It was derived from an analysis of the reasons for the success of most enemy break-throughs. The principal factors to be considered were the following:

a. The annihilation of front-line troops by mass concentration on points along the main line of resistance;

b. The neutralization or destruction of the German artillery by heavy counterbattery fire and continuous air attacks;

c. The elimination of command staffs by air attacks and surprise fire on command posts up to army level;

d. The harassing of reserves by artillery fire and air attacks on their assembly areas;

e. The disruption of the routes of communication to the front which delayed movements of reserves and cut off supply;

f. The massed armored thrusts in depth which enabled the Russians to obtain freedom of maneuver.

For obvious reasons the task of the defender was to neutralize these enemy tactics or at least to reduce them to tolerable proportions. One of the panzer armies in the eastern theater devised the following defense measures and employed them successfully:

a. There were two ways of preventing the annihilation of the frontline troops: either by constructing bombproof and shellproof positions or by withdrawing the forward units in time to evade the devastating barrages. Since the construction of shellproof positions required an expenditure of time and materials beyond the German capabilities, the adoption of evasive tactics was the only solution. Such evasive tactics had already been employed during the last stage of World War I. The forward positions were evacuated shortly before an imminent attack and the defending troops moved far enough to the rear into a new and even stronger line to force the enemy to regroup his forces, always a time-consuming maneuver. The difficulties encountered by the enemy before he was able to resume the attack were to be enhanced by demolitions in the inter- mediate terrain. These evasive tactics were tried out in 1918 in the West when the German combat forces withdrew to the Hindenburg Position and in the South on the Italian front along the Piave River. The loss of some ground which was involved in the application of these tactics was a well-considered sacrifice. But to achieve a permanent gain was possible only if the new positions could be held without fail. Another method of evading fire concentration and a subsequent break-through was the adoption of elastic defense tactics in a deeply echeloned system of machine gun strong points which, however, often lacked the necessary resiliency to stop a major enemy attack.

A method frequently applied by the Germans as another form of evasion can best be compared with saber-fencing tactics. A cut is warded off by sudden retirement with appropriate guard, followed by an immediate counterthrust which will permit the fencer to regain his former position. Like the fencer, the forces holding the threatened sector of the front executed a surprise withdrawal at the last moment. They moved far enough to the rear so that the blow would miss them, the pursuing enemy could be repelled, and the initial position could be regained by a counterthrust. In order to satisfy these requirements, the terrain in which the pursuing enemy was to be intercepted had to be well chosen and systematically prepared in order that the withdrawing forces could resume the defense within a few hours. It was therefore neither possible nor essential to withdraw the front-line units so far to the rear that they were out of reach of enemy guns. Past experience indicated that the enemy fired his concentrations only on the main line of resistance and on strong points in the zone of resistance. For this reason it was absolutely necessary to evacuate this zone. Depending on the terrain and local fortifications, it was usually quite sufficient to withdraw the most forward troops 900 to 2,200 yards. Here was the forward edge of the battle position, a well-camouflaged organized system of defense that took advantage of all favorable terrain features. Numerous strong points and sizable local reserves were distributed throughout the positions which extended back to the artillery emplacements and even beyond. In a camouflaged area behind the artillery were the general reserves of corps and army. By following this procedure, targets were so well dispersed that fire from as many as a thousand guns directed at so large an area could cause only local damage but could never wipe out entire units.

b. If the German artillery was to avoid neutralization and escape destruction it had to switch to alternate emplacements in the battle position at the decisive moment. In addition the artillery also had to use alternate observation posts. These alternate positions had to be prepared well in advance, provided with ammunition, and equipped with a smoothly functioning wire and radio communication system. Additional battery positions and observation posts had to be reconnoitered and organized in depth so that they would be ready for immediate occupancy and utilization in case of emergency. This was to guarantee continuous support for the infantry even in the event of a reverse since only the flexible employment of artillery units which were always intact and ready to strike promised a successful defense. Furthermore, each battery had to establish two or three additional alternate positions and one or two dummy positions and had to fire from them with at least one registration gun in order to determine firing data for every emplacement. Altogether between five and eight positions had to be prepared by each battery. The Russian build-up allowed sufficient time for such extensive preliminary work and the Germans could therefore devote several weeks to these preparations.

c. All necessary precautions had to be taken to protect the command staffs and their communication system from destruction by artillery preparations and the ensuing general attack. For that reason no command staff from battalion up to army was permitted to stay at the command post it occupied before the start of the enemy attack. Each staff had to prepare a well-camouflaged, shellproof command post away from inhabited communities and was required to install a telephone switchboard in a separate bunker. Communications with the command post had to be assured by wire, radio, visual signals, dispatch riders, or runners, and in an emergency by a combination of these various means of communication. Telephone wires had to be laid in such manner that they could not easily be cut by fire or tracked vehicles; wherever possible they were laid along ditches and swampy depressions or strung on trees. Radio trucks had to be dug into the ground in inconspicuous places, protected against fragments, and well camouflaged before the attack started. Then strict radio silence had to be enforced.

d. Before the general attack, all reserves had to leave their billeting areas and move into the battle-position quarters which had to be well camouflaged, outside inhabited communities, and ready for immediate use. Telephone, radio, and other communication media had to be readily available.

e. The routes of communication to the front were of vital importance and therefore had to be kept open under all circumstances. Bottlenecks had to be avoided, defective stretches of road made serviceable even in inclement weather, and strict traffic control imposed for two-way traffic. Alternate bridges had to be built in suitable places away from the existing ones and provided with approach roads. At least two alternative routes had to be determined through each community so that convoys could detour narrow streets whenever there was danger of air attacks.

f. One of the major problems was to intercept massed armored attacks and prevent break-throughs. This involved extensive countermeasures which could only gradually be enforced and slowly integrated into the defense system.

First of all the terrain particularly suited for an armored break-through was mined to a quite unusual extent. Selecting such areas and mining them with due consideration for Russian tactical doctrine presented little difficulty to an experienced panzer expert. The numerous mine fields were to be laid in depth and width in a checkerboard pattern in such a manner that the Germans armored units could detour them on the basis of information received. All signs designating mine fields were removed prior to the enemy attack. No mines were laid in front of the German main line of resistance because the enemy could have removed them and used them for his own purposes before the start of the attack. The main battle position was mined in depth up to fifteen miles to the rear. Prior to the major offensive in the area east of Lvov during the summer of 1944, the sector where the main attack thrust was expected was mined with 160,000 antipersonnel and 200,000 antitank mines within the zone defense. This was the first time that the Germans applied zone defense tactics of the type described in this study.

The most forward divisional antitank guns had to take up positions approximately one mile behind the main line of resistance. The bulk of the artillery and numerous medium antitank and antiaircraft guns were to form centers of gravity behind the forward guns up to twelve miles in depth. In addition, all roads suitable for sudden armored thrusts in depth were blocked by tank obstacles, captured immobile antitank guns, and antiaircraft guns emplaced at all important points up to a depth of twenty-five miles. In case of critical developments numerous self-propelled antitank guns were to reinforce the defense. To camouflage these guns, tank ditches had to be dug and approach roads built in suitable terrain.

The army reserves had to be sufficiently strong to support the front and stop the enemy in case he suddenly shifted his main effort and turned his tanks to an adjacent sector which had not been prepared according to zone defense principles. For instance, during the battle near Lvov the army commander held in reserve five strong panzer divisions which he had withdrawn from sectors that were not in immediate danger. Two of them were to support the front in the center of gravity and the three strongest were to be instantly committed to stop any armored thrust elsewhere in case the enemy shifted his point of main effort. The two divisions assigned to the center of gravity were expected to be able to lend them assistance in due course. The reserves formed mobile battle groups and equipped them with many antitank and assault guns in order to enable them to give immediate support to frontline sectors threatened by sudden disintegration. In most cases these battle groups consisted of reconnaissance or motorcycle battalions reinforced by antitank and assault gun battalions which were held in instant readiness and formed advance detachments of their respective divisions.

The task of indoctrinating the unit commanders in all the essential zone defense measures was far from easy. After detailed briefings, map exercises, and tactical walks, they not only grasped the idea but became thoroughly convinced of the expediency and feasibility of the plan and lent their enthusiastic support to its execution. Discussions and training exercises continued down the line to the smallest units.

The next step was to put these measures to their practical test and examine them in the light of experience. Starting with individual arms, these tests were later extended to larger units. Finally, zone defense tactics were adopted and enforced by entire divisions and corps. The tremendous effort entailed in these preparations was to pay high dividends.

The fencer derives an advantage from cutting into his opponent's sequence when the latter intends to strike because the attacker usually exposes himself on that occasion. This intercepting blow was also included in the zone defense tactics. Since the enemy moved his forces close to his most advanced positions and massed them before jumping off to attack, he exposed himself to concentrated surprise fire from all artillery pieces and rocket launchers. Two basic loads of every type of ammunition had been set aside for just that purpose.

The most difficult and critical problem was to determine the correct time for withdrawing to the battle position. If too late a moment was chosen, the safety measures against the annihilation of the combat forces by an enemy barrage would have remained ineffective. The front-line units and intermediate commands alone were unable to gather sufficient positive clues regarding the hostile intentions to enable the higher echelons to draw the correct conclusions as to when the enemy attack would begin. This can be easily understood since their observation of enemy activities were restricted to the most advanced areas of the front. But well-organized combat intelligence and constant air observation, co-ordinated by the army commander in person, gathered so much information on enemy preparations and covered his rear areas so completely that the H Hour for the attack could be determined with a high degree of accuracy. The most reliable information was secured by radio interception. As much as 70 percent of all reliable information was obtained from this source.

The improvised defense system was first applied in the summer of 1944 in the battle of Lvov and for the second time in January 1945 during the second battle for East Prussia. In both instances the Russians attacked at precisely the point and in exactly the manner expected by the army commander who devised this zone defense system. H Hour for the enemy attack in East Prussia was determined to the exact day and hour. In the battle near Lvov, however, the enemy started his offensive two days later than expected. Interrogation of prisoners confirmed that the attack was postponed by two days at the last moment. As a result the evasive maneuver had to be repeated on three successive nights. On the first day the Russians either did not notice the withdrawal because German rear guards left in the forward positions simulated the weak routine harassing fire or they lacked time to react to this sudden change. On the second day they attacked several evacuated positions with combat teams up to regimental strength and pushed back the rear guards.

Even this turn of events was foreseen in the original plan. Strong counterthrusts supported by massed artillery fire from the regular firing positions sealed off the enemy penetrations and at dusk the former main line of resistance was once again occupied by the infantry. As expected, the enemy resumed his attacks during the night to find out whether the Germans would continue to occupy the positions. When these night attacks had been repelled everywhere and the Russians had convinced themselves that the positions were held by their full complements, the fighting broke off and the front calmed down. After midnight the positions were evacuated for the third time and, when the enemy fire concentration was unleashed at dawn, it hit empty positions. The units that had moved into the battle position suffered hardly any losses and, supported by assault guns and one battalion of Royal Tiger tanks, they were able to drive back nearly all Russian forces which had advanced beyond the empty positions. The artillery preserved its entire fire power because the shelling and air bombardment hit the empty

battery positions which assumed the role of dummies. Not a single gun, not
a single command post was hit. The telephone communications from army
down to regiment suffered no disruption. But the former positions that had
been evacuated were in poor shape. The towns were badly damaged by air
attacks, and the debris of bombed buildings blocked the main roads in several villages. Nevertheless, the traffic continued to move along the previously
designated alternate routes and was stopped only intermittently whenever
the enemy air force scored direct hits on convoys.

The reserves were left untouched by the air attacks directed against them
since they had moved to locations that were unknown to the enemy. The
advancing Russian infantry was hit by the defensive fire of an artillery and
rocket launcher brigade which was fully intact and well supplied with
ammunition. When the enemy infantry attempted to disperse and take cover it
walked straight into the mine fields which had been laid behind the German
main line of resistance. This took the momentum out of the attack and prevented the Russian infantry from concentrating its effort in one direction. The
advance slowed down and became hesitant. Practically all territorial gains had
to be abandoned by the Russians when the German troops that had evaded the
destructive effect of the initial barrage started to counterattack later during the
day. The distress signals sent out by the Russian infantry brought their armor to
the scene. Like a cataract released by the sudden opening of a dam, the massed
armor poured across the Seret River into the historic battle ground of
Yaroslavichi where exactly thirty years before, during the summer of 1914,
Austro-Hungarian and Russian cavalry divisions had clashed head on in the last
major cavalry charge in history.

History repeated itself. Once again the Russians had numerical superiority
and once again the battle ended in a draw. In 1914 the defender achieved this
result by the use of new machine gun and artillery tactics whereas in 1944 he
introduced zone defense tactics to overcome his inferiority. On the very first day
of the armored attack, the enemy lost eighty-five tanks in the mine fields. The
number of tanks lost increased rapidly when the armored thrust came within
reach of the antitank guns and was brought to a halt. The losses assumed truly
disastrous proportions when the German panzer divisions proceeded to
counterattack.

In 1914 as in 1944 the battles for Lvov were not decided by the cavalry
charge or the armored thrust near Yaroslavichi but by a major Russian break-
through north of Lvov in the adjacent army sector to which the enemy shifted
his main effort. Unfortunately for the Germans in 1944, the SS panzer corps
with the three strongest panzer divisions had previously been transferred to the
Western Front because the Allies had meanwhile landed in France. For this
reason sufficient forces were no longer available to stop the Russian armored
drive in the new area of penetration.

Improvised Fortresses

By 1944, after the Germans had suffered a succession of defeats, Hitler frequently tried to reverse the tide by the arbitrary designation of fortresses. In the face of an imminent enemy attack, many towns suddenly became improvised fortresses and had to suffer encirclement and siege as if they were well-equipped strongholds that had been systematically constructed and provisioned over a number of years. A commander was appointed for each fortress, given absolute powers, and put under a special oath. He thereby received authority of life and death over all persons within his jurisdiction and could employ them as he saw fit, even though most of them were merely passing through his territory. These men and their equipment were frequently the only resources at the disposal of the commander who actually was forced to pick them off the streets.

Thus, the city of Kolberg was declared a fortress early in March 1945 when the battle for Pomerania was in full swing. The small city was overcrowded with wounded, the railroad station filled with hospital trains. Columns of refugee carts blocked the roads and enemy tanks were only twenty-five miles off. Precisely at that moment the newly appointed fortress commander who was entirely unfamiliar with the situation was flown in by plane. He was not acquainted with the duties of a fortress commander and had to be briefed in detail. The fortress was absolutely defenseless. Hitler's attention was called to this fact, but he nevertheless decided that Kolberg must be held as a fortress under all circumstances. In his reply Hitler stated that the Spandau depot would receive instructions to immediately dispatch twelve new antitank guns to Kolberg by rail. This was at a time when the single-track railroad line to Kolberg was completely blocked and enemy tanks were expected to appear in the immediate vicinity of the city within a few hours. Obviously, the antitank guns never arrived. The commander was forced to pick his defense force and weapons from the streets. Indiscriminately everybody and everything moving through the city was stopped, whether they were Luftwaffe, naval personnel, damaged tanks, antiaircraft, antitank, or artillery guns, and integrated into the fortress defenses.

It was difficult to imagine why Hitler decided that this former small coastal fort should be defended, unless for historical reasons. In modern times, however, the events that occurred in Napoleon's day could not possibly be repeated. However, the enemy seemed to be impressed by the glorious past of the city because his approach was slow and hesitant. The first Russian attack was delayed for two days, but the defensive tactics employed by the Germans soon revealed their weakness and after only a few days the enemy captured the city. Most of the entirely improvised garrison was rescued by the Navy.

The location of some of the fortresses was so unfavorable that their defense seemed hopeless from the outset. Despite all remonstrances, even these places had to be held at all cost. For instance, Brody, a small town in eastern Galicia completely surrounded by woods, was located in a valley without observation facilities. Dominated by a nearby plateau in enemy hands, the town was under complete enemy observation and at the mercy of his artillery. At one point the woods even reached up to the edge of the town. Because of the lack of space, there was not even a suitable area for the artillery emplacements in case of a siege. In order to avoid an imminent disaster, the army commander circumvented Hitler's orders and adopted tactics that prevented a siege of the town.

The situation at Ternopol was similar; there the garrison held out bravely for one month only to succumb for lack of rations and ammunition after an attempt to break the siege had bogged down in the mud.

By the end of January 1945 one of the German panzer armies had three of its best divisions in Fortress Koenigsberg, two in Fortress Memel, and only the two weakest at its disposal for operations in the field. At this decisive time an entire army group with the best available troops was hemmed in in Kurland and eliminated from participation in the defense of the German homeland because it had strict orders to hold out in place.

These tactics were championed by Hitler in person and enforced with all the authoritative powers at his disposal. In the end they obstructed all operational freedom and devoured the very substance of the German Army until there was no army left.

But the picture was entirely different whenever the encircled forces broke out and remained intact. In February 1943 Kharkov was surrounded by enemy armies and ordered to hold out in a hopeless situation. In his last telephone message the corps commander called attention to the seriousness of the situation and stated emphatically that the only choice was between losing the city alone or losing the city with all the troops in it. The reply was that 'Kharkov must be held to the last man.' On the following morning a second order came through by teletype stating that 'Kharkov must be held to the last man but the defenders must not allow themselves to be encircled.' On the strength of this ambiguous order, the second part of which precluded the first, the encircled corps took immediate steps for a breakout to the rear without the knowledge or approval of army. After two days of hard fighting, which ended with the loss of several hundred motor vehicles, this corps rejoined the German lines. The decision proved to be correct for, together with some divisions detrained in the Poltava area under its protection, the corps was able to launch a counterattack only one month later, recapture Kharkov and Belgorod, and reach the upper Donets.

This example demonstrates very convincingly that it is not of decisive importance to hold a town at all cost but rather to have some forces available for further operations.

Defensive Improvisations in East Prussia

As the danger of an invasion of eastern Germany loomed toward the end of 1944, tens of thousands of civilians were mobilized to construct a number of continuous defense lines in East Prussia. Everywhere people could be seen digging trenches and defense positions. Altogether twelve main defense lines and switch positions were constructed, many of which were well equipped. Perhaps their most outstanding feature was the construction of improvised machine gun emplacements which were very practical and consisted of two large concrete pipes. One pipe stood upright in the ground and served as the gun emplacement proper whereas the horizontal pipe was connected to the base of the upright one and employed as a personnel shelter. This improvisation offered shelter against tanks, could be constructed in a minimum of time, was easy to transport, and highly effective.

In addition to these defensive positions a continuous antitank ditch was constructed which cut across all roads. Temporary bridges, ready for immediate demolition in case of emergency, spanned the ditch where it cut through the roads. Some 18,000 laborers were diverted to the construction of this antitank ditch alone, although they were badly needed to build fortified defensive zones. In order that such zones could be prepared at least in the most essential areas, every man belonging to reserve, service, supply, or headquarters units was assigned his daily quota of obligatory digging that was measured in cubic feet. If necessary the work had to be done at night. To get these positions ready for immediate winter occupancy, the rear echelon units as well as Volkssturm battalions moved into the positions to make the quarters livable. Slit trenches were dug along the roads and antitank and machine gun nests were prepared at all important points. Perimeter defenses were established around every village and hamlet.

The over-all effect of these numerous, fully integrated defense installations was to transform the most vulnerable northeastern part of Germany into one great fortress area. Although some of the defensive positions never played any part in the subsequent fighting, others proved very useful during the battle for East Prussia. If they failed to change the fate of that doomed province, it was due to the entirely insufficient number of troops and to the inadequacy of the weapons which could be mustered for its defense.

CHAPTER 3

Troop Movements

Furlough and Troop Trains under Partisan Attacks

Precautionary measures for the protection of railroads had to be stepped up because of increasing partisan activities in the East. Furlough and troop trains moving over railroad lines which crossed partisan-infested forests were organized as combat units. When a man was sent on furlough he had to carry his rifle until he reached a designated station. He left it there and picked it up on his return trip. The transport commander was simultaneously combat commander, the ranking man in every car was car commander. Demolition of tracks combined with raids from the forests which came close to the lines on both sides were to be expected at all times, particularly at night. In case of a surprise attack or upon a specific alarm signal, the occupants of all cars were instructed to jump off – even-numbered cars to the left, odd-numbered to the right – and to repel the attack. A few assault detachments and a small reserve remained at the disposal of the transport commander in case of a special emergency.

An interesting incident occurred in November 1942 when 6th Panzer Division was moved to the area south of Stalingrad after its rehabilitation in Brittany. The division was loaded on seventy-eight trains of approximately fifty cars each. Each train was organized for combat in accordance with the above-mentioned procedure. Numerous raids and surprise attacks occurred during the trip through the marshy forests. Only a few trains got through the Pripyat region without incident. Most of the attacks were directed against the trains hauling tanks and artillery, and fierce fighting broke out in each instance. One artillery battalion commander and several men were killed and a number of officers and men wounded. The trains were greatly delayed and many of them had to be rerouted. During the ten-day trip they were mixed up and arrived at their destination in improper order and long overdue. A special problem was created by the fact that the trains loaded with artillery and tanks arrived last because twenty such trains were attacked by partisans, some of them repeatedly. This matériel was urgently needed because, from the time when the first train unloaded at Kotelnikovo, the division was under enemy artillery fire and the railroad station was attacked by dismounted cavalry. To secure and enlarge the detraining area required additional fighting. The division had to detrain where the enemy was assembling his forces because there was no continuous German front in this area after the encirclement of Stalingrad. It was due only to enemy hesitation that the units, which had just been unloaded and lacked heavy weapons support, did not get into serious trouble. The enemy started his attack on the assembly area of the completely isolated division immediately after the arrival of the trains carrying the German tanks. On 5 December 1942 an entire Russian cavalry corps with sixty-four tanks drove into the flank of the assembly area south of the Aksay River and achieved a penetration. But during the night the German tanks were unloaded close to the enemy. Some of them were detrained outside the railroad station and prepared for the counterthrust. On 6 December the bulk of the division with 160 tanks attacked the enemy's flank near Pokhlebin, cut off his retreat, and pushed him against the steep banks of the unfordable Aksay. The Russians suffered a crushing defeat from which only small remnants of the corps and six tanks were able to escape.

The Commitment of Furlough Battalions

A few weeks later when the Russians broke through along the Don, the Germans attempted to establish a new front along the Donets River. The situation was serious. The forces available were weak because several armies put in the field by Germany's allies had suddenly collapsed. Every German unit, every German soldier was urgently needed to strengthen the front.

Upon returning from furlough members of units enclosed in the Stalingrad pocket were stopped at Kamensk Shakhtinski on the Donets, assembled, organized into a battalion, and immediately committed along the Donets east of the city. A young first lieutenant was appointed battalion commander and noncommissioned officers commanded the companies. The men came from various units and arms. They did not know their leaders who in turn did not know their men. Equipped with rifles and only a few machine guns, they were to defend a six-mile sector along the river.

The Russians soon spotted this weak sector and, covered by tanks and artillery, crossed the Donets with greatly superior forces and attacked the battalion. They broke through the thinly manned front at various points and advanced swiftly toward the south. The infantry division to which the battalion was attached was involved in heavy defensive battles and could not provide any help. But mobile reserves of the 6th Panzer Division which held the sector adjacent to the east moved up quickly and attacked the enemy from the rear. Within a few hours the hostile force was destroyed and its remnants captured or shattered. After a few more hours the furlough battalion which had suffered heavy casualties was reassembled. It was immediately disbanded and the men were assigned to their basic arms within the panzer division, where their capacities could again be fully utilized. Every individual member of the furlough battalion was a battle-tested front-line soldier. But hastily assembled in an improvised unit, without the essential heavy weapons, these men could not be utilized in accordance with their abilities. The battalion was doomed in this unequal battle.

The formation of furlough battalions was an unavoidable expedient in critical situations, but it really meant the improper expenditure of good combat soldiers. For this reason furlough battalions had to be dissolved as quickly as possible and the men returned to their original units.

CHAPTER 4

Combat Arms

Infantry

In pursuit, German and enemy forces alike found it expedient to mount on tanks. This improvisation proved effective on innumerable occasions when a defeated enemy was to be pursued. For instance, when 6th Panzer Division spearheaded the drive of Army Group North during the first days of July 1941, it broke through the pillbox-studded Stalin Line after two days of fighting (map 2). The enemy offered renewed resistance farther to the northeast but after a few hours the Russians were dislodged from the fortified frontier zone and dispersed into the surrounding forests. In order to take possession of three major bridges before their destruction, it was necessary to prevent the enemy from gaining another foothold. Spearhead panzer units, composed of some fifty tanks with infantry mounted, pursued the retreating Russians relentlessly, occupied the bridges, and – meeting with little resistance – reached the day's objective, the city of Ostrov, within three hours.

Another good example was the battle of annihilation fought southeast of Plavskoye in the Army Group Center sector. It started in the middle of November 1941 when an enemy cavalry division attacked the exposed flank of the army group. Assault guns were to disperse the enemy formations and infantry was to annihilate his forces completely. In order to move the infantry straight into the depth of the battlefield together with the assault guns, volunteers from infantry units mounted the assault guns and, hanging on like grapes on a vine, rode into the enemy lines with all guns ablaze. The enemy cavalry division was obliterated.

In both instances the enemy was totally vanquished and shattered. The completeness of the success of this improvisation can be traced to the panic spread in the enemy ranks by the German tanks. But whenever the enemy was firmly entrenched in front or on the flanks, this venture turned out to be dangerous and costly. During the later years of the war this improvisation was generally discontinued because of heavy casualties caused by antitank weapons and air attacks. Moreover, it was superseded by the introduction of armored personnel carriers.

The Russians also used this expedient repeatedly and found it a fast means of transportation. But whenever they encountered German resistance they always suffered heavy casualties from machine gun fire. For that reason they discontinued this practice when they came close to the German lines.

Artillery

In position warfare daily fire direction exercises carried out by the artillery and infantry howitzers assumed great significance. During these exercises all wire and radio communications were prohibited for extended periods. As substitutes field expedients had to be used to maintain communications between observation posts and gun positions. Some of the media employed were signals transmitted by discs, inscriptions on blackboards read with the help of field glasses, mounted messengers, runners, and relayed messages. Much time was devoted to training in Morse code transmission by signal lamps.

Since the German infantry units were usually understrength the Russians were often able to infiltrate through their defense lines. The artillery positions therefore had to be fortified and constructed as strong points in the depth of the defensive zone. The artillerymen had to be given advanced infantry training and were issued extra machine guns and hand grenades whenever possible. The gun crews had to be ready to make counterthrusts which were specified in the combat orders of each battery.

Such a system of strong points proved effective during the summer of 1943 when the Germans were engaged in heavy defensive battles west of Kharkov. The artillery troops intercepted an enemy force which had infiltrated through sunflower fields. For a while the situation looked very critical but the artillerymen, fighting a delaying action, gained sufficient time for the launching of a counterattack which led to the annihilation of the enemy forces.

Some German commands on the Russian front issued orders prohibiting their artillery from firing on enemy command posts. The enemy was to feel secure and was to establish a network of communication lines and observation posts based on his command posts and was not to suffer any interference during that time. But the destruction of uncovered command posts was to be prepared in such a manner that it could be carried out instantaneously in accordance with the demands of the tactical situation. The sudden elimination of enemy command installations never failed to produce a favorable effect on offensive or defensive operations.

Flat trajectory fire from howitzers proved very effective in clearing tree tops in forest fighting. In one instance, during operations near Leningrad in the autumn of 1942, marshy terrain prevented the howitzers from going into position to deliver flat trajectory fire and to assist in the penetration of a large wooded area. The following tactics were therefore employed to cross the wooded region: all artillery pieces, heavy infantry howitzers, antiaircraft guns, and ground support planes were temporarily subordinated to the artillery commander so that he could exercise centralized fire direction. Heavy rolling barrages systematically raked the woods and cleared lanes in one sector after another. For this purpose the wooded zone was divided into 1,600-foot squares which, in turn, were subdivided into 400-foot squares. Artillery, infantry, and

Luftwaffe units marked identical squares on their maps. According to the attack plan one square after another was raked by heavy concentrations either from front to rear or from rear to front or alternately, but always in conformity with the requests of the assault troops. Smoke shells were interspersed to obstruct the enemy's vision and prevent him from conducting a systematic defense of the forest. The forward assault units were withdrawn a few hundred yards shortly before H Hour to enable the artillery to soften up the enemy positions without endangering the infantry. The delay caused by this withdrawal was made up by the immediate launching of the attack as soon as the fire lifted. During the course of the assault the advancing infantry closely followed each shift of fire, moving into each square as soon as it had been cleared, and proceeded to mop it up.

The detection of German artillery positions by enemy observation was sometimes made more difficult by camouflaging the firing report with the help of an improvised device that simulated detonations. At the beginning of the war most observation battalions were equipped with such simulating devices, but later on only few of them were available and those few were inadequate for actual deception because of the great variety of guns used in counterbattery fire and for infantry support. Actual deception of the enemy artillery observation could only be achieved if the deceptive firing report sounded like the detonation of a real gun both to the enemy ear and to his sound-ranging equipment. A close similarity between the actual and the deceptive report was achieved with the assistance of engineer specialists who built a makeshift detonation device which was thoroughly tested behind the front. The amount of explosives used in this device was regulated in accordance with data provided by the sound-ranging check points. These experiments were continued until the instruments finally showed that the detonations could have originated from 150-mm. field howitzers or 210-mm. howitzers. Furthermore it was established that the most effective deception could be achieved by placing the detonation device approximately one mile to the front of the battery which was to be protected but never on its sides or to its rear.

The results of these experiments were confirmed in 1942, when it was necessary to deceive the enemy about the positions and strength of the German artillery in the Volkhov sector of Army Group North. There the 818th Artillery Regiment was faced by numerically superior Russian artillery in extremely narrow positions hemmed in by woods, marshes, and impassable terrain. Deception was essential in order to protect the positions from counterbattery fire and air attacks and to divert the enemy fire by misdirecting it into unoccupied territory. For some time the impact areas of the enemy fire in the immediate vicinity of the detonation devices gave the impression that the improvisation had served its purpose and that the enemy had been deceived, at least for a while. Yet, some caution against over-estimating the effect on an alert and well-trained enemy may well be indicated. Although the accuracy of his observation can often be frustrated by distorting the sound patterns at his control points, the continuous deception of the enemy requires the introduction of a few additional improvisations which might present inconveniences to the artillery units applying them. These are:

a. Several men would have to be permanently assigned to servicing the detonation device and maintaining telephone communications with the gun emplacements. In co-ordinating the simulated detonations to the actual gun reports it is necessary to pay careful attention to the velocity-of-sound factor.

b. The dummy positions must have the outward appearance of fully occupied firing positions. This can be achieved by burning wood fires that leave traces of smoke in the air and show up on air reconnaissance photos.

c. It will be helpful if the camouflage materials are frequently renewed, particularly in the event that tree trunks are supposed to represent guns.

In the field of sound deception, which assumed particular importance when a weak force faced a considerably stronger enemy, several other expedients proved quite effective:

a. Co-ordinating the fire of several batteries or battalions by issuing simultaneous fire commands over the wire or radio fire direction system in order to prevent the enemy from identifying individual emplacements.

b. Moving individual guns out of the firing positions and including these roving guns in the fire-command system.

c. Combining a medium battery with a light howitzer battery for simultaneous firing, particularly during the registration fire by sound and flash methods which provided the data for firing for effect, since these preliminaries always took time and were easily observed by the enemy.

Critical ammunition shortages forced the artillery to fire almost exclusively on observed point targets. In view of the circumstances this produced better results than firing on area targets with insufficient ammunition. Harassing fire by sudden concentrations was also excluded. Instead, slow fire by single pieces from many batteries had to be carried out simultaneously according to a precise firing plan. The advantage of this method was that it could be continued all through the night and that enemy communications to the front could thus be seriously hampered and more effectively disrupted than by intermittent concentrations. This expedient was successfully applied at Sevastopol in 1942. According to intercepted radio messages all Russian supply movements had come to a standstill during the nights preceding the German assault.

In many instances the Germans were painfully short of artillery for area targets while the Russians always had plenty of multi-barreled rocket launchers and long-range heavy mortars. These were the most suitable weapons to cover an area with surprise fire and to protect flanks.

During position warfare the Germans made up for this deficiency by flexible artillery tactics which included many improvisations. They fired mass concentrations on single point targets when all batteries within range would fire one round. If, for instance, eighty batteries were within range of a target, it would be hit by eighty rounds on one single command. As a result, the individual batteries achieved a maximum concentration on a given area with a minimum expenditure of ammunition. The effect was excellent and this procedure had the additional advantage of frustrating all enemy attempts to detect the location of individual batteries by sound range.

Whenever there was a shortage of antitank guns and whenever defensive sectors were overextended, field howitzers and antiaircraft guns were used as antitank weapons by the Germans. They were emplaced in rear area strong points and were given the mission of stopping at point-blank range all enemy tanks and assault forces which might break through. The field howitzer batteries frequently consisted of only three guns which, however, proved fully sufficient for routine missions particularly when ammunition was in good supply. A Russian cavalry division which had broken through in the 97th Light Infantry Division sector in the winter of 1941 was routed by field-howitzer fire from all directions.

On 26 July 1941 another German infantry division committed its entire artillery regiment for antitank defense against an enemy corps north of Lvov. After the Russians lost a large number of tanks they were no longer in a position to continue the attack. In later years armored break-through attempts repeatedly failed due to the improvised antitank defense system of the artillery. The standing operating procedure for light artillery batteries prescribed that only three guns were assigned to purely artillery missions whereas the fourth was to be employed as antitank weapon.

Although the inaccuracy resulting from wide dispersion made rocket launchers generally unsuitable as antitank weapons, they occasionally proved effective in massed fire. Thus, during the fighting around Minsk in July 1941, an armored thrust launched by the Russians from the woods south of the city was stopped with the assistance of two rocket launcher batteries. In massed fire they scored some direct hits on tanks and succeeded in shooting the turret off one tank.

Massed fire by several rocket launcher battalions against an enemy armored attack echeloned in depth had a particularly strong impact on enemy morale. During the fighting near Voronezh in mid-July 1942 an armored thrust, launched by the Russians from cover of nearby forests, ground to a halt in the face of rocket-launcher fire. Several tanks attempting to infiltrate through gullies were stopped by the fire of some 300-mm. mobile launchers.

Particularly in this case the psychological effect was greater than the material damage. The tanks stopped and the crews dismounted and ran away. The other tanks which formed the main spearhead turned back in the face of 320-mm. incendiary rockets. Actually, rocket launchers were not intended for fire on point targets or the destruction of tanks.

Combat Engineers as Infantry

When critical situations developed in wide sectors the Germans were often forced to employ combat engineer units as infantry. But this expedient backfired because many essential and almost irreplaceable engineer specialists were lost in combat. This wasteful dissipation of valuable personnel had to be repeated over and over again despite the fact that the responsible commanders were fully aware of its disadvantages. Necessity knows no laws; in critical situations every available man had to be committed at the front. The employment of combat engineers as infantry was very tempting because they were trained for combat and also because they were exceptionally good soldiers. Many commanders were prompted to commit them as infantry when the situation did not fully justify the change. This was all the more regrettable since it was none other than the infantry which had to pay for the improper utilization of the engineers. In extreme emergencies it was of course necessary to use engineer units as infantry. On many occasions the courage and staunchness of the engineers saved the day. For example, when the enemy broke through southwest of Rzhev in 1942, a corps engineer regiment, all engineer units of one division, and even all the construction engineer companies and some of the road-building battalions from the vicinity were committed to stop the Russian thrust into the rear of Ninth Army. The engineers halted the enemy advance and allowed the tactical command sufficient time for countermeasures which eliminated the danger (map 2).

CHAPTER 5

Indispensable Expedients

The German supply and transportation system in Russia was greatly dependent on improvisations because of the peculiarities of terrain and climate. From the outset of the campaign, supply columns were improvised with motor vehicles of every type which had been requisitioned from private owners. They did not fully replace standard military columns since some of the vehicles were in poor condition and therefore of little service. In addition, the problem of replacing spare parts for so many different types of trucks caused incessant difficulties. Yet, most of these vehicles were in service for many years and some of them lasted for the duration of the war.

The *Panje* Column

In Russia, motorized transportation was useless many months of the year. During winter and muddy periods the entire supply and transportation system would have been completely paralyzed if supply columns of *Panje* wagons or *Panje* sleighs had not come to the rescue. These vehicles were in use throughout the Russian campaign and were looked upon as vital for the prosecution of the war.

When the German armored and motorized units swept across the dusty plains of Russia during the summer of 1941, nobody paid much attention to the insignificant little peasant horses of the Russian steppe. The tankers and truck drivers could not fail to notice the industrious little animals pulling heavily loaded peasant wagons cross-country whenever they were pushed off the road by the modern mechanical giants. They were looked upon sympathetically, but what was their performance compared to that of the steel colossi and multiton carriers? Any comparison obviously was out of the question. Many a man dismissed them with a disdainful gesture and the words: 'A hundred years behind the times.' Even next to the heavy cold-blooded draft horses and the tall mounts of the infantry divisions their dwarfish cousins seemed slightly ridiculous and insignificant.

A few months later the *Panje* horse was judged quite differently. It came into sudden demand during the muddy season when no motor vehicle could operate and any number of cold-blooded horses could not move the heavy guns and ammunition. How were the advance elements to be supplied when they were stranded without provisions? By *Panje* columns. Who brought the urgently needed ammunition to the front when the organic divisional supply columns were stuck in the mud as far as fifty miles to the rear of the advance elements? Again the *Panje* column. Who was capable of moving gasoline from the railheads to the mechanical colossi even through the deepest mud? The *Panje* horse. By what means of transportation were the badly wounded to be transported when the most modern ambulances could no longer advance in the mud? The answer was always the *Panje* horse and wagon. From then on they became faithful, indispensable companions of the field forces. In winter the *Panje* horse proved even more essential. The *Panje* sleigh became the universal means of transportation when motor vehicles were incapacitated and roads were snowbound or nonexistent. During the first months of 1942 some panzer divisions had as many as 2,000 *Panje* horses but hardly a single serviceable motor vehicle. For that reason they received the nickname '*Panje* divisions.' This unexpected turn of events made the veterinarian the busiest man in any panzer division.

A good idea of the role played by the *Panje* horse may be gathered from an incident which occurred to the 51st Rocket Launcher Regiment when it was moved into the Vitebsk area in January 1942. After having lost most of its vehicles during the battles for Moscow, the regiment was in the midst of reorganization when it was suddenly called upon to participate in the defense against a major enemy break-through at Toropets. The organic prime movers were either unserviceable or had been lost in previous battles. Only a few trucks in poor condition were available. Snowstorms and high snowdrifts at a temperature of $-22°F$ impeded all motor traffic on the roads. Enemy spearheads were approaching the vicinity of Vitebsk, Velizh, and Velikiye Luki.

In this emergency two rocket launcher batteries were hurriedly mounted on sleighs. Each battery of six 150-mm. launchers was assigned seventy-five *Panje* horses and three ammunition sleighs for each launcher. After they had crossed the frozen Dvina River the two batteries were committed for the relief of Velizh as part of a reinforced corps. Because of the heavy weight of the ammunition – each projectile weighed approximately 110 pounds – the few remaining trucks had to use the Vitebsk-Velizh highway after it had been cleared of snow and mines. During this emergency march the local model of low, small sleighs usually drawn by one or two *Panje* horses proved to be the only effective means of transportation. The large sleighs supplied by the German Army were too heavy and far too wide for the narrow tracks made by native sleighs. Moreover the harness of the *Panje* horses which had to be used in this emergency were suitable for only limited loads. Despite very difficult terrain conditions the rocket launcher batteries reached the city in time to relieve it. On the other hand, four medium howitzers drawn by heavy German horses never reached their destination.

There was not a single German military agency in Russia which was not forced to employ *Panje* vehicles or columns during winter, not even excepting the Luftwaffe. German mechanization had not made sufficient progress to cope with the Russian mud or terrain conditions in winter As a result German motor vehicles were incapable of replacing native means of transportation despite the fact that the latter were 'a century behind the times.'

The Corduroy Road

War could never have been waged in the vast swamp regions of Russia had they not been made accessible by improvised corduroy roads. These were the most important static improvisation of the entire Russian campaign and many operations in swampy forests and in the mud of northern and central Russia were feasible only because of the construction of such roads. The first corduroy road was built soon after the Germans crossed into European Russia; the last one during the westward retreat across the German border. In the intervening period hundreds of miles of corduroy road had to be built or repaired during the muddy seasons in order to move up supplies and heavy equipment. At the beginning of the war it was often sufficient to construct a corduroy road 25 to 100 yards long to get hundreds of bogged-down vehicles back on the move.

During the thrust on Leningrad in mid-July 1941 an entire panzer corps bogged down in the swampy forests, separating the corps from the Luga River. For several days the corps was unable to assist its hardpressed advanced elements which were surrounded in a bridgehead on the other side of the river. Only corduroy roads built with considerable effort could restore the former mobility of the corps. In another instance, in 1942, Eleventh Army had to abandon a planned offensive in the direction of the Neva River because corduroy roads could not be built in time.

The swamps along the Volkhov River were impassable because there were no usable roads. The construction of corduroy roads was the only means of overcoming such terrain difficulties. Since Russia lacks rock and gravel but has an abundance of timber in the central and northern parts, the construction of concrete or paved roads was impossible and corduroy roads became the only feasible substitute.

In constructing these roads it was important to select logs about ten inches in diameter and place them in several layers. As in the superstructure of a bridge, stringers, double layers of crossed logs, and siderail lashings had to be used. The guard rails had to be wired because nails could not be used. The cross logs had to be topped with a layer of sand – not dirt – or, when no sand was available, with cinders or rubble. Time and personnel permitting, the top layer of logs was to be levelled off. Only such thoroughly constructed corduroy roads could stand the strain of constant traffic.

The crossing of the many small swamps found along almost any Russian road caused many special difficulties. It was at these points that the supply convoys got stuck when the heavy trucks of the motor transportation regiments sank in.

As a result, serious traffic disruptions lasting many hours and sometimes even several days occurred quite frequently. Over and over again the convoy commanders made the same mistake of failing to wait until the roadbed was repaired by the construction of corduroy roads. Instead, they believed that they could force their way through. The flat swampy stretches, which could have been repaired within a relatively short time before they were completely torn up, were soon in such a condition that their restoration became extremely difficult. The road had to be closed to all traffic since it had become impassable and the swampy stretches obstructed the flow of traffic. Frequently repair work could not be undertaken in time because the road construction engineers had no motor transportation and therefore arrived too late at crucial points. In general, the construction of a corduroy road proved sufficient to bridge small swamps. But whenever swamps were too deep a regular bridge had to be built across them.

Corduroy roads had a detrimental effect on the speed of movements since they slowed down traffic. The average march performance of foot troops dropped to two miles an hour whereas motor vehicles could cover about five miles an hour. Traveling along a corduroy road on foot or by motor was very strenuous, and equipment, especially sensitive instruments, suffered from incessant concussions. These roads complicated and slowed urgent movements of reserves in critical situations.

In the Leningrad area there was not a single serviceable hard-surface road leading east toward the German front (map 6). In this sector the local army commander was wholly dependent upon two long corduroy roads that covered a total distance of eighty miles. Since they were the only arteries for troop movements and supply traffic, they were used by day and night and their maintenance therefore presented many problems.

In the vicinity of Leningrad two types of construction were commonly used: the heavy corduroy road built over a foundation of five log stringers and the light one which was placed directly on the ground. The two layers of cross logs forming the roadway consisted of logs about five inches in diameter that were secured on both ends by guard rails which in turn were anchored to the ground by drift pins and wire loops. The road was just wide enough for one truck because longer logs could not be procured. Turnouts were built at 1000-yard intervals. Special traffic-regulating detachments directed all movements along these roads.

CHAPTER 6

Other Expedients

Improvisations in the Construction of Bridges

In European Russia temporary bridges were built almost exclusively of wood because iron and steel were scarce. In general, the first construction was a wooden emergency bridge which was not secure against the danger of floods. Later on, this bridge was usually replaced by a permanent structure above flood level. Whenever it was possible, attempts were made to construct double-track bridges. GHQ engineers, bridge-construction engineers, or ordinary construction battalions were usually employed for the building of the first temporary bridges. The bridges above flood level were built by bridge-construction battalions and Organization Todt [paramilitary construction organization of the Nazi Party, auxiliary to the Wehrmacht] personnel. The local civilian population served as auxiliaries and were paid for their services.

During the spring of 1942 one division was ordered to move from Kiev across the Seim River to the east. The floods were assumed to have receded by then, but this was not the case and no bridges above flood level were available. A low emergency bridge had to be quickly constructed. No engineer units were within reach because they were all at the front. There was therefore no other choice but to recall one competent officer and some technicians from the front and to build a 600-foot bridge and a 450-yard corduroy approach road with the help of local civilian labor. The work was completed within five days with the help of 500 women volunteers. These native women were well paid and fed; they performed their heavy work in the best of spirits.

The hauling of the essential lumber and the procurement of nails and iron straps always constituted great problems, mainly because the engineers were chronically short of organic vehicles. Timber-and-nail stringers had to be substituted for the long steel I-beams which were not available.

Improvised Road Maintenance

Army and paramilitary construction units were responsible for keeping roads and highways in serviceable condition. This meant hard work and required a lot of manpower, particularly in spring. Special roads were reserved for armored vehicles and maintained with particular care. Along these roads the construction units had to build bridges or fords for heavy tanks and assault guns since the existing ones usually could not carry such heavy loads. These improvised methods of improving the road net facilitated quick movements of entire units and reinforcements which were to be transferred from one sector to another. They contributed decisively to the success of many defensive and offensive operations.

Deceptive Supply Movements

Supply vehicles were frequently dispatched along certain routes to order to deceive the enemy and make him believe that these movements meant the relief or arrival of troop units. Dust raised by motor or horse-drawn vehicles behind the front lines also deceived the enemy. The vehicles dragged tree trunks or brushwood along the roads in order to raise more dust.

Invasion Barges as Means of Transportation

During the course of preparations for a landing in England in the late summer of 1940, the Germans built invasion barges, the so-called Siebel ferries, in record time and put them through various tests. These ferries were equipped with four 88-mm. guns and an appropriate number of 20-mm. Flak guns which could be fired at air, land, or naval targets. Powered by obsolete aircraft engines, these ferries reached a speed of four knots. They were actually used for transportation on Lake Ladoga, in the Mediterranean, and in the Straits of Kerch where they performed well.

Transportation over Frozen Waterways

Most rivers in European Russia freeze during winter and the ice was frequently used as a roadbed for supply routes. For this purpose the roadway was reinforced by blocks of ice and, whenever the ice grew thinner, by rafts. Such improvised supply routes across the long rivers could be found in all parts of the Russian theater. Leningrad, for instance, was supplied over ice roads during many months of the year and, during the later stage of the siege, even by a railroad that crossed the deeply-frozen Lake Ladoga. The Russians also used their most important inland waterway, the Volga, as a main traffic artery for motor vehicles and sleighs during the winter months.

In East Prussia the entire supply of Fourth Army moved over ice bridges across the Frisches Haff in February 1945. Moreover, during the winter 1944–45, elements of Third Army were supplied with rations, ammunition, and equipment over an ice route across the Kurisches Haff.

Fuel Conservation Expedients

Forced to apply strict conservation measures because of the gasoline shortage, which gradually increased during the war, the Germans introduced wood-gas generators in ever greater numbers. At first these were installed on supply trucks used in the zone of the interior. Fuel conservation measures had to be imposed on combat units soon afterward but the conversion to wood-gas generators was impracticable for tactical reasons. The railroads had to carry all supply as close as possible to the front and were used even for minor local troop movements. In the Tilsit area in East Prussia ration and ammunition trains moved as close as 500 yards behind the front line. On the lower Memel front a narrow-gauge lateral supply railroad was built at 500-yard distance from the main line of resistance.

These measures alone were far from sufficient. The field forces therefore introduced expedients on their own initiative. Every empty truck had to take a second empty in tow. With the exception of certain staff cars no passenger vehicles were allowed to undertake individual trips. Passenger vehicles had to be towed by trucks even during troop movements. These and some other similar measures subsequently became standing operating procedure and their enforcement was strictly supervised. They did not alleviate the over-all gasoline and oil shortage but it was only by their enforcement that it was at all possible to maintain the most essential motor traffic.

Railroad Tank Cars Towed Across the Baltic (Map 5)

Continuous air attacks during 1944–45 drained Germany's fuel reserves and reduced her means of transportation. The heavy losses of tank cars caused a great shortage of vehicles capable of transporting fuel by rail. Seventy tank cars immobilized in Memel were therefore urgently needed. But it was no longer possible to move them out of Memel because the city was surrounded by Russian forces. Nor were there any suitable vessels on hand that could transport tank cars across the sea. Various expedients were considered in an effort to find a way out but none promised success. Finally an engineer officer calculated that empty tank cars could float on the sea if they were sealed airtight. On-the-spot experiments immediately confirmed this theory. Local naval units instantly received orders to tow all the tank cars from Memel across the Baltic to the nearest port with railroad facilities. Despite all doubts expressed by the Navy, the army commander insisted on the execution of this order. The first vessel with five tank cars in tow arrived in Pillau, west of Koenigsberg, in the fall of 1944 after a night journey of 110 miles across a fairly calm sea. The cars were undamaged upon arrival and were put into service without delay. Thereafter these phantom voyages continued in the same manner night after night with the number of cars in tow varying between eight to ten per convoy. Everything went according to plan. Only toward the end of these curious railroad-sea convoys was it found that several cars had broken loose because of heavy seas and had floated away from their towing vessel. They caused considerable excitement in coastal shipping when they were first discovered and reported as enemy submarines. Naval planes and patrol boats immediately put to sea to observe this enemy threat from closer range. To everyone's relief the dangerous submarines turned out to be the turret-like superstructures of the tank cars which had been lost at night and were now rocking on the high seas. The runaways were soon caught and towed into port.

CHAPTER 7

Supply by Airlift and Aerial Delivery Containers

The First German Experiments

For the Germans, dropping supplies by parachute to encircled units from battalion to army strength had all the characteristics of improvised operations. At the beginning of the first winter in Russia, the Army High Command asked the Luftwaffe to give immediate assistance to isolated or temporarily encircled units by dropping rations, medical supplies, and ammunition in aerial delivery containers which were originally designed for the supply of parachute units in action. In most cases these missions were successfully accomplished in a spirit of unhesitating co-operation between the services.

The need for the first airlift operation arose in 1942, when major elements of Eighteenth Army were trapped in the Demyansk pocket and Hitler ordered that they be supplied by air. The First Air Force was given this mission and assigned three groups of Junkers transport planes as well as some cargo gliders to carry it out. The chief supply officer of the air force formed a special air transport staff which, in co-operation with the responsible army agencies, carried out the supply operations in accordance with requests received from the encircled units.

An adequate airstrip was available within the pocket. The surrounding terrain could be used as a parachute drop zone. The enemy territory to be crossed was narrow and fighter cover was available throughout the flight and during the take-off from the airstrip. There were but few days on which the airlift was interrupted by snow storms, the formation of ice, or fog on the ground. Under such favorable circumstances it was not too difficult to maintain the fighting strength of the encircled forces.

On return flights the carrying capacity of the aircraft was taxed to the utmost since they were loaded with sick and wounded, official and soldiers' mail, and sometimes even with scarce matériel in need of repair. Although few planes were lost through enemy action, the rate of attrition from wear and tear was very high, requiring constant replacement of the transport planes. Because of increased demands by other sectors of the front and the low rate of production, it was even necessary to employ training planes in order to fill the gaps that developed.

In addition to regular airlift operations, aerial delivery containers were dropped by bombers to various isolated units which were in immediate need of supply. In round-the-clock flights the bombers dropped their containers at the lowest possible altitudes despite strongly increased antiaircraft fire. These missions were very costly and put the personnel to a severe test. During February 1942, I Air Corps flew 1,725 bomber sorties in direct support of ground operations and 800 supply missions for the Army; by March the supply missions required 1,104 bomber flights. These figures clearly indicate that great numbers of bombers were diverted from their original purpose and employed in an improvised supply operation.

The Demyansk pocket was eventually relieved and in the opinion of top-level Army experts the air supply operations had been of decisive importance in enabling the encircled forces to hold out.

The Stalingrad Airlift

As a result of the above experience Hitler ordered that Sixth Army, which was encircled in Stalingrad during the winter of 1942, be supplied by air. Goering accepted the assignment without opposition although his assistants raised strong objections. The Fourth Air Force was charged with the mission of transporting 500 tons of supplies per day to a suitable airfield near Stalingrad. The experiences of the past winter indicated that only 50 percent of the planes could be fully operational at any given time and that therefore 1,000 transport aircraft carrying an average load of one ton each were required. This calculation did not take into account adverse weather conditions or losses by enemy action. Germany had just about that many transport planes but they were scattered all over Europe. The organizational machinery needed to concentrate most of these planes in the Stalingrad sector, and to improvise the essential procurement and transportation measures, reached truly gigantic proportions.

The circumstances surrounding this venture clearly indicated that it was doomed to failure and Luftwaffe experts therefore seemed extremely skeptical. That their misgivings were justified became obvious when the Russians continued their advance and captured most of the departure airfields within easy reach. As a result many aircraft were lost while they were grounded for repairs. The approach flights led over an ever-widening strip of enemy-held territory which soon extended beyond the range of German fighter cover. Losses in men and matériel were replaced by crews and aircraft from the training commands, so that virtually all training of bomber crews came to a standstill during the winter of 1942–43. By the following spring the Stalingrad airlift accounted for the loss of 240 training crews and 365 training aircraft. The training program did not recover from the effects of these losses until 1944.

Inclement weather also played its part. Heavy snowstorms disrupted all air operations for days on end. Russian fighter and antiaircraft strength increased steadily. Nevertheless, the German crews did their utmost to accomplish their mission which, however, was far beyond their capabilities. The amount of supplies which eventually reached Sixth Army was small and could not avert the impending disaster.

Airlift operations in support of entire armies constitute a task which can only be accomplished after careful planning and preparation and then only by an air force which has all the necessary means at its disposal.

CHAPTER 8

Supply and Transportation Problems in the Arctic

Most of the supply and transportation problems in the arctic were caused by terrain difficulties, by the virtual absence of routes of communication, by the arctic winter weather with its abundance of snow and ice, and finally by the fact that all sea traffic from Germany to northern Finland was dependent on the navigability of the Baltic. From this arose the need for numerous improvisations.

In the absence of roads that could be used as traffic arteries, the transportation problem could be solved only by the use of very narrow conveyances which could move across open country, through swamps of little depth, and through snow. The ideal means of transportation was the Finnish cart, a narrow two-wheeled vehicle drawn by a small horse. In addition the Germans used self-sprung drag sleds formed of tree forks, which the Finns called *purillas*, pack animals, and human pack bearers. Reindeer served as draft animals during the winter. These reindeers were purchased with the assistance of local experts and given some time to get accustomed to the German soldiers who were to be their new handlers. With its highly developed sense of smell the reindeer does not take to strangers and is likely to run away. For the transitional period of adjustment it was therefore decided to hire the Lapps who had hitherto handled the reindeer. The next step was to train the troops in the handling and care of these animals. In summer the reindeer roam on the open range like any other wild game and can only be classified as such, whereas in winter they become domesticated animals. Even the methods of harnessing and driving reindeer are unusual and must be learned. Each division received one reindeer transport column with fifty reindeer for the primary purpose of facilitating the supply of raiding detachments and reconnaissance patrols. Partly because of foreign exchange considerations the Germans employed relatively few reindeer whereas the Russians organized an entire reindeer division and committed it in mid-winter after executing a major enveloping maneuver on the southern flank of the German arctic front. In this operation the Russian troops and all their equipment were transported on reindeer sleds.

During the unusually severe winter of 1941–42 the Baltic Sea was frozen over for several months and it was not until several weeks afterward that freight traffic was partly restored. Outside the icebound Finnish ports supplies were transshipped to lighters for which a narrow traffic lane could be kept open by a light ice breaker. At times these lighters were unable to come alongside the freighters. In such instances supplies had to be transferred to the lighters over boardwalks laid across the ice. This additional handling had to be taken into account in the packaging of supplies at their points of origin.

Supply by aircraft was an emergency measure to be employed only when all other means had failed. Under the terrain conditions encountered in the arctic, landings in winter could be made on the frozen surface of lakes, whereas in summer the use of medium and larger-sized land-based aircraft was altogether out of the question. Special crews therefore had to be trained for dropping supplies by parachute. Airlift operations also proved extremely valuable for speeding up the evacuation of wounded from the arctic wilderness.

CHAPTER 9

Clothing and Equipment

Improvisations of clothing became necessary when the German Army was suddenly faced with the prospect of a winter campaign in Russia. To alleviate the lack of adequate clothing during the winter of 1941–42, several divisions helped themselves by organizing large sewing workrooms in near-by Russian cities. From used blankets and old clothing, local workers produced flannel waistbands, ear muffs, waistcoats, footcloths, and mittens with separate thumbs and index fingers. Sheepskins were tanned and transformed into coats for sentries and a limited number of felt boots were manufactured in small Russian workshops. It was possible to requisition fur garments and felt boots from local inhabitants for a small number of men. Some winter clothing was also acquired from dead enemy soldiers. Fur-lined coats, warm underwear, gloves, and ear muffs of regular winter issue did not arrive from Germany until the early spring of 1942. During the first crucial winter the available supply was sufficient for only a small percentage of the forces. The clothing of the great majority of men was not nearly adequate since few of them had more than one item of winter clothes. Whoever possessed extra underwear wore one set on top of the other. All supplies of underclothing in the divisional and army dumps were issued. Eventually every man was able to protect his head and ears to some extent by using rags and waistbands.

Effective relief gradually reached the front once the so-called fur collection campaign got under way throughout the Reich. This campaign was by far the greatest and most valuable improvisation in the field of clothing. Even though the outfits were of varied appearance they fulfilled their purpose. If it had been started earlier many casualties could have been prevented during the severe winter of 1941–42.

At the beginning of the war the German armed forces were quite unfamiliar with the geographic data and climatic conditions of the far north. German clothing and equipment allowances failed to take into account the peculiarities of warfare in the arctic. The troop sent to this theater were unable to operate effectively until they were issued the same clothing and equipment as mountain divisions. This consisted of laced mountain boots instead of standard infantry boots, mountain trousers and tunics instead of regular issue, visored mountain caps with turn-down ear and neck protectors instead of the ordinary field caps, and rucksacks in the place of field packs. Every man was issued complete skiing equipment.

Intermediate and lower commands improvised many other items of clothing and equipment but most of them were of little consequence or of limited application and are therefore not mentioned in this study.

CHAPTER 10

Shelter

The construction of temporary shelters assumed great importance during the fighting in the far north. A lean-to, set against the wind, topped with branches and twigs, served as shelter for raiding detachments in the arctic winter. To obtain heat two logs were split lengthwise, placed on top of one another at the entrance to the shelter and set afire. This reflecting fire produced sufficient heat even in low temperatures. In many instances igloos were built and used as emergency shelters. Portable Finnish plywood structures and Swedish canvas tents were provided as semipermanent shelters to protect personnel from the rigors of the arctic winter. Motor vehicles and the recoil fluids in guns were kept from freezing by the use of various kinds of stoves of improvised construction.

CHAPTER 11

Weapons

There were few improvisations in the field of weapons. The field forces made minor improvements but never went as far as to create new weapons. Captured weapons were not popular with the field forces but frequently had to be used, in order to compensate for German shortages. Captured artillery pieces were organized into batteries and battalions or employed individually. Most of the time they were committed on secondary fronts or in the depth of the battle position as antitank weapons. Their performance was rarely equal to that of German guns. For many of these pieces no firing data were available, others had no sighting devices, and still others were without adequate transportation facilities. Whenever several types of captured guns were assigned to one unit, as in the Crimea and other secondary theaters, the defects and difficulties multiplied in proportion to the variety of types. Lack of ammunition soon put an end to the employment of many of these weapons.

One of the exceptions to the above observations was the Russian heavy mortar which was very popular with the Germans. This weapon was easy to operate, effective, and justly feared. Captured Russian mortars were often organized into batteries and committed at the front with German crews. By request of the field forces, mortars of the same type were produced in Germany in 1944. Even then they could not be issued at all or only in limited quantities because the necessary ammunition was not available at the front.

Painting silhouettes of the most common types of enemy tanks in front view and profile on the shields of artillery and antitank guns proved a very practical antitank defense aid. The vulnerable points were marked in red. In addition there was a warning sign on the shield: 'Observe carefully, take good cover, and open fire at a maximum range of 1,000 yards.' The distances were indicated by markers on the ground at 200-yard intervals in all directions so that reference points for the exact distance were always available.

As the standard German antitank weapons proved ineffective against the Russian T34, light howitzers as well as captured Russian 76-mm. guns were used as direct-fire weapons against tanks. In addition, hand grenades and mines were produced locally and used as makeshift antitank weapons. During periods of position warfare, the engineers prepared large quantities of wooden-box mines. The bodies were made of impregnated wood and the mines were fired by pressure. The introduction of the *Panzerfaust* – a recoilless antitank grenade and launcher, both expendable – completely superseded previous improvisations in the field of antitank weapons.

Sunflower oil proved excellent for the care of weapons. During the winter of 1941–42 sunflower oil was the only available lubricant which would permit proper functioning of weapons in the cold climate that prevailed on the Russian front. Unfortunately it was produced only in the southern regions and even there not in sufficient quantities.

In general, the existing German weapons were adequate for arctic operations. The need for additional antiaircraft weapons was met by mounting light artillery pieces, barrels pointing upward, on revolving platforms. For operations against Russian raiding parties on the Kandalaksha front, captured Russian tanks were placed on flanged-wheel cars and thus transformed into armored cars on rail. Cross-country mobility was stressed in the choice of weapons but not all requirements could be met. To increase the mobility of the artillery, one pack artillery battalion replaced a field howitzer battalion in each artillery regiment. Later the arctic theater was assigned a recoilless gun battalion. Although this battalion was not nearly so mobile as the pack howitzer units, it was more suitable than ordinary light artillery. Moreover the number of mortars was greatly increased in order to make the infantry more independent of artillery support in difficult terrain. Most rifles issued to the infantry were replaced by submachine guns because the former proved ineffective during combat in the wilderness.

CHAPTER 12

Technical Training for Arctic Conditions

The improvisation of arctic clothing, equipment, and weapons had to be complemented by special training. The most important objective in this technical training was to make an indefatigable and accomplished skier of every soldier, regardless of where he might be employed. The German training methods deviated from the Finnish since the Finns stressed cross-country skiing. Accustomed to the use of skis as a means of locomotion from their early childhood, the Finns were capable of covering distances of twenty-five to thirty miles a day even during heavy snowstorms. The German skiing technique always emphasized downhill runs. The type of bindings used by the two nations fully expressed the difference between their skiing techniques. Finnish skis merely had a loop to hold the pointed boot whereas the Germans used a regular binding like the Kandahar and mountain boots with toe plates and grooved heels. The Finnish binding did not permit the execution of speed turns while the German binding which had a tight hold on the foot made it impossible to discard the skis instantaneously whenever the tactical situation required it. Although the Finnish method had great advantages in the arctic, where the downhill technique is of little use and where one can easily dispense with speed turns, German skiing instruction continued to follow the Alpine method. The training program included certain theoretical courses such as those on the proper treatment of skis, on the best way to dress in arctic temperatures, and on protecting oneself from frostbite. Special instruction in the handling and firing of weapons by troops on skis played an important part. The training program was standardized throughout the entire theater; it culminated in a field exercise under combat conditions continuing several days and in winter sports competition.

Every replacement assigned to the Kandalaksha front first had to undergo a two-month special training course at Kairala in order to adjust himself to the living and combat conditions of the arctic. The local command had issued explicit directives for this orientation course, including examples of the proper tactics to be employed in the wilderness north of the Arctic Circle. These directives were brought up to date by the inclusion of the most recent tactical lessons, above all in small unit actions. Thus, for instance, pamphlets were issued on the subject of long-distance marches, march security, combat and reconnaissance patrols, outposts, strong points, guard duty, combat intelligence, movement of supply through enemy-infested areas, and operations in snow and ice as well as in primeval forests and swamps.

This type of training was designed to adjust a newcomer to his environment and its peculiar climatic features. Moreover it was to stimulate and further the soldier's natural affinity to primeval forests and vast spaces and to assist him in orienting himself, tracking down the enemy, avoiding ambush, and interpreting footprints and ski tracks. In fact, it was a kind of 'Cowboys-and-Indians' training course. Proper attention was devoted to everyday problems such as passing the night in the open in the arctic winter, constructing a brushwood shelter or an igloo, building a reflecting fire out of split logs, finding food in the wilderness, and applying first aid in case of accident or battle injury. A newcomer had to acquire a great deal of knowledge on such subjects before he was qualified to be assigned to a combat unit without jeopardizing himself and his comrades. The numerous field exercises often lasted several days and took place at great distances from the training center. They were conducted under the continuous threat of enemy raids and almost without noticing it, the novices to arctic warfare became adjusted to the peculiarities of fighting and living in the extreme north. Whenever the combat troops were transferred to quiet sectors, they continued to receive supplementary training which ranged from improving their skiing technique to the proper care of weapons, equipment, clothing, and rations, and included protective measures against frostbite. Courses in the proper treatment of reindeer had to be repeated over and over again in order to prevent the loss of any of these animals which were so difficult to replace. Thus even the experienced combat soldiers in the far north could always acquire additional knowledge.

CHAPTER 13

Improvised Front-Line Propaganda

During the Russian campaign the Germans made extensive use of frontline propaganda and achieved remarkable results in many cases. The following incident occurred during the winter of 1941–42 when 6th Panzer Division launched a series of limited objective attacks to the west to secure the lines of communication of the German units facing the main Russian assault from the east (see *Snail Offensive*, chapter 1). In this instance, front-line propaganda was improvised very effectively after the second thrust. Among the many wounded and dead Russians collected on the battlefield was Vera, an eighteen-year-old female sergeant. After a few hours treatment for shock, she recovered from her horrible experience which she compared to the 'end of the world'. Vera was a medical auxiliary with the battalion that had held the main strong point and had been completely annihilated with the exception of one officer and fourteen enlisted personnel.

During her first days as a prisoner of war she was under a severe emotional strain. Her interrogation confirmed other intelligence on enemy dispositions gathered from statements of other prisoners. By her own admission she was a member of *Komsomol* [the Russian communist youth organization], that is to say, a convinced Communist. Before she was evacuated with the next transport of prisoners she innocently requested permission to return to her former regiment. Asked for the reason for her request, she replied in a serious and calm tone: 'I want to tell my comrades that it is hopeless to fight against such weapons and that the Germans will treat them well. They should come over to the German side.' Asked whether she had any other reasons for returning, she answered: 'Yes, I would like to save the life of my friend who is still over there.' To the question of whether this was not a subterfuge to escape from the Germans, she replied: 'No, I have already stated that I shall return and bring along my friend.'

Since she could not possibly give away any German secrets and her self-assured statements seemed trustworthy, her request was granted. Dressed in civilian clothes she crossed the German lines at a point opposite the sector held by her former regiment. German scouts escorted her through the deep, snow-covered forest to a place close to the enemy outposts. She promised to return at the same point once her mission was accomplished.

Several days passed but the girl did not return. After twelve days many people expressed doubts as to her true intentions. But on the fourteenth day the designated front sector reported the arrival of two Russian deserters, one of whom was a woman. It was Vera and her companion. Half exhausted from the long march through the deep masses of melting snow, they arrived at the command post. Vera had an interesting story to tell.

After her return to the Russian lines Vera was immediately interrogated by a *Politruk* [low-ranking political officer] who doubted the veracity of her statements when she told him that she had been treated well by the Germans and was able to escape in civilian clothes because of the carelessness of her guards. For five days and nights she was imprisoned in an ice bunker in the company of criminals under sentence of death and was fed bread and water. When she was questioned again she repeated her previous statements. As a result she was returned to her former regiment, given another uniform and assigned to a front-line battalion as a medical auxiliary. This battalion was waiting for the arrival of urgently needed replacements since it had lost its entire manpower with the exception of one lieutenant and a few soldiers. After she was initiated in her duties she took the lieutenant's map and compass and went to the front. There she surprised a Russian sergeant while he was reading a German propaganda leaflet and persuaded him to desert by telling him of her own good experience with the Germans. She talked to a few more men and told them the same story. They believed her and the story spread like wildfire.

One hour after Vera's return to the German lines the remnants of the sergeant's unit consisting of six men and one machine gun arrived at the point where she had crossed and surrendered. They had overheard the conversation between Vera and the sergeant and decided to follow their example. For several days groups of two to three deserters arrived daily at various points along the front. This provided the division with exact information on enemy intentions and facilitated the planning of further attacks.

With regard to the effect of propaganda leaflets dropped from the air, Vera stated that they were hardly ever read by Russian soldiers because such an offense was punishable by death. Moreover the contents were not believed because of the intensive counterpropaganda to which the commissars subjected them. But she was certain that her former comrades would believe anything she wrote in personal letters. Her idea was taken up and soon this valuable correspondence was in full swing. German patrols delivered her hand-written letters at various points in the forest near Russian outposts and attached them to branches in the trees. They were easily recognizable by their red markings. The results were unmistakable since the number of deserters doubled within a short time. When, in addition, her voice was recorded and transmitted over loudspeakers near the enemy lines, the number of deserters along the entire sector increased so much that it exceeded 400 only three weeks after the start of this improvised propaganda campaign. This figure was much higher than the combined total of deserters on all other sectors of the entire army front. The idea of using Vera as the mainstay of this propaganda campaign proved very effective.

Four days later a few bottles of liquor made a powerful propaganda improvisation that eliminated the danger of a local enemy penetration. After a German attack with limited objective the enemy attempted several strong counterthrusts. The situation became very tense when several Russian tanks penetrated the German lines and the last reserves had to be committed. The tanks were destroyed but some of the enemy infantry succeeded in infiltrating through the German lines. Not many Russians got through at first but more and more followed. In this difficult situation the local German commander sent a civilian with several bottles of liquor to the Russian soldiers behind his line and invited them to taste these samples. They were told that they could drink to their heart's content if they decided to come over unarmed. Slightly inebriated by the first bottles they began to arrive hesitantly and in small groups without arms. As soon as the first men had convinced themselves that the Germans had no intention of killing them, about fifty additional Russians turned up to receive their liquor. They indulged so heavily that they forgot all about their weapons, quite apart from the fact that they were physically incapable of returning to them. Meanwhile a strong German detachment picked up the abandoned weapons and stopped all further enemy infiltration attempts.

CHAPTER 14

The Manpower Problem

The Situation at the Outbreak of War

Improvisations in the field of manpower were rarely necessary as long as the war took a normal course and the nation was capable of providing the men needed for new combat units and as replacements. The situation changed when the manpower reserves at home began to run low and special measures had to be taken to make up for the serious shortage of replacements. Even at the beginning of the war, the Germans had to resort to some organizational improvisations, particularly to strengthen the defenses in the West.

At the outbreak of war in 1939, the frontier defense command of St Wendel in the Saar was ordered to defend that sector of the West Wall which extended from Mettlach to Saarbruecken. Only a very small force of regular troops was available. It consisted of frontier guard units stationed in the Saar prior to the war. To a frontage of seventy-five miles there were altogether two battalions to every twelve miles. Reinforcement by second-wave divisions could not be expected for about fourteen days, whereas first-wave divisions were to be made available later on after the conclusion of the Polish Campaign. The number of available antitank guns and artillery pieces of every caliber was ample but there were no gun crews. To form these crews, conscripts from near-by towns who were in the older age groups were to be drafted directly instead of being inducted through regular channels. No preparations of any kind could be made because the frontier defense command was not notified before mobilization. Consequently quite a few of the men had received different mobilization orders and had already left to join their units. Others had been removed from their homes during the evacuation of those districts of the Saar territory that were closest to the front. Nevertheless, crews for the antitank guns were formed without delay and given hasty two-day instruction courses at their gun positions. Sufficient personnel could be found even for the artillery guns which were organized to form reserve batteries, although the men drafted for this purpose had been trained with entirely different guns.

On the other hand it was impossible to find suitable battery commanders or technical specialists. These reserve batteries were therefore attached to batteries of regular artillery battalions which were part of the frontier defense command. Local border patrol personnel were organized into a regiment with four battalions in order to increase the defensive strength of the infantry and, above all, to obtain personnel acquainted with terrain conditions. Each battalion was assigned to one of the four subsectors along the Saar River. This measure alone amounted to a doubling of the infantry forces and meant the addition of particularly qualified personnel since all the border patrolmen were former noncommissioned officers of the 100,000-man Army.

Even the second-wave divisions activated at the outbreak of the war might be termed improvisations. In addition to a certain number of reservists, many other men had been called up to fill the divisions' ranks. Some of these men had merely undergone a short, eight-week basic training course during the last few years. Others had served during World War I and had never since taken part in any military exercise; their average age was around forty-five. During the winter of 1939–40 the enemy granted the Germans sufficient time for further preparations during which these divisions were consolidated and trained and the men belonging to older age groups were reassigned to service units.

The Luftwaffe Field Divisions

The Luftwaffe was still in the development stage when the war began and was experimenting with various forms of aerial warfare. During the course of its operations it was often faced with missions that could only be solved by improvisations. This study describes only those major improvisations in which the Luftwaffe was closely connected with ground operations.

One of the best known Luftwaffe improvisations was the creation of Luftwaffe field divisions. In 1941 the Luftwaffe was at full personnel strength as it was to be greatly expanded after the anticipated rapid conclusion of the Russian campaign. Not only did these plans fail to materialize but, during the winter of 1941–42, the Army was faced with the first major manpower shortage when it ran out of combat troops. On various sectors of the Eastern Front local commanders took the initiative of quickly organizing and committing provisional units composed of Luftwaffe ground personnel, construction battalions, and signal communication units in ground combat. Shoulder to shoulder with Army units, most of them gave a good account of themselves.

As a further step in this direction, Adolf Hitler ordered the transfer of seven divisions from the Luftwaffe to the Army. Goering, the commander in chief of the Luftwaffe, always jealously concerned with his prestige and possibly hoping for a more favorable turn in events, suggested that these divisions remain under the jurisdiction of the Luftwaffe and be subordinated to the Army only in tactical matters. This suggestion was adopted and the Luftwaffe organized ground combat divisions under its own jurisdiction. The personnel of these divisions met with the highest physical standards but the training of the commissioned and noncommissioned officers was totally inadequate for the purposes of ground fighting. The care of weapons and horses left much to be desired. Since the Army was taxed to the utmost, it could provide few instructors and little equipment. Consequently these divisions were sent into combat after receiving only superficial training. They fought as bravely as most other units but their casualty rate was above normal. To the very end of the war, these divisions continued to present a never-ending series of problems to both the Army and the Luftwaffe with the latter obliged to provide a continuous flow of replacements. Time and again the Army had to transfer commissioned and noncommissioned officers to these divisions and provide additional instruction and training so they could serve their purpose.

The consensus is that this improvisation was ineffectual. Despite great devotion and heroism displayed by individual divisions, it would have been preferable to ignore prestige matters and place this valuable personnel at the disposal of the army without attaching any strings. The policy was not reversed until the last stage of the war when transfers of personnel from the Luftwaffe to the Army finally became unconditional.

Maintenance of Combat Efficiency

Delays in the arrival of replacements occurred very early in the Russian campaign. The combat strength of some infantry companies often dropped to an unbearably low level. The first stop-gap measure to be introduced was to screen all supply and service units for men who were fit for front-line duty. When these units were no longer in a position to provide suitable men, others with little or no training were called upon. They were transferred to the infantry as long as they could somehow meet the physical requirements. Since proper training facilities were rarely available, the combat efficiency of the front-line units suffered considerably by the employment of such replacements. Another expedient was to form rifle companies with surplus personnel from artillery, antitank, or armored units that had lost their equipment and to commit them as infantry.

Many artillery and signal units were forced to release commissioned and noncommissioned officer personnel to the infantry and these arms were soon short of technicians and leaders. Any further transfers were therefore out of the question. In such instances the infantry units short of the minimum number of leaders had to be merged. The personnel and training situation of the field forces improved only after each division was assigned its own field replacement training battalion which guaranteed a satisfactory flow of replacements. During position warfare the divisions in the field were then able to raise the training standards by organizing a variety of courses, but the shortage of combat units frequently forced the command to commit these training battalions as temporary combat units. During the last stage of the war, training and replacement divisions of the various armies as well as Army service schools were often called into action in emergencies. As a result, training organizations that had been built up under great difficulties were repeatedly torn apart and destroyed.

Maintaining the combat efficiency of the infantry divisions despite their continuous commitment and the impossibility of relieving entire divisions presented a special problem. When the fighting raged with full fury for several consecutive weeks, it was impossible to relieve the front-line units by reserves because the situation usually was too critical. Only too often the troops were forced to continue fighting until they were completely exhausted. In order to have at least some small but well-rested assault detachment available, the units alternated in withdrawing a small number of soldiers from the thick of the fighting to give them two or three days' rest behind the lines. For the same purpose headquarters and higher echelon supply personnel up to and including army staffs were committed at the front in rotation.

Since transportation to and from Germany was often disrupted, leaves and furloughs had to be frozen for long periods. Whenever the situation permitted, armies, corps, and divisions therefore established rest camps for the men who were due furloughs. These camps were invaluable in maintaining the combat efficiency and morale of the troops. Another improvisation was the introduction of so-called sponsorships at higher headquarters. Certain staff officers maintained constant personal contact with specific combat units and took them under their wings. Moreover, up to 10 percent of the personnel assigned to headquarters staffs rotated with their comrades at the front to allow them to go on leave or to a rest camp. These measures were of benefit to the troops and improved the relationship between headquarters staffs and combat units.

A very successful improvisation was the introduction of rehabilitation units. Soldiers who had been sentenced to serve extended prison terms but who showed promise of reforming were not relieved of front-line duty but put on parole and transferred to improvised rehabilitation platoons, companies, or battalions. These were committed at critical points of the front. The rehabilitation units had particularly efficient commissioned and noncommissioned officers and gave a good account of themselves. This very effective improvisation soon became a permanent institution which received unanimous approval and was accepted as a good solution not only by the prisoners but also by the officers to whose units they were assigned. In 1944 one of these rehabilitation battalions fought exceptionally well in the encircled fortress of Ternopol in eastern Galicia. When the town fell a number of noncommissioned officers and men of this battalion fought their way back to their own lines under great hazards and hardships.

The organization of indigenous units was another improvisation designed to strengthen German fighting power. Such units were organized in occupied territories and friendly countries, especially by the Waffen-SS [combat arm of the SS; in effect a partial duplication of the German Army]. They relieved German units of minor duties and were also frequently committed as combat units. Their performance at the front was far below the standard of German troops. For this reason the front-line troops usually objected to the employment of indigenous units. On the other hand, many volunteers from prisoner-of-war camps were employed as auxiliaries to replace soldiers transferred from supply and service units. In general they were quite dependable and useful.

Late in the war, when few or no replacements were available, all divisions in the field had to use some of their service troops to form emergency alert units. These were originally intended for the defense of strong points of towns in their rear areas or as security detachments for rear positions; but frequently they had to be committed in the front lines to close a gap and sometimes even for the purpose of local counterattacks.

As another emergency measure, convalescent furloughs granted to sick or wounded soldiers were severely curtailed in order to shorten all periods of absence from the front. But, since it was obvious that combat units could only use fully recovered men, most local military authorities failed to comply with these regulations. They also showed great reluctance in carrying out another order which pertained to the induction of men in advanced age groups who were also affected by the draft because the age limit had been raised. It was felt that these older men ought to remain in their civilian occupations where they would be able to serve the nation much better than as soldiers.

The Employment of Women in the Armed Forces

The employment of women with the German field forces was not as widespread as among enemy armed forces. During the latter part of the war women were used as clerical and signal communication auxiliaries at German forward headquarters. They took over these duties from men who were thereby released for combat. These women soon became familiar with living conditions at the front and settled down to do an excellent job. In the arctic the possibilities for employing women were very limited. In that region army headquarters was the lowest echelon to which the auxiliaries were ever assigned. The Russians on the Kandalaksha front, however, had divisional signal battalions exclusively composed of female personnel. Female radio operators were frequently identified as members of small Russian commando and sabotage teams dropped by parachute in the arctic. Generally these detachments consisted of one female radio operator and eight men.

In Germany proper the program of substituting female for male military personnel met with a great deal of opposition because it ran counter to well-established military traditions. The responsible administrative officials were very hesitant in introducing this new program but as the war progressed the increasing manpower shortage imposed the extensive utilization of women in a variety of military jobs.

One of the first measures was to employ women as instructors at riding and driving schools and as grooms at remount depots. They were also used as maintenance crews for aircraft at training centers, as parachute riggers, and as refueling personnel at airfields. A great number of women were employed as antiaircraft auxiliaries at fixed Flak installations throughout Germany. Toward the end of the war the percentage of female personnel in several searchlight units rose to 90 percent.

The Russians often used women to work as laborers on construction projects. In one instance some women captured near Orel told the story of a Russian improvisation to provide urgently needed laborers for work on fortifications. The impending German advance on Bryansk in 1941 was to be stopped by a strong belt of fortifications at the approaches to the city. For this purpose 100,000 laborers had to be recruited without delay. Among them were women from the Caucasus who had been hotel employees. One day the entire personnel of the hotel were suddenly ordered to assemble in the backyard. Not allowed to return to their rooms, they were marched to the railroad station where a train was waiting to take them to Bryansk. The work on the fortifications around the city took four weeks. At the end of that period all laborers were released on the spot and left to their fate.

The organization of the Finnish *Lottas* shows how the employment of women can raise a country's fighting power by releasing men. The *Lotta-Svaerd*, a sister organization of the Finnish security corps, had a membership of over 100,000 women and girls. During the war they performed all military duties which could possibly be taken over by a woman, regardless of the proximity of the enemy. *Lottas* were encountered in field kitchens of companies in the front lines. The commander of a Finnish border infantry battalion in a very exposed sector of the arctic front used a *Lotta* as battalion clerk and interpreter. The Finns also employed young boys in army uniforms as messengers and for similar duties.

CHAPTER 15

The Organization of Special Units

Staffs

ecial command staffs are often needed to carry out certain types of improvisations. A wise commander will anticipate such situations by keeping special staffs at his disposal for any emergency. This is only possible if all staffs not absolutely essential at the front or in rear area assignments are actually pulled out and thereby made available to the command. The Germans might have accomplished a lot more in this respect. For instance, the commander of XXXVI Mountain Corps was under the impression that a corps staff was not needed on the Kandalaksha front and might be put to better use elsewhere. He suggested that a divisional staff with an expanded supply branch would be quite adequate to exercise the tactical command functions in this area. Although he submitted several suggestions along these lines, they were quickly turned down by army. In similar cases it should always be possible to transfer such a staff without delay, if necessary by air, to a point where it might be urgently needed.

In many instances a command staff had to be suddenly improvised to take over some special mission. After the Stalingrad disaster the staff of XI Infantry Corps was reconstituted from an unassigned corps staff which was hastily organized in the beginning of February 1943. Formed in the area north of Kharkov, it consisted of one general and several general staff officers who happened to be in this area on an inspection trip. The staff was to assume command over three German divisions which had been committed to strengthen sectors formerly held by Hungarian and Rumanian forces. These divisions were without higher headquarters after the collapse of Germany's allies on the Stalingrad front. The lower echelons of the staff were picked from the field units, and a Hungarian signal battalion, later replaced by a small German unit, took care of signal communications. The initial difficulties were gradually overcome. It took five months and required numerous reassignments and organizational changes to transform the improvised corps staff into a regular one. Other corps staffs were improvised in a similar manner and their deficiencies were eliminated step by step until they finally became fully organized corps staffs.

In one instance the improvisation of two special traffic regulating staffs made it possible to withdraw ten divisions and thousands of refugees across the Dnepr River (map 7). During the course of the large-scale Russian counteroffensive in August–September 1943, the enemy advanced rapidly from the Belgorod area toward Kiev, and Army Group South had to be withdrawn behind the Dnepr. The crossing of the river, which was 2,500–3,500 feet wide in this area, was complicated by the fact that only a few bridges were left standing. Some of the bridges were threatened by the enemy advance while others had been reached by the Russians before the arrival of the German troops. Every possible step had to be taken to delay the enemy advance and simultaneously accelerate the crossing of the German units over the few remaining bridges.

The long wooden bridge at Kremenchug alone had to serve as a crossing point for ten divisions, six of which were panzer divisions. The XI Infantry Corps was put in charge of the river crossing and was assigned two special staffs to assist in this mission. One staff had to make certain that the march order was observed on the north bank and had to enforce one-way traffic in order to ensure a steady flow of approaching units. The other special staff was employed on the south bank of the river at Kryukov with the mission of assuring the rapid debouchment of the divisions. Although the mission sounded simple enough, its execution presented all manner of difficulties. Even before the previously scheduled withdrawal of garrison installations and unwieldy army and army group supply units had been completed, the situation demanded that the panzer divisions cross immediately. Some Russian parachute troops had meanwhile landed on the other side of the river and their ground forces had begun to cross the river upstream. Only motorized units were capable of reaching the south bank of the river between the bridges in time to restore the situation. In order to give the panzer divisions precedence over other units, it was necessary to stop all traffic and clear the roads for the tanks. For five days mixed columns of all arms extending over many miles camped in the adjacent fields or, wherever this was impossible because of the many swamps, they kept to the side of the road and waited for the signal that would allow them to continue on their way. Their campfires were close to their foxholes. Alongside these columns, or trapped between them, were streams of refugees and herds of cattle.

Only radical measures against traffic violators of all kinds made it possible to put the panzer divisions at the head of the columns. Even more difficult than the approach to the 2,500-foot highway bridge was the exit on the south bank because the streets of Kryukov were very narrow and winding. In addition, the drivers had a tendency to slow down once they had reached safety on the south bank or to stop altogether to obtain information on the whereabouts of their parent unit. This had a delaying effect and was therefore very harmful. The attempts of mixed convoys to find the right branch of the road and turn off immediately after crossing the bridge also caused major delays. The drivers seemed to forget that many thousands of vehicles behind them were waiting to cross the river. To overcome this difficulty all units were ordered to continue on the highway to the south for twenty miles from the bridge without regard to resulting detours. Drastic steps had to be taken to enforce this order and many control points and even airplanes had to supervise the flow of traffic.

The two special staffs worked with perfect co-ordination and during the first days directed 5,000 to 7,000 motor vehicles a day across the river. Later this rate was stepped up to an average of 8,000 to 10,000 and within ten days a total of 70,000 motor vehicles had crossed the highway bridge.

Simultaneously, three infantry divisions with their horse-drawn vehicles as well as the trains of two additional infantry divisions crossed the river on a railroad bridge covered with planks. Alongside this bridge engineers built an improvised floating bridge for the crossing of the 30,000 civilian vehicles that were routed through the Kremenchug area during the same period.

The special staffs also regulated the traffic across these two improvised bridges. It was particularly difficult to designate the approach routes to the bridges in such a manner that the columns would not cut across each other or, where that was unavoidable, to establish intersections at points where cross-traffic would cause the least disturbance.

Regulation and control of the river crossing topped all other tactical considerations for ten days. Despite so many difficulties, all divisions crossed successfully with their vehicles and it was even possible to get the slow-moving evacuation transports and various supply columns across the river. The rear guards held out long after the time limit set by army and saw to it that even the last immobilized tanks were moved across the highway bridge. Several tanks were coupled by cables and towed by prime movers although permission for their demolition had been given several days before. At Poltava, twelve freight trains loaded with tanks and other valuable equipment stood ready for demolition because enemy tanks had already cut the railroad track connecting Poltava with Kremenchug. A counterattack by German armor cleared the line sufficiently to allow all twelve trains to pass the threatened points and reach Kremenchug.

The two infantry divisions whose trains had been put across the river at Kremenchug had to cross the Dnepr fifteen miles downstream. Some of the civilian columns and most of the herds of cattle were diverted to that crossing point. None of the engineer units in the area had any standard military bridging equipment, motor boats, pneumatic pontoons, or civilian shipping facilities. For this reason the two divisions had to resort to whatever expedients they could devise at the time. The last remaining fishing boats were assembled, floats were built from old logs and native wagons without wheels, and some mill boats anchored along the banks were used as ferries.

With these improvised craft soldiers and civilians were moved across the river with all their equipment and possessions. Wagons that were unsuitable for use as ferries were disassembled, floated across, and reassembled on the south bank. Tied to the various makeshift ferries, the horses swam across without resistance. Herd after herd of cattle was driven into the water, but the animals repeatedly shied away from the 2,500-foot-wide river. Only when led oxen were willing to precede them did the mass of the cattle follow into the river accompanied by shouting peasants crossing in boats in both flanks. Slowly and with deafening roars the cattle waded across the 700 to 1,000-foot-wide shallows. Then they suddenly sank into the navigation channel and with heads up swam silently through the very deep and up to 1,000-foot-wide channel until they could set foot again about 350 to 500 feet before reaching the other bank. Herd after herd, 800 to 1,000 head of cattle each, was driven across the slow-flowing river. Even though some herds had been on the move for a month and had covered distances of 125 to 200 miles, there were no casualties. A total of 64,000 horses and more than 80,000 head of cattle swam the Dnepr. The young animals followed separately on large, boarded-up ferries. This completely improvised measure contributed greatly to relieving the bridges at Kremenchug and proved very effective.

The successful completion of the difficult mission may be attributed to the fact that the dual responsibility for the conduct of operations and for the technical problems of the river crossing was vested in the local corps commander. By this arrangement all tactical and technical measures were coordinated under a single man. But a considerable part of the success is to be credited to the efficient special staffs and to the additional crossing facilities – both major organizational improvisations. Yet all these efforts could have been frustrated had the enemy used strong air forces at the right time. However, they were not effectively committed until 90 percent of the forces had completed the crossing. Then a Russian bomber scored a direct hit on the detonation device installed on the highway bridge which had been readied for demolition. The charge was set off and the bridge was destroyed. At that time, however, the loss of the bridge was not particularly serious because the rear guard tanks and assault guns were able to withdraw across the railroad bridge which remained intact. Before this attack enemy air activity was negligible, and only one light bomb scored a direct hit on the highway bridge. It merely pierced the surface without damaging the vital bridge structure. The vehicles bypassed the small hole which was covered up within one hour. The flow of traffic was not interrupted.

Special Formations

A certain number of the organizational improvisations mentioned in this chapter deserved to be permanently incorporated into the tables of organization and equipment of the units concerned. But only a few were officially adopted because manpower and matériel shortages usually prevented the introduction of far-reaching changes. In order to overcome some of the chronical deficiencies, the infantry corps and divisions were forced to use a number of expedients. When they were on the defensive and had to hold overextended front-line sectors without motorized units, they scraped together all the available motor transportation to have at least one motorized battalion or just one company for emergency purposes. These elements used *Panje* wagons during the muddy season and sleighs during the winter. By this improvisation the command had mobile reserves on hand even though they were small.

The formation of so-called *Korps Abteilungen* {provisional corps} was an emergency measure that was also helpful in deceiving the enemy. Remnants of three divisions which had been badly mauled in difficult extended battles were merged into one division with each of the original divisions forming one regiment. The new division was designated *Korps Abteilung* and distinguished by a letter A, B, C, etc. Each provisional corps carried the corps insignia and each infantry regiment was designated by the number of its former division. The regiments drew their replacements from the Wehrkreis of their original divisions. [The Wehrkreis was the basic military area in Germany, resembling somewhat the prewar U.S. Corps Area; it had the additional functions of administering conscription policies and furnishing replacements to specific units whose home stations were located in the Wehrkreis.]

The provisional corps had the combat value of an infantry division and fought equally well. The merger had the advantage that the staffs of two divisions with all their organic units became available for reassignment to new divisions or could be used as special staffs or for some other purpose. On the other hand, the new regiments could not be used as battle-tested cadre for newly-organized units. This disadvantage outweighed all benefits that could be expected from the formation of *Korps Abteilungen*. The field forces resented this measure as well as the policy of giving preference to the organization of new divisions with inadequate cadres instead of providing experienced, though weary, front-line divisions with replacements to restore their former striking power. Whenever a new division without sufficiently experienced cadre was suddenly committed in a major battle in the Eastern theater – as happened only too often – it just melted away like snow in the midday sun. The field forces unanimously requested that the battle-tested divisions be reorganized. Yet, as a rule, new inexperienced divisions were sent to the front despite all the damage caused by this procedure.

The provisional corps may have fulfilled their purpose as a temporary measure, but in the long run they proved to be a handicap rather than an asset. If the purpose of this expedient was to eliminate divisions that had not performed well in combat, it would have been better to dissolve them entirely and not to preserve them in parts.

The German experiments with the employment of task forces were more conclusive. In one instance an improvised task force, organized for a specific purpose, played a decisive role in the annihilation battle near Plavskoye in November 1941. The enemy had moved up an armored brigade, which the Germans were unable to match at that time since their panzer forces were heavily engaged in the vicinity of Tula and no armored units of divisional or brigade strength could be withdrawn from that sector. In this emergency Second Panzer Army entrusted a brigadier general on the staff of XXIV Panzer Corps with the mission of improvising a panzer brigade. Time was of the essence. Discussions with other agencies were no longer feasible and, in any event, they would have been fruitless. For this reason army released some panzer units to the improvised brigade. Equipped with ample authority, the brigade commander succeeded in assembling his force within a few hours. In addition to the panzer units assigned by army, he picked up some motorized artillery and other combat units on his way to the front and brought them along. Other units volunteered to join his task force.

The next day the commitment of the brigade led to a decisive victory. The battle southeast of Plavskoye was won with very heavy casualties to the enemy. Most elements of the improvised brigade could then be returned to their parent units. This example shows that the success of an improvisation greatly depends upon the man who is charged with its execution. Responsible commanders must therefore always keep in mind who is best suited to carry out an improvisation if they want to avoid the mistake of selecting an officer just because he happens to be available. This is of particular importance whenever an improvisation may have decisive influence on the entire situation.

The formation of more or less independent regimental combat teams often became necessary in view of the vastness of European Russia and its terrain conditions. The composition of these teams was usually adapted to local requirements which meant that organized operational units such as divisions had to be split into two or more improvised forces. This measure proved expedient in specific situations which occurred quite frequently in Russia, but was applied only on exceptional occasions because maximum striking power could be assured solely by committing an entire division as one unit. Regimental combat teams were effective whenever they were employed to turn the tide of battle at a decisive point.

A railroad combat team was improvised when the German offensive reached Orel in 1941 and two Russian armored trains were captured intact at the railroad station. One infantry regiment, some artillery, Flak, and railroad engineer elements were loaded on captured railroad trains and attached to the armored trains manned by German crews. This improvised combat team made a thrust to the south in the direction of Kursk and succeeded in surprising the Russians. Within two days the combat team reached Ponyri on the way to Kursk and took firm possession of the railroad lines after some small-scale fighting. Thus the unit contributed materially to the success of an operation which resulted in the capture of Kursk during the muddy period of 1941.

Flying columns were committed for the same purpose as combat teams. In most instances these were motorized units compc⸴ of elements from various branches and their strength and structure depended on the mission they were to receive. For instance, in 1941 the 97th Light Infantry Division left its rear elements in the assembly area and improvised a flying column with truck transportation from its service units. This column was composed of three motorized units – one infantry battalion, one artillery battery, and one antitank battalion. By its quick action and deep enveloping maneuvers it spared the follow-up division many casualties.

In another instance a flying column was committed in the Kerch Peninsula immediately after the German break-through of the Parpach Line during the Crimean Campaign. The same evening the column reached the Tartar Wall, a fortified line west of Kerch, and captured the enemy positions. The crucial point for the recapture of the peninsula was thereby once again in German hands. The 132d Infantry Division which followed in the rear could never have reached this point in time.

An interesting improvisation took place in the arctic when a mountain pack bearer battalion was transformed into a mountain infantry battalion. The mountain pack bearer battalion was composed of men in advanced age groups who hailed from the Alps. They were gradually replaced by younger men and the battalion was transformed into a combat unit. Clothing and equipment were appropriate. All members of the unit were experienced skiers but, since they needed specialized training, they were withdrawn from the line for a two-month period. Upon completion of the training this battalion was capable of difficult independent missions in the arctic wilderness.

At the outset of the campaign north of the Arctic Circle it became clear that formations of a special type were required. In the midst of operations, however, any kind of large-scale reorganization was out of the question. As a modest beginning the command decided to experiment with the formation of a swamp battalion which was to be particularly qualified for independent small-unit action in the arctic. Since there was no precedent for the formation of such a unit, it was organized by selecting young soldiers in excellent physical condition who were experienced skiers. They were issued the same clothing and equipment as mountain infantry troops. This proved so effective that all combat troops in the arctic were subsequently equipped in the same manner. A few captured trucks were to provide the battalion with motorized transportation. The men soon gained confidence and adjusted themselves to the difficult conditions prevailing in the arctic wilderness. The Finns provided instructors and gave some welcome assistance. When XXXVI Mountain Corps applied for official recognition of the unit, the request was approved and the battalion was designated a bicycle battalion. A shipment of bicycles promptly arrived; needless to say, they were absolutely useless in the arctic. Following another request the battalion was finally redesignated as an independent motorized infantry battalion. It was issued command cars and *Volkswagen* [the German version of the jeep] which had proved extremely useful in the snow and on the poor, narrow, rocky roads. Now the battalion was truly mobile. Later when the Finnish units which had been attached to corps were pulled out, the new battalion carried out difficult combat and reconnaissance patrols in the arctic virgin forests and barren wastes north of the Arctic Circle.

Last-Ditch Improvisations

THE LEUTHEN PROJECT

When the Russian armies poured across Germany's eastern borders in the beginning of 1945, the Army High Command introduced a major improvisation, the LEUTHEN Project, which constituted a radical change in the Army's replacement and training policy. To the German mind Leuthen, a small town in Silesia where Frederick the Great had won a major battle with improvised forces, was the symbol of a victorious last-ditch stand. It was probably for this reason that the Army selected the term Leuthen to designate this project. The plan foresaw that all training units of the entire replacement army were to be transferred and assigned to the field forces as soon as the code word LEUTHEN was transmitted to them. In immediate proximity of the front these training units were to be subjected to a more realistic combat training than they could possibly receive in the zone of the interior. Moreover, they were to serve as security forces in rear area positions or defense lines. The original idea was therefore both sound and practical, but it should have been put into effect much sooner, when the front was still stable. What actually prompted the execution of the LEUTHEN Project at that late stage, whether it was still the original intention as officially proclaimed or rather the steadily deteriorating situation on the fighting fronts, must be left to conjecture. In reality all the LEUTHEN units were immediately committed and thrown into the thick of fighting in critical situations.

What did the LEUTHEN units look like? In every Wehrkreis there were a number of training and replacement units of various arms which were under the command of division staffs. The men who had completed their training and were ready for combat duty were in the replacement units. The training units were composed of recently inducted recruits who were to be prepared for combat by undergoing an eight-week basic training course. Upon receiving the code word LEUTHEN, the division staffs were to move out with all training units that had completed one to seven weeks of training.

One of the units alerted in this manner was the Special Administrative

Division 413 which consisted of several training battalions, a regimental headquarters, an artillery battalion with an odd assortment of guns, and elements of an engineer and a signal battalion. As a tactical unit, the division was really no more than a reinforced infantry regiment commanded by an elderly general with a small staff. Needless to state, it was absolutely incapable of any combat assignment. The cadre up to the division commander consisted of personnel unfit for combat because of sickness, injury, or for lack of tactical qualifications. Most of the noncommissioned officers had suffered combat injuries of such severity that they were barely fit for garrison duty. Some of the men were entirely untrained, others had completed one half to three quarters of their basic training. Some of them were unarmed because the number of weapons provided for training units did not suffice to arm every soldier. In addition, the various formations had absolutely no organic transportation. There were no more horses than those needed for the normal garrison functions and the division had no field kitchens since the food had always been prepared in the permanent garrison kitchens. The clothing and equipment were equally defective. Quite a few soldiers, for instance, could not be issued garrison belts. In general, everything was in exactly the condition to be expected from a home station in times of stress where shortages have become the rule rather than the exception.

When the LEUTHEN division moved out it was therefore no more than an improvisation of the poorest sort. This might not have mattered so much had the division undergone a rigid training schedule far behind the lines. But even while it was on the approach march to its destination, one of its battalions was shifted from the Main River valley to Hammelburg where a small enemy armored force had broken through. The remainder of the division was immediately sent into combat and annihilated.

In summarizing, one may state that the LEUTHEN Project was doomed from the outset because it was applied in a situation for which it was entirely unsuited.

OTHER DESPERATE MEASURES

In view of the extremely heavy losses of manpower, the shortage of weapons, and the precarious condition of the transportation system, the situation of the German Army became so critical that the need for improvisations grew even more urgent during the last few weeks of the war. The organizational improvisations of that period were a far cry from those introduced during earlier stages. In many cases the selection and training of replacements was makeshift. Equipment of all types was totally inadequate and consisted of whatever was left over or could be picked up. Since no guns were available, the organization of new artillery units was practically impossible. Whatever new infantry units were organized during this period were of limited capability in the field. In

Bavaria, for instance, the last regular activation of a new infantry division took place in November 1944. What followed thereafter was pure improvisation, not so much because of the shortage of trained replacements, but because of the inadequate supply of weapons and equipment.

Although the organization of new divisions had become impossible, replacement units were sent to the front until the beginning of March 1945. Then even this function could no longer be accomplished. Each Wehrkreis assumed command over its replacements, organized a few emergency infantry battalions and transferred them to the nearest tactical command. Many well-trained soldiers were still available but, because of the serious shortage of infantry heavy weapons, it was no longer possible to organize entire machine gun companies. The battalions were therefore composed of a small battalion staff and four rifle companies. Each company had one machine gun platoon with two heavy machine guns and a few locally requisitioned wood-gas-burning trucks, one of which carried a cook stove. The few artillery battalions organized during this period were composed of a great variety of guns. No two batteries were alike and every section had guns of different caliber.

During that period occurred a very significant incident which demonstrated the effects of the improper utilization of administrative personnel. Several first-rate panzer battalions were in the process of rehabilitation at the Grafenwoehr troop training grounds in Bavaria. When enemy armored spearheads approached the area, a corps commander responsible for a near-by sector of the front ordered the staff of the training center to assume the tactical command of the panzer battalions and stop the enemy advance. The commander of the training center was a general well along in years who had always handled administrative assignments very competently but had never during his long career commanded a panzer unit. His staff was composed of elderly reserve officers and ordnance specialists. Their leadership spelled disaster for the panzer battalions.

The numerous organizational improvisations introduced during that period were only stop-gap measures applied in time of extreme emergency. Since most of them were adopted to overcome purely local critical situations they are of little consequence in a study of this type.

CHAPTER 16

Political Measures Introduced by the National Socialist Party

Civilian Labor Procurement

During the years preceding the outbreak of the war, civilian labor procurement had to be improvised on a large scale for the construction of fortifications. Even at the time when the West Wall was under construction, the allocation of manpower was essentially an improvisation of gigantic proportions. Receiving unusually high pay and enjoying a variety of other benefits, hundreds of thousands of men were employed by the Todt Organization and moved from one building project to the next. Not everything that was built at that time was beyond criticism, yet some of the achievement of the years 1938–39 would not have been possible without these improvisations. Toward the end of the war another improvised labor force was formed to construct additional fortifications in the west. This time it consisted of entire Hitler Youth units, of men who were in age groups subject to labor conscription but too old for military service, and of men who were no longer fit for combat.

The improvisations introduced during that period had highly political aspects. They were directed by laymen some of whom had never seen military service and whose technical knowledge was very limited. They were unaware of the major importance of matériel in military planning and were inclined to confound a temporary surge of enthusiasm – such as undoubtedly existed among the Hitler Youth Combat Units – with real fighting ability. These Party functionaries were under the erroneous impression that their own fanaticism was shared by everybody and that this alone would make up for all the shortages and deficiencies which characterize all last-minute improvisations. On the other hand, there was little opportunity for preventive measures at a time when only painstaking efforts could conceal the exiting chaos. The Volkssturm might perhaps have presented such an opportunity if only it had been drawn up as a levee en masse with long-range material preparations and if entirely different slogans had been used for the mental and spiritual conditioning of the people.

The Volkssturm

The most extensive improvisation undertaken by the National Socialist Party was the mobilization of the Volkssturm during the last few months of the war. The idea was to call on the last forces of resistance the German people were capable of mustering. A misunderstood and misinterpreted tradition built on memories of 1813 may also have played its part in the minds of some Party officials.

The Volkssturm included all men up to the highest age groups as long as they were capable of bearing arms and were not already serving with the armed forces. This might have provided a broad basis for successfully mobilizing whatever fighting strength had not yet been tapped if there had not been a complete lack of weapons, clothing, and equipment. Whereas clothing and equipment might conceivably be improvised, this does not hold true of arming hundreds of thousands or even millions of men. The Wehrmacht could spare nothing. At the same time it became more and more obvious that the para-military Party formations had hoarded and hidden weapons and ammunition, but in view of the large number of Volkssturm draftees these weapons were of little help. Then, a Party official had the idea of manufacturing simplified Volkssturm rifles with barrels he could 'procure' from some factories in Saxony. This plan was also of little consequence. Thus the whole project of staging an armed levee en masse was doomed from the very outset.

Leadership and training were two of the other problems to be solved. Among the men of the Volkssturm were many veterans of World War I. Although there had been many changes in the field of tactics, these men had sufficient military background to cope with the simple missions of which the Volkssturm was capable. To provide adequate training was a more difficult matter. Men who differed widely in age, former branch of service, or type of training, as well as men without any training whatsoever, were attending military drill periods in their spare time, as a rule on Sundays. Occasionally, in towns with local garrisons, one or two instructors were provided by regular army units. That was all the assistance the Wehrmacht could give because it had no men to spare. Moreover the Volkssturm was a Party improvisation and probably deliberately kept apart from the Wehrmacht from its initial organization.

Only when actually committed in combat was the Volkssturm to be placed under the tactical control of the Wehrmacht and fight in conjunction with the regular field forces. There was no reason for great expectations. The call to arms for an extended tour of duty was to be locally restricted. The men were to be called upon only if the enemy threatened their home county and even then they were to be used exclusively for local defense. Even that was almost too much to expect. When, toward the end of the war, entire Volkssturm battalions were committed far away from their homes on the Eastern Front, this emergency measure was contrary to the spirit and original mission of the Volkssturm and could only lead to failure.

Guard duty and local security assignments were practically the only missions for which the Volkssturm was really qualified. Its composition, its limited training, and the fact that no more than rifles and in some cases only pistols and hand grenades could be issued as weapons, precluded its commitment in real combat operations. Since it was incapable of withstanding critical situations, the Volkssturm could only become a liability and threat to the troops it was to join in battle. Its proper mission was to construct and guard road blocks. Important psychological considerations spoke against restricting Volkssturm units to purely local commitment. Surely the primary interest of the men resided in inflicting a minimum of war damage to their home towns where their families lived. Thus, it was safe to assume that the Volkssturm men would prefer to avoid any last-ditch stand in the immediate vicinity of their home towns. The tactical commanders therefore took the precaution to suggest that road blocks and fortifications should be erected at a sufficient distance from any community in order to spare it the effects of combat action. Later orders from higher headquarters specified that no Volkssturm units should be committed any closer than thirty miles from their immediate home towns. This, however, meant a complete reversal of the basic principle of restricting the Volkssturm men to the defense of their immediate home territories.

In East Prussia the Volkssturm did a better job than anywhere else. It was there that the idea of the Volkssturm levy had originated since East Prussia was the first German province directly threatened by the enemy. There the organization and training of the Volkssturm made the greatest progress.

East Prussia alone raised thirty-two Volkssturm battalions. All of these remained in that province even when, in November 1944, the civilian population from the northern districts had to be evacuated. After that, most of the Volkssturm units were used to prepare reserve battle positions in the rear area for a possible withdrawal of the combat troops who in turn provided instructors for the Volkssturm battalions. Months of continuous instruction raised their standard of training to such a degree that a number of Volkssturm battalions were able to carry out limited combat missions. A few of these so-called special employment units were equipped with a sufficient number of modern weapons such as the most recent 75-mm. antitank guns, the latest model machine guns, and some older-type small-caliber antiaircraft guns. Some of them even had adequate motor transportation. The units were composed of a small percentage of World War I veterans with the rest about equally divided between 16-and 17-year old youngsters and elderly men from 60 to 75. Some of the battalions were under the command of former staff officers who had distinguished themselves in World War I but were now afflicted with various physical disabilities. The majority of the battalions were short of weapons, equipment, and training, and their employment in actual combat operations was out of the question. It was planned to integrate them into the field forces only in case of a general withdrawal of the lines.

From the outset this was recognized as a serious handicap which, however, could not be corrected since the Army had no jurisdiction over these formations. Time and again the Army requested that the battalions be immediately disbanded and all Volkssturm men fit for combat duty be transferred to the field forces. Yet every one of these requests was flatly rejected by the Party. Thus, during the latter part of January 1945 when the front began to give way, most of the Volkssturm battalions employed in East Prussia were of no use to the Army. Wherever they did not disintegrate altogether, they suffered heavy casualties. But contrary to standing orders, a few battalions had been moved up into combat alongside seasoned field units during the preceding weeks and these battalions gave a good account of themselves. Special mention is due to Volkssturm Battalion Labiau which fought as part of a division improvised from service troops. Three times the battalion was dislodged, but in every instance it succeeded in recapturing its original position by launching counterattacks. In this bitter struggle the battalion commander and most of his troops remained on the field of battle.

At another time the Volkssturm performed less well. Showing much zeal in military matters, Party headquarters in East Prussia produced its own 75-mm. antitank guns with iron-wheeled gun mounts and conducted short training courses to familiarize members of the Volkssturm organization with the weapon. By the end of January 1945, the situation near Tapiau east of Koenigsberg was obscure (map 5). There, the personnel of an Army ordnance school was engaged in bitter fighting against advancing enemy armor. The commanding officer of the ordnance school had been killed and Tapiau had changed hands several times but was held by German troops at that moment. Rumor had it that enemy tanks had broken through and were advancing on Koenigsberg. Thereupon Party headquarters improvised an antitank gun battalion with twenty new 75-mm. antitank guns from its training school and dispatched it to the area east of Koenigsberg to take up positions for the protection of that city. At sundown strong armored formations suddenly came into sight opposite the antitank gun position. This impressive spectacle caused such a state of terror among the inexperienced gun crews that they left their guns and ran for cover in all directions. Their leader, a young first lieutenant, tried in vain to stop them. Assisted by a few instructors he succeeded in getting some of the guns ready for action and was just about to open fire when he realized to his surprise that he was facing German tanks. It was the 5th Panzer Division which, after heavy tank fighting in the area east of Tapiau, had succeeded in breaking through the enemy lines and was now assembling in this area in compliance with its orders. For once the failure of an improvisation was of distinct advantage.

Paramilitary Units During the Last Stage of the War

Toward the very end of the war the Party organized certain tactical units which were to be committed in the field. Political considerations predominated and outweighed all others. For some time past, elements of the Reich Labor Service had served as antiaircraft units. Since there were absolutely no other forces available, elements of labor service battalions were employed to defend the road blocks they had previously constructed.

Hitler Youth Combat Units, organized during the last weeks of the war, were assigned to the field forces on various sectors of the front. Their special task was the pursuit and destruction of enemy tanks with the help of bazookas and *Panzerfausts*. Just before the end of the war, Party Secretary Bormann attempted to organize an Adolf Hitler Volunteer Corps.

The accomplishments of these various paramilitary units are unknown to the authors.

CHAPTER 17

Are Improvisations Inevitable?

A considerable number of the improvisations described in the preceding chapters could undoubtedly have been avoided by normal advance planning. Other improvisations could have been minimized by preparatory measures of a general nature which could have been further developed if and when the need arose. A third category of improvisations could not have been even generally anticipated because they were caused by such abnormal conditions or extraordinary circumstances.

Avoidable Improvisations

In an attempt to avoid improvisations one must search for and examine all the problems that may possibly confront an armed force in future wars. First of all it is necessary to determine the probable theaters of war. Nowadays any conflict is likely to assume the proportions of a global war if it transcends the limits of a purely local police action. Prior to World War II the Germans did not think far enough ahead. When, for instance, the Armed Forces Academy needed maps of Finland, it was discovered that the available supply of such maps at the Map Service of the Reich War Ministry was inadequate.

The next step is the acquisition of a thorough knowledge of the potential theaters of war, a knowledge not limited to their broad geographic or military-geographic features, but which includes above all their climatic conditions. In every geographic region the native mode of life is determined by the climatic conditions. For obvious reasons this influence is especially pronounced in the many fields of military activity. Strategy and tactics, organization, weapons, munitions, equipment, clothing, food, training, replacements, billeting and many other factors are strongly affected.

Moreover, a great deal may be learned in advance about one's potential enemy. Differences between his armed forces and one's own are usually not fortuitous but rather reflect a discrepancy in the military policy of the two nations. The observation of any striking deviations from standard procedures should therefore give rise to speculation about their inherent causes. This will make it possible to decide upon the appropriate measures which must be introduced in every military sphere in case of an armed conflict with that country. Friendly nations which are subject to the same climatic conditions as

118

those of the potential enemy may serve as a source of useful information in peacetime.

Senior commanders in the armed forces and military specialists in all important fields must acquire firsthand knowledge of the climate and terrain as well as the social, economic, political, and military conditions in any potential theater of war or at least in those neutral or friendly countries which show similar characteristics. On the basis of their own observations, these men must determine what is essential for the conduct of military operations. Firsthand personal impressions are indispensable; they may be supplemented by the study of pertinent books and documents and by consultation with private citizens who are likely to have a sound judgment of foreign countries.

Military history is another source of valuable information. It is never too late to determine the reasons for the success or the failure of past operations. Many of the decisive factors have retained their validity throughout the years and their effect on military operations in our time would be very much the same as in the past.

In view of the foregoing, the Germans were in a good position to learn the general as well as the climatic conditions of European Russia and the far north. If they actually acquired this knowledge, the Germans certainly failed to draw the proper conclusions for their military policy. Instead, they were forced to use improvisations because of the lack of advance planning and preparations. If they did not get that information in the first place, they were obviously guilty of neglect. For instance, the Finns might have told them that ordinary flat-country divisions are not suitable for fighting in the impenetrable forests, the rocky labyrinths, and the swamps and marshes of the arctic. Perhaps German planners were still too deeply entrenched in Central European military traditions. Also, the military were not sufficiently familiar with foreign lands and particularly with countries whose climatic conditions differed from the German. As a result they were lacking in proper personal understanding of what was to be expected. They probably took matters too lightly at the outset. In the field of tactics and logistics in European Russia and the arctic, better preparations might have been made before military operations began. Many improvisations pertaining to tactics and logistics could have been foreseen, in particular those which developed into permanent institutions and were eventually incorporated in German standing operating procedures.

Thus if improvisations are to be avoided, one of the essential prerequisites is the logical application of any knowledge possessed or acquired about a potential theater of war. It may happen that a country becomes involved in a war by surprise; in that event the top-level military leadership must act immediately and take appropriate steps to master the situation. It is wrong to wait until the field forces begin to help themselves by introducing improvisations which in some cases may be the wrong ones and difficult to eradicate. After weighing the requirements against the available emergency resources, all spheres of the war effort must immediately be adjusted to the new situation by concerted action. This will prevent many adverse psychological effects which may otherwise easily disrupt the confident relationship between the top-level command and the field forces.

Unavoidable Improvisations and their Minimization

A different category of improvisation will be unavoidable whenever an unexpected or unpredictable situation produces the need for extraordinary tactical or logistical measures. A number of the improvisations mentioned in the preceding chapters could not have been avoided, even if adequate preparations had been made. The need arose so suddenly or was so localized that preparations carried out elsewhere could not be used in time to remedy the situation. Logistic preparations, for example, will prove effective only if mobile transportation is readily available in case of a sudden break-down in the movement of supplies. For this purpose higher headquarters may resort to airlift, truck, railroad, or inland water transportation. Such preparations must be made well in advance in order to assure immediate availability of stand-by transportation of the above-mentioned types in sufficient numbers and within reasonable distance.

In situations which require immediate emergency measures there is at first no choice but to improvise extemporaneously. If such improvisations are enforced for some time, it will be possible to correct their deficiencies gradually and to introduce systematic improvements.

Improvisations in the fields of weapons, ammunition, equipment, clothing, or rations can rarely be avoided since it is impossible to anticipate all requirements. In some instances stop-gap measures may well consist of emergency purchases of consumer goods, but a general solution can be found only if the rigid system of standards and specifications adhered to in military procurement can be modified and adjusted to the flexible methods applied by private industry. It would then become possible to provide suitable equipment for specific needs in time, thereby eliminating many improvisations. It goes without saying that one cannot possibly mass produce arctic equipment in peacetime in expectation of an armed conflict in the arctic at some time in the future.

Improvisations in Extreme Emergency

In times of extreme emergency, improvisations must be approached from a different point of view and applied with other standards than those used during other periods of the war. In such situations preparatory measures hardly enter the picture because then it is a matter of living from hand to mouth while being catapulted from one crisis to the next. The pressure of time assumes tremendous proportions. Obviously no country at war will ever expect to be faced by a situation such as that with which the Germans had to cope during the closing days of the last war. Much less will any country attempt to prepare for such an emergency.

CHAPTER 18

The Relative Value of Improvisations

The preceding chapters give a fairly detailed account of German military improvisations and indicate their relative value in a variety of situations. By presenting numerous examples, an attempt has been made to demonstrate why certain improvisations served their purpose whereas others failed. This presentation should enable the reader to draw a number of conclusions that have general validity. The most obvious conclusion is that, because of their always-present inherent defects, improvisations should be avoided altogether whenever possible. On the other hand, some of the improvisations presented in this study were absolutely essential and proved effective. For instance, it would have been absolutely impossible to conduct operations in the arctic or to control the supply situation in the Russian theater, had not improvisations been introduced. That many of them were eventually accepted as standing operating procedures simply indicates that they should never have been improvisations. Their success was based on the fact that they were initiated and carried out by experts and that the essential prerequisites for putting them into effect existed in these specific cases.

The failure of any improvisation could be attributed either to the lack of proper planning or to the fact that it had been introduced at a time when the necessary means to implement it were no longer available. In many instances its failure could be traced to the laymen who were charged with the responsibility for its execution. All these factors predominated during the last stage of the war when a great number of improvisations failed to meet expectations.

In general, however, improvisations proved effective provided the right men were selected for their implementation and provided they were enforced with the best available matériel and the firm determination to achieve the intended military purpose.

An observer who looks at the Russian campaign in retrospect will come to the conclusion that the multitude of improvisations which were employed far exceeded what Moltke once designated as a 'system of expedients' in a tactical sense. Actually, the Germans were forced to introduce the first improvisations as soon as they crossed the eastern border. The farther they advanced into Russia the more expedients they had to devise. The number rose by leaps and bounds when operations began to be hampered first by mud and swamps and later by snow and ice. During the last stage of the war, improvisations permeated every compartment of the war effort both within Germany and at the front. At the culminating point expedients assumed the proportion of an avalanche, the momentum of which eventually buried the entire military machine. Improvisations could never be expected to compensate for the lack of vision and the fundamental blunders of German leadership. It is no exaggeration to state that the entire Russian campaign will go down in history as one gigantic improvisation.

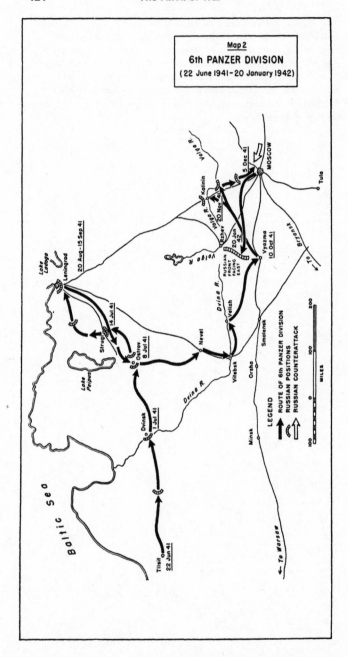

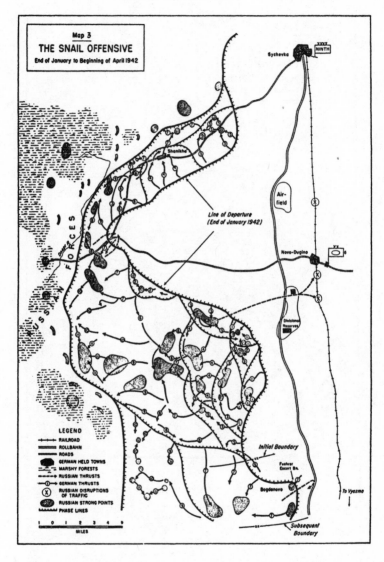

Map 3

THE SNAIL OFFENSIVE

End of January to Beginning of April 1942

LEGEND
RAILROAD
ROLLBAHN
ROADS
GERMAN HELD TOWNS
MARSHY FORESTS
RUSSIAN THRUSTS
GERMAN THRUSTS
RUSSIAN DISRUPTIONS OF TRAFFIC
RUSSIAN STRONG POINTS
PHASE LINES

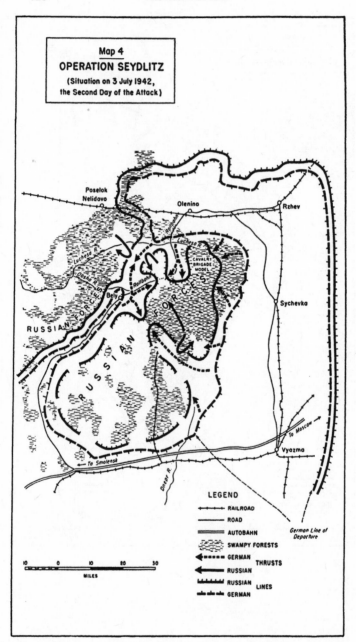

Map 4

OPERATION SEYDLITZ

(Situation on 3 July 1942,
the Second Day of the Attack)

LEGEND

+++++	RAILROAD
———	ROAD
≡≡≡	AUTOBAHN
⋯⋯	SWAMPY FORESTS
◄⋯⋯	GERMAN THRUSTS
◄———	RUSSIAN
┴┴┴┴	RUSSIAN LINES
━ ━ ━	GERMAN

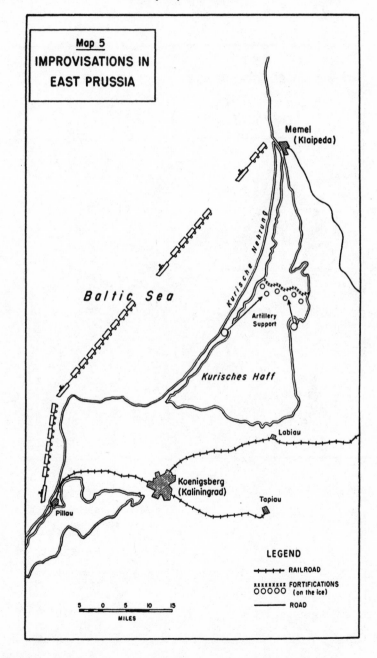

Map 5
IMPROVISATIONS IN
EAST PRUSSIA

Memel
(Klaipeda)

Kurische Nehrung

Baltic Sea

Artillery
Support

Kurisches Haff

Labiau

Koenigsberg
(Kaliningrad)

Tapiau

Pillau

LEGEND

+++++++ RAILROAD

xxxxxxxxx FORTIFICATIONS
OOOOO (on the ice)

——— ROAD

5   0   5   10   15
MILES

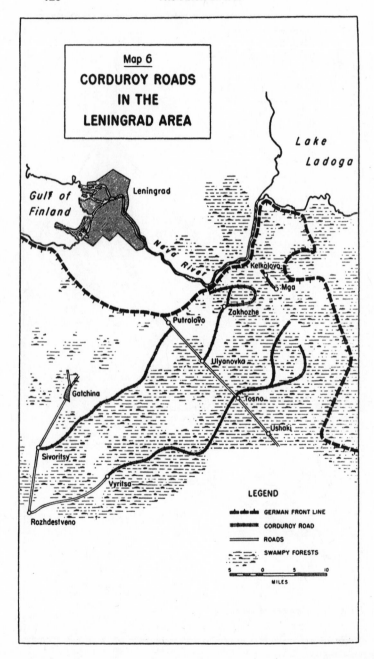

Map 6

CORDUROY ROADS
IN THE
LENINGRAD AREA

Lake Ladoga

Gulf of Finland

Leningrad

Neva River

Kelkolovo

Mga

Zakhozhe

Putrolovo

Ulyanovka

Gatchina

Tosno

Ushaki

Sivoritsy

Vyritsa

Rozhdestveno

LEGEND

GERMAN FRONT LINE
CORDUROY ROAD
ROADS
SWAMPY FORESTS

5   0   5   10

MILES

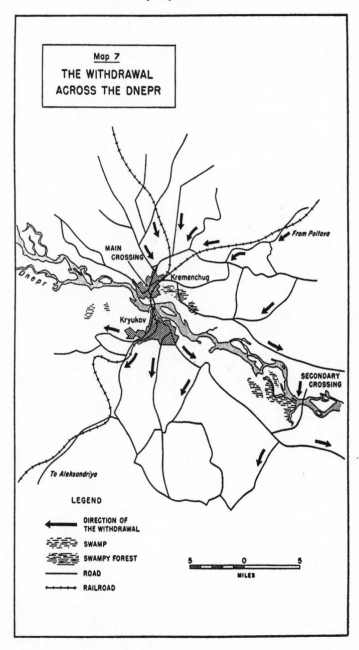

Map 7

THE WITHDRAWAL
ACROSS THE DNEPR

From Poltava

MAIN
CROSSING

Kremenchug

Dnepr

Kryukov

SECONDARY
CROSSING

To Aleksandriya

LEGEND

→ DIRECTION OF
   THE WITHDRAWAL
   SWAMP
   SWAMPY FOREST
── ROAD
┼─┼─┼ RAILROAD

5   0   5
      MILES

Part Two

German Defense Tactics against Russian Break-throughs

By GENERALOBERST ERHARD RAUSS

Commander, 4th and 3rd Panzer Armies

Introduction

By means of short narratives based on actual experience, this study endeavors to describe the characteristics of Russian break-throughs and the countermeasures employed by the Germans. No attempt has been made to present anything like a complete picture. Since these reports were written from memory, some of the dates and figures may be inaccurate. A few combat narratives contain other than strictly tactical details in an effort to convey some of the emotional factors which affected the actions of troop commanders and their men in different situations.

Each of the following chapters deals with one of the more frequently employed tactics to prevent or contain break-throughs. It should be pointed out, however, that only in rare instances was one single method used. Most often one tactical measure predominated in an operation, with two or three others, or even more, complementing it. During extended defensive operations even the predominant method changed occasionally. The use of a combination of defense tactics without preponderance of any one often proved effective. On many occasions the parent unit employed one specific defense method while its subordinate units had to use other tactics. No two situations were alike, and each had to be treated on its own merits. The selection of the type of defensive tactics depended on the intuitive perception of the commander in the field as well as upon the circumstances.

CHAPTER 19

Frontal Counterattack

One of the simplest methods of sealing off a break-through or eliminating a penetration is the frontal counterattack. Usually, such a counterattack can be launched only if the break-through is minor and can be localized, and if both shoulders are secure. Moreover, sufficient reserves must be available to close the breach by a quick counterthrust before the enemy is able to widen the gap. Once hostile preparations for a break-through have been clearly recognized, it is most effective to move the reserves close to the rear of the threatened sector. While the reserves must be close enough for instantaneous effective employment, they should be sufficiently removed from the front line so as not to forfeit prematurely their freedom of maneuver. In their assembly areas the reserves must be concealed from enemy observation and air attacks and must not be exposed to hostile preparation fire. Obviously, reserves should have maximum fire power and mobility; armored divisions come closest to these requirements because they combine tremendous striking force with concentrated fire power. Infantry supported by assault guns will often restore the situation so long as the break-through is local.

A counterattack is far more complicated if, before its effect is felt by the enemy, the shoulders begin to crumble, the breach is widened, and the enemy attack gains ground in depth. But even in this event, it is best to maintain the tactical integrity of the reserve so that upon commitment it can overrun the enemy infantry in one powerful thrust and regain the key positions of the former line. Only then should attempts be made to close the smaller gaps by flanking actions. As a countermeasure against the disintegration of the shoulders and as support to the flanking actions, it will prove effective to protect the open flanks of the break-through area with artillery and to assemble small local reserves behind them. Frequently one infantry company supported by assault guns will suffice for this purpose.

It would be a mistake to attempt to close an extensive breach across its entire width by overextending the attack frontage of the main reserve force. A counterattack delivered under such circumstances would not have sufficient striking power and would be in danger of losing its punch and bogging down before it reached its objective. On the other hand, a delayed commitment of the reserves will result in an expansion of the breach; then, the counterattacking force will be faced with an entirely new situation with which it will be unable to cope alone. Such a delay often leads to heavy losses which can only be offset by committing additional forces.

Whenever the enemy achieves a major break-through that causes the collapse of a wide sector of the front (thirty miles or more), the local reserves will always be insufficient to close the gap by frontal counterattack. Piecemeal commitment of individual divisions in a gap of this width will simply lead to their engulfment by the advancing hostile avalanche. Only a strong force consisting of several corps will be able to stem the tide and halt the enemy advance in the depth of the defense or to close the gap by a counterattack. There will usually be a considerable time lapse, however, before a force of such strength can be released from other sectors and moved to the break-through area. Meanwhile, attempts must be made to narrow the breach by withdrawing to a shorter line and by strengthening the resistance in the sectors adjacent to the gap.

The German offensive to recapture Kharkov and Belgorod presents a good example of a frontal counterattack. By 23 November 1942 the Russians had closed the ring around Stalingrad and started the most powerful winter offensive of the war. Advancing rapidly, they annihilated in quick succession the Romanian, Italian, and Hungarian units along the Chir and Don Rivers and opened a 350-mile gap in the German front This breach was equal to the total length of the western front in World War I. Initially, only isolated German divisions, committed in support of the allied and satellite forces, stood in the way of the Russians, like the stays of a corset. The bulk of the German reserves, including five fully equipped panzer divisions, were tied down in western Europe because of the invasion of North Africa by Allied forces. Some of these divisions later appeared on the eastern front. The German armies in the Caucasus, in danger of being cut off, were forced to withdraw. Their motorized units, mainly First Panzer Army, were committed along the Donets in order to strengthen the southern wing of Army Group Don. North of the gap, the Second Army was forced to evacuate Voronezh and the Don front, and its southern wing was pushed far back to the west. Gradually, two-thirds of the entire Eastern Front began to sway and crumble. Russian pressure mounted constantly and the only solution was to withdraw farther and farther to the west. The Russians poured in a never ending stream of hastily reorganized divisions and continued their drive. Three hostile armies converged on Kharkov and in mid-February 1943 succeeded in capturing this important traffic center by a concentric attack (map 9). But their next thrust, aimed at Poltava, ground to a halt 30 miles short of the city because the Soviet troops were too exhausted to continue. Now they placed all their hopes in the Third Tank Army commanded by their most capable tank expert, General Popov. In mid-February Popov advanced practically without resistance in the direction northwest of Dnepropetrovsk with the apparent intention of reaching the Dnepr bend. His objective was to cross the Dnepr before the German forces were able to build up their defenses along the river, but it soon became obvious that his forces lacked the necessary drive. Meanwhile, the Germans were building up strength for a frontal counterattack.

The divisions arriving from the West detrained at Poltava behind a defensive screen established by Provisional Corps Rauss. This corps held the line with three infantry divisions and the reconnaissance regiment of the 3d SS Panzer Division. Its other motorized elements, the Panzer Division Grossdeutschland and the Fuehrer Escort Battalion, were in rest areas west of Poltava, close to the front. They formed a mobile reserve to be committed in the event that the enemy attempted to capture Poltava by an enveloping thrust through the gap to the north. The Russians actually tried to outflank Poltava, but this danger was eliminated by German infantry supported by the reconnaissance regiment and tactical Luftwaffe units. During these actions the enemy showed definite signs of weakness and exhaustion, and the time for a major counterattack seemed to be approaching.

Quick action was indicated since the snow was beginning to thaw. Mud formed on the ground and soon all movements would become impossible. But deep down the soil was solidly frozen. Cold nights prevented a quick thaw and favored movements during the early morning hours. Meanwhile, the battle-weary German front-line troops were granted a short breathing spell and given the opportunity to integrate newly arrived replacements and equipment.

By 10 March 1943 the counterattack forces stood ready to jump off; their morale was excellent. The main effort was placed on the southern wing where terrain conditions favored the employment of armor. Here, the Grossdeutschland Division was assembled and given the mission of attacking toward Valki. Adjacent on the left, the 320th Infantry Division jumped off after a preparation from all guns of two divisions, supported by corps artillery. The infantry penetrated the enemy positions, mopped up a strong point on the main Poltava–Kharkov highway, and pushed the enemy beyond a flooded brook on the other side of the town. This normally insignificant watercourse had suddenly grown into a raging torrent which brought the attack to an unexpected halt after a gain of only one mile. The tanks of the Grossdeutschland Division attempted to overcome the swift current farther upstream and finally succeeded in crossing after several hours. More than eighty tanks broke through the second enemy position on the east bank of the brook and rolled toward Valki. Soon an improvised bridge was thrown across the brook and the attack regained its momentum. In the sector adjacent to the north, the 167th and 168th Infantry Divisions penetrated the enemy positions after heavy fighting, captured a number of villages, and attempted to establish contact with the LI Infantry Corps on the left. The reinforced reconnaissance regiment, committed between the 320th and the 167th Divisions, closed in on the enemy positions situated in the woods and penetrated deep into the forest. Its tanks advanced along the railroad tracks running parallel to the woods. By afternoon Corps Rauss was making progress along its entire front and kept the crumbling enemy forces on the move.

On the second day of the thrust the corps committed all its forces in a concentric attack on Bogodukhov. For this purpose the corps zone was narrowed to 10 miles. Its width had already been reduced from 60 to 25 miles by the end of the first day. The enemy forces holding Bogodukhov were unable to resist the onslaught of the German ground troops which were closely supported by the Luftwaffe. The city fell after brief house-to-house fighting. Corps Rauss then established contact with the spearheads of the I SS Panzer Corps which had just entered Olshany, fifteen miles southeast of Bogodukhov. After annihilating strong enemy forces in the Olshany area, the panzer corps turned to the east to envelop Kharkov and cut off the enemy's route of withdrawal to the north.

While the main force of Provisional Corps Rauss was to advance northward in an attempt to establish contact with the LI Corps and thereby cut off the enemy forces in the Akhtyrka area, the 320th Division was to screen the pivoting movement of the I SS Panzer Corps. Ever increasing mud and floods slowed the advance at every step. Although all bridges across the swollen Vorskla, Udy, and Lopan Rivers had been destroyed, the infantry and panzer units were nevertheless able to reach their daily objectives. Many motor vehicles and horse-drawn artillery pieces, however, bogged down along the way. On the other hand, the considerably lighter artillery of the Russians and their *Panje* [Russian peasant] wagons pulled through everywhere and escaped the German advance.

The Grossdeutschland Division carried the main effort and reached the upper Vorskla, with the 167th Division following closely. Since the LI Corps on the southern wing of Second Army lagged far behind, no contact with that corps could be established and the enemy around Akhtyrka escaped encirclement. The continuation of the operation by a thrust on Tomarovka required the panzer forces to pivot to the east, changing the direction of their advance. They were replaced by elements of the 167th Division which were to hold a line facing north to provide flank cover. The advance toward Tomarovka was delayed because territorial gains toward the east automatically led to an extension of the open flank.

By the second day of this eastward thrust, the strong 167th Division was almost entirely immobilized along the flank. The arrival of LI Corps had to be awaited before the eastward thrust could be resumed. Army Groups Center and South ran along the Vorskla River. The Army High Command, responsible for co-ordinating the operations of the two army groups, was too far removed, and its decisions therefore were too slow to keep abreast of the fast-moving events at the front. Finally, the Army High Command ordered LI Corps to relieve the

167th Division. The advance continued and the Grossdeutschland Division entered Tomarovka. On its approach to the town, the division destroyed a considerable number of Russian tanks while many undamaged ones, which had bogged down in the mud, were retrieved and turned against the enemy.

It was in this action that Tiger tanks engaged the Russian T34's for the first time; the results were more than gratifying for the Germans. For instance, two Tigers, acting as an armored point, destroyed a pack of T34's. Normally the Russian tanks would stand in ambush at the hitherto safe distance of 1,350 yards and wait for the German tanks to expose themselves upon their exit from a village. They would then take the German tanks under fire while the Panthers were still outranged. Until now, these tactics had been foolproof. This time, however, the Russians had miscalculated. Instead of leaving the village, the Tigers took up well-camouflaged positions and made full use of their longer range. Within a short time they knocked out sixteen T34's which were sitting in open terrain and, when the others turned about, the Tigers pursued the fleeing Russians and destroyed eighteen more tanks. It was observed that the 88-mm. armor-piercing shells had such a terrific impact that they ripped off the turrets of many T34's and hurled them several yards. The German soldiers' immediate reaction was to coin the phrase, 'The T34 raises its hat whenever it meets a Tiger.' The performance of the new German tanks was a great morale booster.

Farther to the south, Kharkov was captured by the 1st SS Panzer Division after four days of street fighting during which Tigers again played a decisive role. The 2d SS Panzer Division turned north, advanced on Belgorod, captured the city, and linked up with the Grossdeutschland Division which had thrust beyond Tomarovka. The capture of the two cities secured the anchors of the new German line along the Donets. Between these two points two German divisions slowly struggled through the mud in their effort to reach the west bank of the river.

The Russian elements that were able to cross the Donets were badly mauled. German reconnaissance units, advancing beyond the river, met with little resistance. Even though the German attack divisions were fully capable of continuing their drive, the over-all situation and the prevailing mud made it inadvisable.

The objective of the frontal counterattack had been achieved. The breach, open for four months, was closed and the greatest Russian winter offensive was stopped. After suffering a defeat of gigantic proportions, the Germans once again held a continuous line anchored on the Donets River.

CHAPTER 20

Flank Attack

The defender will often find it expedient to attack the flank of an enemy penetration with the objective of cutting off and destroying the hostile forces that have broken through. Such tactics are effective only when a secure shoulder provides the defender with a springboard for an attack which is launched straight across the gap to the other shoulder, or when a natural obstacle, such as a large body of water or a swamp, serves as an anvil against which he can crush the attacker. An effective flank attack requires a balanced force with adequate striking power whose strength need not necessarily exceed one-third of the total enemy forces committed in the break-through. The more powerful and mobile the force, the quicker the defender will attain his objective. Unsupported infantry is incapable of mounting a successful flank attack against an armored penetration. In such a situation infantry must always be supported by strong assault gun and armored units as well as sizable antitank forces.

The defender who attacks the flank of an enemy penetration runs the risk of exposing his own flank and must therefore take this factor into account when he plans the counterattack. The danger is usually less serious than anticipated because, during the initial stages of the break-through, the attacker usually commits his forces almost exclusively along the axis of advance without giving much attention to his flanks. These rush tactics are practical, however, only so long as the defender has neither the means nor the opportunity for immediate, effective counteraction. During their invasion of Russia in 1941, for instance, the Germans did not present the Russians with any such opening. On the other hand, during the Russian counteroffenses in 1942, the German command always had strong armored forces at its disposal, making it inadvisable for the enemy to be careless in exposing his flanks. Bitter experience was to teach the Russian that flanks must be protected until he finally made them so tank-proof that they could only be overpowered with heavy casualties. For this reason the German flank attacks gradually lost their sting after 1943 and were more often repulsed.

Flank attacks are particularly effective when employed to eliminate hostile river crossings. The forces which cross first can usually be shattered or wiped out without too much difficulty because they rarely have adequate defensive protection. This happened, for instance, along the Teterev in December 1943. (See Chapter 21.) The defender will find it much more difficult, well-nigh impossible, to eliminate a strongly fortified enemy bridgehead which has adequate fire support from the far bank of the river.

At the beginning of April 1944, the Germans launched a flank attack which proved very effective in remedying a precarious situation. After heavy winter fighting in eastern Galicia and Podolia, the Fourth Panzer Army, with three corps, was on a line extending from Kovel in the north, through Brody, to Berezhany in the south (map 10). The Russian encirclement of Brody was imminent. There was a gap between that town and the army's left wing, and the army right flank was exposed. The so-called fortress Ternopol, 18 miles to the front of the south wing, had been encircled for ten days. The First Panzer Army, forming a roving pocket, was moving north of the Dnestr River toward the gap on Fourth Panzer Army's southern flank. Strong Russian forces were driving westward past the pocket on both sides of the river.

Although the over-all situation was far from satisfactory, the Fourth Panzer Army had at least stopped its retrograde movement. The army was intact after many critical battles and had inflicted heavy losses upon the enemy during the winter. Despite evident battle weariness, the Russians continued their attempts to take Brody in order to gain a route to Lvov. They did succeed in encircling the city on several occasions. The encirclements were broken each time by the provisional armored Task Force Friebe, made up of one battalion of Tigers and one of Panthers. This task force, augmented by a rocket projector brigade equipped with 900 late-type launchers, destroyed the enemy while he was still in his assembly area preparing the final all-out attack. The Russians abandoned the siege of Brody and, in a most unusual change of tactics, used their newly arrived forces to form a continuous front line opposite the army center. The XIII Infantry Corps followed suit and linked up with the XLII Infantry Corps to the north, thus closing the gap north of Brody. The armored task force was now available for other missions.

The army's exposed right flank was under light attack. The Russians captured a few villages, but they were promptly retaken by local reserves supported by an armored battalion which moved freely along the flank. The army front was intact and the southern flank, though exposed, was secure.

Still, the Russian forces which had bypassed the roving pocket continued their westward drive. Their armored spearheads south of the Dnestr entered Stanislav, and those to the north of the river approached the fortified area around the Galich bridgehead. Quickly gathered German infantry, together with advance elements of the Hungarian First Army, which was assembling in the Stanislav–Nadvornaya area, drove the enemy out of Stanislav after street fighting. North of the river, however, the enemy, hampered only by muddy terrain, reached the Zlota Lipa valley. His axis of advance pointed toward the Drohobycz oil fields.

The forward elements of the forces in the pocket had by now reached the Chortkuv area. The Fourth Panzer Army was given the mission of relieving the First Panzer Army by a flank attack, and it received strong reinforcements for the execution of this task. The flank attack was to be launched to the southeast from Berezhany, while a secondary thrust to the Dnestr was to pinch off and destroy the Russian infantry divisions which had penetrated as far as the Galich area.

As a preliminary step, the first elements of the 100th Light Infantry Division, detraining in the army rear area, were ordered to capture the terrain south of Berezhany. Elements of another infantry division were to take the area south of Rogatin. Both of these operations were designed to secure the unloading of II SS Panzer Corps, which had been transferred from Italy. Within a few days after detraining the corps was ready to jump off. Aware of the threat to their flank, the Russians used all their available air power to harass the assembly of the German forces which were restricted to the only two usable roads in the area. This enemy interference, however, was negligible compared to the difficulties presented by the muddy terrain.

The 100th Light Infantry Division was to clear the way for the decisive thrust, with the panzer corps following close behind. The only available all-weather road permitting major mechanized movements led via Podgaytse to Buchach. The infantry had the mission of capturing heavily defended Podgaytse to open the road for the panzer thrust. Hardly had the enemy screening force been dislodged from the wooded heights south of Berezhany, when the infantry ran into huge snowdrifts which covered the entire road to a depth of several feet along 200- to 500-yard stretches. It was impossible to bypass these obstacles because of the rugged, snow-covered terrain on both sides of the road. Security guards were posted and the combat troops, equipped only with intrenching tools and a few locally procured shovels, began to clear the snow. After several hours of steady work, a single lane was opened and around noon it was possible to move up the artillery and tanks which were essential for the impending operation against Podgaytse.

Despite the delay, the infantry took the strongly organized high ground in front of Podgaytse the same day. The division's Tiger battalion knocked out the T34's and antitank gun positions which defended the entrance to the town, but in so doing completely blocked its own advance. The main entrance alone was clogged by sixteen disabled Russian tanks and, as the infantry edged forward in house-to-house fighting, the wrecks were towed off, pushed aside, or blown up. By late evening the Tigers had thrust across the town, knocking out thirty-six additional tanks in their advance. The infantry mopped up during the night and on the next morning turned eastward toward the Strypa River to secure the left flank of the panzer corps and to make way for its advance.

The 10th SS Panzer Division now took the lead, with 100 tanks spearheading the movement. At the southern edge of Podgaytse the division ran into strong resistance from skillfully concealed antitank guns which were too well entrenched to be attacked frontally and could not be bypassed because of the deep water ditches, ravines, and swamps on both sides of the road. After close reconnaissance, the guns were finally knocked out one by one with concentrated panzer and artillery fire. The way cleared, the tanks rolled forward. To avoid further delay, the division commander decided to drive cross-country to Buchach, but the route taken for a short cut proved to be a quagmire. Only the division commander with five lead tanks got through. Although he was able to establish contact with the spearheads of the First Panzer Army, this achievement served no practical purpose as long as the highway from Podgaytse to Buchach was still in enemy hands. The hasty decision to leave this highway delayed the operation and cut off the division commander from his troops. Their tanks bogged down, the panzer troops, fighting as infantry under the corps commander, undertook the clearance of the highway. Hostile antitank fire interfered with their advance, and the Soviets offered strong resistance in the villages along the road. But, subjected to increasing pressure both from the panzer corps and the infantry division approaching from the Galich area, their efforts were in vain. That evening, near the bend of the road west of Buchach, the Russian infantry divisions fleeing eastward along the Dnestr were blocked off, hurled against the river, and destroyed with the help of newly arrived infantry forces. The attack units regrouped and then turned eastward. On 5 April Buchach was reached, and the axis of withdrawal of the encircled army was cleared. The Russians did not readily yield the prize which was being wrung from their grasp. In fierce pursuit they tried to cross the swollen Strypa to cut the escape artery, but they were no match for the liberating forces. Whenever they got across the river, they were immediately thrown back.

By mid-April the right wing of the Fourth Panzer Army had deployed behind the Strypa, and the front, anchored on the Dnestr to the south, included a bridgehead across the Strypa opposite Buchach. On this line fixed positions were organized. The objective of the flank attack – stabilization of the front in eastern Galicia – was attained with the liberation of the First Panzer Amy from encirclement and its reintegration into the German defense system.

In another instance, hostile armored forces opened a 20-mile gap through which the Russians poured reinforcements. The German command wanted to close the breach by a flank attack but had only one panzer division for this purpose. The division was much too weak for this mission, all the more since the enemy had committed strong forces to widen the gap and was protecting his southern flank with powerful armored and antitank units. The operation was therefore divided into several phases. As an initial step the crumbling shoulder south of the gap was strengthened, and then a preliminary panzer attack narrowed the breach to ten miles. Immediately after its replacement by infantry units, the panzer division was ready for the main phase of the operation – the closing of the gap. In a surprise night attack against the enemy flank, the mechanized infantry overcame the tank and antitank cover, and the German tanks, immediately following, succeeded in closing the gap. Furious enemy attacks against the newly established defense line were repelled, but now the northern anchor, held by a recently activated division, gave way in the face of heavily mounting pressure. Finally, this danger was eliminated by the timely arrival of reinforcements. This example clearly demonstrates the effectiveness of a well-executed flank attack even though it may have to be carried out with comparatively weak tank forces. The importance of securing the shoulders at the base of a break-through is only too obvious.

The flank attack is very frequently used in local counterattacks and is an integral part of many large-scale defensive operations. A break-through on a very wide frontage by overwhelmingly superior armor cannot be eliminated by a flank attack even though strong tank forces may be available to the defender, because the attacker usually protects his interior flanks with adequate armor and antitank gun fronts. But even if the flank attack should surmount this obstacle, the attacker still has sufficient time to shift strong tank units from his main effort to the threatened interior flank in order to eliminate the danger. Under the most favorable circumstances, the defender's armored units may be able to divert the attacker's main force by compelling him to establish a new defense line on his flank. This happened west of Kiev in November 1943 when the Germans first succeeded in thwarting the enemy's attack plan, but later saw their own plans frustrated. The result was an extension of their own front line which tied down the German reserves committed in the flank attack. Moreover, by leaving their own flank open, the Germans encouraged the Russians to press their attacks in that direction.

Frequently, the threat of a flank attack by armored forces will alarm the attacker so much that he will halt his offensive in order to avoid the annihilation of those of his forces which have broken through. He will be especially apprehensive if, only shortly before, he has suffered a severe blow by a flank attack or some other armored thrust. During the German relief thrust toward Stalingrad, for instance, panzer forces turned against the flank of the advancing Russian infantry, who fled panic-stricken. This was not surprising since earlier that month a Russian cavalry corps had been annihilated by a flank attack of a strong panzer division at Pokhlebin on the Aksay River and two Russian infantry divisions had been routed north of the river by similar methods (see Department of the Army Pamphlet No. 20–230, Russian Combat Methods in World War II, pp. 69 ff).

CHAPTER 21

Spoiling Attack

The spoiling attack – a surprise thrust into the enemy attack preparations – is a very effective, though rare, operation. Its purpose is to disorganize the enemy's assembly and thereby delay and weaken his offensive or to force him to launch his attack at a less vulnerable point.

Such an attack from the defensive can be undertaken only under certain conditions. The enemy assembly area must be easily accessible to a surprise thrust, and the defender must have strong armored reserves on hand. The terrain and road net must facilitate quick maneuver under cover of darkness. All attack plans must be concealed from the enemy, or he must be deceived with regard to the real intentions. For this reason, it is imperative that one act without delay.

These prerequisites existed only on rare occasions. However, the Germans were presented with a perfect opportunity to exploit them at the beginning of November 1943 (map 11). The Russians had broken through north of Kiev, and there were indications that they intended to envelop the northern wing of Army Group South. The forces at the disposal of the First Ukrainian Front were insufficient to attain this objective. The Soviets advanced sixty miles to the west, captured the important railroad junction of Fastov, neutralized Zhitomir, and encircled the LIX Infantry Corps in Korosten. But a German flank attack by armored units forced the Russians to pull back across the Teterev. Although Zhitomir was relieved, Fastov remained in enemy hands, and the siege of Korosten continued. The Fourth Panzer Army front, which had faced east before the Russian offensive, gave way and was now facing north. Both the German and the Russian flanks were open to the west. Because of their inability to close this gap, the Germans extended an open invitation to the Russians, to continue their offensive in order to exploit the success they had hitherto achieved. They had a unique opportunity to execute a wide envelopment out of their assembly area north of Zhitomir. Troop concentrations and road repairs performed behind the hostile lines indicated the imminent resumption of the Soviet offensive which would first threaten the Fourth Panzer Army and subsequently the entire army group.

The situation called for immediate action, and the Germans therefore decided to avert the threat by striking the flank of the hostile attack preparations with strong panzer forces. The XLVIII Panzer Corps, with the 1st SS, 7th, and 1st Panzer Divisions, was withdrawn from the front and assembled behind the center of the army sector. Meanwhile the approach routes – some of which led through marshy wooded terrain – were reconnoitered, bridges repaired, and the partisan units rampant in the forests dispersed by the security division responsible for this area. Immediately afterward, the combat elements of all three panzer divisions moved out in broad daylight and marched along the main highway through Zhitomir in order to deceive the enemy into believing that strong forces were being shifted to another sector of the front. It was later established that this deception was completely successful. In any event, these preliminary steps were actually inevitable since the movements connected with them had to be executed to enable the Germans to strike deep into the open enemy flank. Without this attempt at deception, the movements would have required two nights, since the approach and assembly of such a strong panzer corps could not be effected in one night. By carrying out the movements by day, they could be timed so that the units reached their turn-off points along the main highway shortly after dusk. By that time half the itinerary had been covered and the movements continued without interruption. The enemy had no opportunity to observe the turning movements of the corps, first to the north, then toward the east.

The entire movement proceeded according to plan without enemy interference. On 4 December 1943, at 0600, all three panzer divisions were poised for attack along the Zhitomir–Korosten highway. At the same time all the GHQ artillery, a rocket-projector brigade with launchers of different calibers up to 320-mm., and an armored train, were moved into position behind the left wing of XIII Infantry Corps on the extreme end of the open flank. These preparations, as well as the concentration of strong reserves behind XIII Corps wing, were to lead the Russians into assuming that the German attack would continue on the army left wing, exactly where it had bogged down the previous month. The Russians were easily convinced of these intentions because their own reaction in similar situations was identical. When a heavy concentration was delivered in this sector at dawn and a German infantry division launched a frontal attack immediately afterward, the enemy felt absolutely certain that his estimates were correct. He shifted strong reserves to this sector and counter-attacked, only to be stopped in his tracks by the concentrated fire of 300 rocket launchers. The Russians were still completely unaware of the impending flank attack. Only after they had moved all available forces and weapons close to the front line, did two German corps comprising five divisions simultaneously attack their right flank. The main thrust was executed by the three divisions of XLVIII Panzer Corps which advanced east toward the Teterev River. Some 1st SS Panzer Division elements were to turn south and attack the Russian forces from the rear. The 7th Panzer Division was to cover the corps left flank and establish contact with LIX Corps, which was breaking out of encircled Korosten.

Completely surprised by this flank attack, the enemy offered little resistance during the first day. The mine fields emplaced by the Russians to protect their open flank were easily discovered from the air and bypassed. The entire flank was crushed and destroyed by the attack from the rear. Within a few hours the German tanks penetrated deep into the enemy artillery emplacements, overran batteries under cover of light ground fog, and destroyed the guns. Since the ground was frozen and covered by only a thin layer of snow, the tanks were able to move quickly and according to schedule. By the end of the first day, the panzer divisions had advanced fifteen to twenty miles into the enemy's flank, taken numerous prisoners, and captured all of his artillery. The LIX Corps had achieved its breakout and established contact with the panzer corps. The Zhitomir–Korosten highway and railroad line were once again in German hands. The completeness of the surprise achieved guaranteed the success of the operation. Only weak remnants of the enemy forces escaped to the east.

The thrust was continued during the second day. But its momentum was greatly impaired by heavy fog and a breakdown of the 1st SS Panzer Division supply system. Even though this division dropped out because of ammunition and fuel shortages, the other divisions advanced twelve more miles. The enemy resistance remained negligible. As the attack progressed, the elements of the XIII Corps gradually joined the panzer corps thrust along the sectors in which the flank attack had swept away all enemy opposition. Farther north, however, the LIX Corps was heavily engaged and progressed only step by step.

It was not until the third day that the first enemy countermeasures were felt, but the few Russian armored and infantry units thrown across the lower Teterev were incapable of withstanding the powerful drive of the panzer corps. The Russians' newly established defenses were quickly overrun and several Soviet tanks destroyed during this action. Armed points of the 1st Panzer Division reached the Teterev south of the railroad bridge. The 69th Infantry Division, operating on the right wing of XIII Corps, crossed the Teterev at Radomyshl and joined the panzer corps advance. On the other hand, the sizable Russian forces remaining in the swampy forests along the Irsha held out so tenaciously that the LIX Corps with its two infantry divisions was unable to overcome their resistance. West of the Teterev, the enemy troops were reduced to a few bridgeheads. During the night, however, these were reinforced to a point where they nearly burst with personnel and equipment. A new enemy army attempted to reverse the tide at any cost.

During the fourth day, heavy enemy attacks struck at the XIII Corps and XLVIII Panzer Corps sectors. Most of them were checked and territorial gains were made by means of armored counterattacks. By the end of the day, however, the center of XIII Corps was in danger of being overrun.

The Germans now decided to eliminate the enemy bridgeheads. On the fifth day of the drive the 1st Panzer Division and the 1st SS Panzer Division formed the jaws of a pincers movement intended to annihilate all enemy forces remaining on the west bank of the Teterev. The weak 7th Panzer Division was to protect the north flank. Desperate enemy attempts to withstand the onslaught of 200 tanks were in vain. One bridgehead after another was crushed or reduced by the powerful drive of the panzer divisions. By noon armored points established contact with the perimeter of the fifth and last enemy bridgehead. The bridges were blown up and the bulk of the enemy equipment, together with many prisoners, fell into German hands. The day culminated in an all-out attack by all available panzer forces and strong elements of XIII Corps against those enemy units which had dented the German lines during the preceding day. It ended in their encirclement and annihilation.

Thus, the first objective of the operation was achieved. The surprise thrust from the defensive penetrated an area forty-five miles in depth and completely destroyed one Russian army and a second one suffered such heavy casualties that it was at least temporarily rendered ineffective. Enemy casualties numbered thousands dead, wounded, or prisoners; more than 200 enemy tanks were destroyed and approximately 800 artillery pieces captured. German losses were light. The front line was shortened and now faced east; it was held solely by German infantry divisions. The XLVIII Panzer Corps was available for another mission.

The second phase of the thrust had the objective of consolidating the German lines. In order to clear the swampy forests along the Irsha of hostile forces and establish direct contact between LIX and XIII Corps, the XLVIII Panzer Corps moved to the Korosten area and launched a pincers attack against the enemy forces in the swamps. Two panzer divisions and *Korpsabteilung* 'E' [a provisional unit of divisional strength formed by three weakened infantry divisions, each organized into one regiment] attacked from Korosten, north of the Irsha, toward the southeast, and the 7th Panzer and 112th Infantry Division thrust from positions south of the river toward the northeast. The northern spearhead, advancing in open terrain along the railroad to Kiev, initially made good progress, whereas the southern thrust was slowed down by heavy fighting in the wooded terrain. Nevertheless, the two armored spearheads established contact by the second day. The marshy forests along the Irsha were still being combed when strong Russian tank formations suddenly launched a flank attack from the north. Soviet armor and infantry also moved up from Kiev. According to statements made by prisoners of war, the Russians anticipated a German offensive to capture Kiev and therefore committed all units available in the area. In view of their limited strength, the Germans had not planned such a large-scale operation, quite apart from the difficulties they would have had in getting through the marshy forests extending between the Teterev and the Dnepr. Actually, the objective of the surprise thrust had been fully achieved, and the intended creation of a continuous infantry front was well under way. In spite of the reckless expenditure of newly arrived armored and infantry forces, the Russian counterattack did not gain any ground. All enemy attacks were repelled after stubborn fighting. On the very first day of the clash, the enemy lost more than eighty tanks. During the following two days, 150 additional tanks were destroyed by the Germans, and the Russian counterattack bogged down eventually. Minor thrusts supported by tanks were directed against the XIII Corps sector but were equally futile.

The consolidating phase of the thrust accentuated the effects of the initial surprise attack. Two additional Russian armies were so badly mauled that they were incapable of offensive action. The acute threat in the area north of Zhitomir was thereby eliminated. A few weeks later the Russian Christmas offensive was launched at a less vulnerable sector of the front, an obvious indication that the enemy had been forced to change his plans.

The spoiling attack therefore achieved the dual purpose of relieving an encircled corps and enabling the Germans to build up a continuous front where previously there had been a wide gap. The annihilation of strong enemy forces was an incidental, though important result of this operation. A frontal counterattack would not have been successful in this case, quite aside from the heavy casualties it would have involved.

Frontal thrusts into enemy attack preparations can be employed only in minor operations. Their success depends on achieving complete surprise as, for instance, during night raids. A singularly well-executed frontal surprise thrust was launched at the beginning of March 1945, when a detachment of young German naval cadets carried out a raid from a bridgehead north of Stettin. Well equipped with *Panzerfausts* [recoilless antitank grenade launchers], they struck at the center of the assembly area of a Russian tank brigade and destroyed all its thirty-six tanks.

CHAPTER 22

Defensive Pincers

Since defensive pincers are the most effective countermeasure against an enemy break-through, they should be applied whenever the tactical situation permits and the necessary forces are available. If these forces have sufficient striking power and mobility, the application of defensive pincers will reverse an unfavorable situation very quickly and decisively. The immediate objective is to seal off the enemy penetration by flank attacks launched simultaneously from both shoulders. Ideally this maneuver should lead to a 'Cannae' – the encirclement and destruction of the enemy force which has broken through.

The jaws of the pincers must attack simultaneously, overcome the hostile flank protection, and link up before enemy countermeasures can become effective. If the jaws do not strike at the same time, the enemy will be given an opportunity to reinforce that interior flank which is not under attack and the maneuver may easily fail. A typical example for such a failure was the Russian pincers attack which was launched during the summer of 1941 in an attempt to eliminate the German bridgehead at Porechye on the Luga. (See Department of the Army Pamphlet No. 20-230, pp. 42ff).

Another indispensable prerequisite for the success of defensive pincers is the close co-ordination of all participating units under one command. In minor actions the exercise of unified command will not meet with any particular difficulties. Complications arise during large-scale operations when some of the participating divisions are separated by long distances and belong to different armies or army groups. In such instances it is expedient to make a single army or army group command responsible for the entire operation. A similar procedure must be followed even in minor actions if the enemy attempts to break through at a sector boundary – a common practice with the Russians.

Defensive pincers can eliminate even comparatively major break-throughs. During the course of such an operation several divisions or corps may regain their freedom of maneuver as, for instance, after the Russian break-through near Belgorod in 1943. At that time the armored wedge which the enemy had driven to a depth of 100 miles was pinched off at the base of the penetration, and his thrust was checked by a pincers movement carried out by two panzer corps, starting from the two opposite shoulders.

When the jaws of the pincers are too weak or the terrain too difficult to tie off the enemy forces that have broken through, protracted fighting involving many critical situations and the formation of curiously shaped front lines will result.

In the Russian campaign this occurred for the first time during the battle along the Volkhov in the winter of 1941–42, when the city of Leningrad came close to extinction, one million civilians being starved or frozen to death. Even the Russian soldiers were inadequately fed and equipped and by the end of the winter half of them were dead.

Faced by this situation, the Soviet leaders decided that Leningrad must be relieved at all cost. For this mission a new command staff was formed under General Merezkov, and the Fifty-ninth and Second Assault Armies, moving up with strong, fresh forces, were integrated into the front line built up along the Volkhov River (map 12). At the same time six divisions from the Leningrad sector were shifted farther east to strengthen the Russian Fifty-fourth Army. After the German spearheads had been withdrawn from Volkhovstroy, fighting continued along a broad front extending from Novgorod to Lodva. Although the German forces dug foxholes and trenches in the frozen swampy forests and snowdrifts, they lacked adequately prepared positions and supply routes.

In this situation, between 10 and 13 January 1942, the Second Assault Army, led by General Vlassov, achieved a break-through across the Volkhov. Five divisions and one ski brigade reached the Novgorod–Chudovo highway and railroad line and pushed back the German screening force along a twenty-mile front. The Germans attempted to re-form their lines along the highway. Islands of resistance in encircled Mostki and in Spasskaya Polist prevented a German rout, but a fifteen-mile gap was opened in the German line, leaving the Russians free access to the rear of the Eighteenth Army. The Second Assault Army struck across no man's land through the forests to the northwest. The attack plan called for cutting the Tosno–Chudovo *Rollbahn* [road designated as a main axis of motorized transportation] and the disruption of the other German supply routes in conjunction with frontal attacks along the Leningrad sector. If the Russians succeeded, most of Eighteenth Army would be lost with only a few remnants escaping to the west. The Russian spearheads advanced 50 miles, meeting virtually no resistance.

The German command and troops performed extraordinary feats during these weeks of extreme danger. Battalions, combat teams, even entire divisions were improvised and thrown into battle. No task was left undone; virgin territory was explored; new expedients were developed. All service forces were employed in combat, troops of other arms suddenly becoming infantrymen. This was a struggle for survival waged simultaneously against an enemy superior in manpower and matériel and against the terrors of a fierce winter. Besides struggling against a cunning enemy, the Germans also had to steel and conquer themselves. Yet the impossible was accomplished. Only 12 miles separated the enemy spearheads from their objectives when they were suddenly stopped, repelled, and shattered. On 25 February one enemy force that had penetrated close to the *Rollbahn* west of Lyuban was cut off from its rear communications and annihilated. A new inner front extending over 120 miles was built up around the Volkhov pocket and connected with the outer front. It ran straight across the marshes north of Lake Ilmen, followed the course of the Oredezh and the railroad tracks connecting Divenskiy with Chudovo. The danger had not yet been overcome.

In view of the latest setback, the Soviet command reduced its objectives, but its new intentions presented an even greater danger. For several weeks the Russian Fifty-fourth Army had attacked the thinly held German line in the swamps south of Lake Ladoga. These attacks were repelled by the 269th Infantry Division and units of XXVIII Corps. The Fifty-fourth Army received additional forces and was given the mission of breaking through at Pogostye and thrusting toward Lyuban. At the same time the Second Assault Army in the pocket stopped its westward drive and assembled its forces south of Lyuban. Strong elements of the Fifty-second and Fifty-ninth Armies followed into the pocket to cover the rear and the flanks of the Russian forces. The Fifty-fourth and Second Assault Armies were to launch a pincers attack, cut off the German I Infantry Corps, and encircle and annihilate it. Once this was accomplished, the road to Leningrad would be open again.

By now the Volkhov pocket held fourteen Russian infantry divisions, supported by three cavalry divisions, seven cavalry brigades, one tank brigade, and five GHQ artillery regiments. The Fifty-fourth Army had reached a strength of twelve divisions. Its striking power centered in an armored force of 200 tanks, most of which were T34's capable of operating under winter conditions. The German defence forces had no equivalent matériel to oppose them. Jumping off on 9 March, the Fifty-fourth Army therefore had no difficulty in penetrating the German lines and widening the gap until it reached ten miles in width and twelve miles in depth. The German infantry formed a human wall in an attempt to stop the enemy. Although its number was at no time more than 3,500, it withstood the onslaught of 90,000 Russians. The German forces yielded ground, lost some engagements, but final victory was theirs because the Russians were denied the opportunity to exploit their local penetrations. The enemy was finally forced to discontinue the offensive three weeks after he had launched his first attack in this sector.

The encircled Second Assault Army was even less successful when it hurled its forces against the German lines forming the northern boundary of the pocket. During several weeks of fierce struggle, the Russians were incapable of overcoming the German resistance. What finally paralyzed them was the disaster that took place to their rear.

On 15 March, elements of I Corps with the SS Police Division in the lead went over to the attack west of Spasskaya Polist and struck at the enemy supply routes. Elements of the XXVIII Corps converged from the south. After great hardships, the German spearheads linked up on 19 March. Even though this ring around the Volkhov pocket could not be fully maintained in the face of incessant counterattacks by superior Russian forces, the escape gap was kept down to approximately two miles. The Russians laid the tracks for two narrow-gage field railways through the gap, but their capacity was insufficient to supply the 180,000 men within the pocket.

When, after a series of attacks and counterattacks, the front was stabilized, the German lines formed a 'finger' cutting across the Russian axis of movement. It was twelve miles long, but in no place more than two to two and a half miles in width. There was not a single point within this finger which could not be swept by enemy heavy weapons fire from the east or from the west.

At first the Soviets made some vain attempts to envelop the finger through the swamps in the rear and cut it off at its base. In April the Russians decided to make an extreme effort. On 29 April the Fifty-ninth Army threw seven infantry regiments and two armored brigades into an attack along a narrow front. Thrusting westward from positions north of Mostki, they were to link with four divisions attacking eastward. This Russian attack had to succeed. Two gaps, each two miles in width, were torn open on either side of the finger which was lacerated to the bone. During the next few days the fortunes of war changed frequently. Finally, undaunted courage and supreme devotion triumphed. By 13 May the Russian regiments which had penetrated the German lines were encircled and shattered, and the former main line of resistance was re-established.

The die was cast. The Volkhov pocket had become untenable for the Russians, and their withdrawal began about 15 May. The cavalry corps farthest to the northwest was withdrawn, the concentration south of Lyuban was dispersed, and medium artillery as well as supply units were pulled out. The Germans soon recognized the enemy intentions. On 22 May German forces launched the pursuit from north and west across mud and slush and reduced the pocket to a twelve-mile square by 30 May. On that day the Germans also sealed the small escape gap and established a blocking position across the Soviet supply route in the vicinity of Myasnoy Bor.

The struggle entered its final phase, a phase which was to last four more weeks. While the German spearheads steadily narrowed the enemy-held territory, the Soviets, with courage born of desperation, furiously sought to extricate themselves from the pocket. In their quest for safety and escape from death, elements of eight divisions repeated their daily attacks in waves of four to six regiments. The Russians pinned their main hope on the Fifty-ninth Army which was to break through from the east. Without interruption this army attacked 2–26 June, delivering a crescendo of fire and hurling ever increasing masses of infantry and tanks into the battle. The carnage reached tremendous proportions. At times it seemed as if the Russians might achieve a break-through after all, but the Germans always succeeded in hurling them back.

Only small groups escaped. The encircled forces were split into several smaller pockets, and all organized resistance of the Second Assault Army ceased by 25 June. The Russian casualties in the pocket amounted to 60,000 dead and prisoners, among the latter General Vlassov and numerous high-ranking commanders and staff officers. Six infantry divisions and six brigades were annihilated. Nine additional divisions were either totally or partially destroyed. The Soviets had suffered terrific losses, expended more than twenty divisions, and spent themselves in vain, six-month effort to break the ring around Leningrad.

Another incomplete pincers movement led to curiously shaped front lines during the fighting near Rzhev in January 1942, where a German pocket separated the main body of enemy forces from a Russian pocket. In this instance the Russian forces in the pocket had only poor supply routes at their disposal, and more than 100,000 men had to subsist for several months under the most precarious circumstances. The Russian cavalry corps, trapped in the swampy forests southwest of Sychevka after its pocket was reduced by the Snail Offensive was in such a pitiful situation that the men first ate the meat and later chewed the hides of their horses to keep from starving. Despite their plight, the Russians refused to consider abandoning their pocket (see Part One, pp. 36ff).

Two additional incomplete pincers movements are worthy of mention. In March 1944, First Panzer Army formed a roving pocket when its pincers attack failed to liberate the encircled German forces near Cherkassy. Finally, during the battle near Lvov in July 1944, the Germans were forced to hold simultaneously two parallel fronts, twenty-five miles apart. The forward front line had a gap which was narrowed to three miles by a pincers attack, whereas the other line was open on the flanks. This extraordinary synthesis of defense lines, as well as the interlocking pockets, were caused by German and Russian pincers, the jaws of which were not completely closed.

Defensive pincers are the preferred method of eliminating an enemy bridgehead. German experience shows that there are no safer tactics for wiping out bridgeheads and inflicting heavy losses on the enemy. Chapter 21 contains a description of the elimination of five newly formed enemy bridgeheads across the Teterev which were wiped out in one day by a pincers attack executed by strong panzer forces.

The most effective pincers attacks are those which, instead of being directed against both flanks, simultaneously envelop the enemy's front and rear. However, the jaw of the pincers that is to strike the hostile rear area is in danger of being attacked in its own rear, as happened, for example, during the Russian defense against the German break-through of the Leningrad line. In this operation the Germans executed two simultaneous pincers attacks. The forward claws pinched off the Russian front line and shattered it while the rear pincers enveloped and inflicted heavy casualties on the armored reserves which had been thrown in to lend assistance (see Department of the Army Pamphlet No. 20-230, pp. 62 ff).

By some extraordinary circumstance it may occasionally be feasible to strike at both enemy flanks and simultaneously envelop his front and rear. This double pincers maneuver will nearly always lead to the complete encirclement and annihilation of the enemy forces. For instance, in March 1943 in the lower Dnepr bend, the pulverizing jaws of a double pincers movement destroyed the Third Russian Tank Army.

The success of pincers attacks is contingent upon the size of the forces available in a given situation. Whenever the tactical situation offers an opportunity for the use of defensive pincers but available forces are insufficient, it will prove more advantageous to assemble all available units and launch a powerful flank attack.

CHAPTER 23

Defense in Place with Mobile Reserves

Even large-scale offensives can be stopped by a defense in place if a number of successive positions are available and the infantry holding the front line has strong artillery, tank, and assault gun support. The reserves must be mobile so they can be shifted from one sector to another in time to prevent or at least contain an enemy penetration. This can be achieved only if the road net is in good condition and sufficient transportation is available.

A conflict entailing simultaneous fighting in different theaters of war and at different fronts within each theater may easily produce a shortage of combat forces which can be overcome only by improvising reserves. In such a situation, security and supply troops, as well as other service units, may have to be committed along extensive, quiet sectors to release combat forces for the formation of reserves. A correct estimate of the enemy's intentions is essential for the timely withdrawal of units from apparently safe sectors.

In the operations near Orsha during the winter of 1943–44, the Germans employed defense-in-place tactics and denied the Russians the use of the Minsk–Smolensk *Rollbahn* for several months. In this instance, railroad and highway communications were excellent, and the mobility of the reserves, together with the construction of defensive positions in depth, prevented a Russian break-through. Used in other sectors, the same tactic proved ineffective when road nets were bad or when the Russians massed a thousand or more tanks to force a break-through, and the Germans had no adequate weapons to oppose them. Had the enemy used such a mass of armor at Orsha, the Germans would have been unable to hold with a defense in place.

Even at Orsha the general situation of Fourth Army was anything but favorable (map 13). By the end of September 1943, the army had just completed a strategic withdrawal from positions east of Smolensk under extreme difficulties. In accordance with orders from Army Group Center, the army was to occupy the Panther position east of the Dnepr in order to deny the Russians access to Orsha, the communication center on the Dnepr, where three railroad lines and the Moscow–Minsk and Leningrad–Kiev highways intersect. The capture of Orsha would have jeopardized the position of Third Panzer Army adjacent to the north and Ninth Army to the south. The Fourth Army sector was seventy-five miles wide and ran from a point ten miles north of the *Rollbahn* to the southern outskirts of Chausy. The army had three corps with eleven divisions whose combat efficiency was greatly reduced by the hard fighting and the withdrawal they had recently undergone. With the exception of one reorganized division, the combat strength of the divisions had dropped to that of regiments, and their weapons and equipment were inadequate. At first the Panther position was very thinly held. With the arrival of replacements and the introduction of various expedients, the army gradually succeeded in building up a fairly adequate defense system.

The construction of the Panther position began in August 1943. In some sectors the position consisted of two parallel trenches, in others of only one. A number of trenches had not been completed by the time the line was occupied and in these sectors the defense system was only a cordon of individual strong points. Tactical wire was strung intermittently and dugouts were few. Natural obstacles had been integrated into the defense line wherever possible. From a tactical point of view, some of the sites were not too well selected because they ran along unsuitable forward slopes. Enemy fire soon led to the abandonment of these positions and forced the Germans to dig in on reverse slopes. Observation was adequate and, though the position was far from perfect, it offered the weakened German forces the possibility of making a stand.

The Russians had followed the German withdrawal very closely. They assembled their forces in front of the position and made careful preparations for a break-through. They did not attack until 12 October and the German troops made good use of this delay to improve their defense area. The German command expected that the immediate objective of the impending Russian attack would be to take Lenino, cut the Orsha–Gorki highway, link up with strong partisan groups operating in the forests northwest of Gorki, turn toward Orsha, and advance along the *Rollbahn* to Minsk.

The reserves of the Fourth Army consisted of several assault gun battalions, some motorized antitank units, GHQ artillery, rocket projector regiments, and engineer and construction units. The success of the defense in place depended upon correctly timing the shift of the mobile elements of these reserves to threatened areas or sectors already under attack. No outside assistance was to be counted on, but the army intended to withdraw battalions, regiments, and even divisions from quiet sectors and move them to critical points once the Russian attack was in full swing. In so doing, the army commander was ready to take great risks in stripping quiet sectors of the front.

The task of shifting these forces was greatly facilitated by the availability of excellent routes of communication. From the lateral highway and railroad line connecting Vitebsk with Orsha and Mogilev, routes branched off to each corps sector. Truck transportation, earmarked for supply functions, was diverted to troop movements. All roads and highways were clearly marked, and construction units maintained them in serviceable condition, a task which was especially difficult in spring and required a lot of manpower. Particular care was given to the marking and maintenance of panzer roads. Special bridges had to be constructed or fords provided for heavy tanks and assault guns because the existing bridges could not carry such loads. Railroad operations were conducted up to points immediately behind the front line.

Instead of giving the weak combat forces a well-deserved rest, the army commander was forced to issue strict orders that all front-line troops work without interruption on improving the forward positions. An exacting, at times even petty, control system had to be imposed by the army to find out where the construction work was lagging and how weak points could be reinforced. By this method the defense system gradually gained depth, and one obstacle after another was constructed. Finally, the Panther position consisted of two continuous trenches and a fortification system protecting the artillery gun positions. As soon as the Panther position was sufficiently strong, several other positions were constructed in the rear. The first two were spaced at six-mile intervals, and the third covered Mogilev, Shklov, Kopys, and Orsha on the Dnepr by the construction of perimeter defenses east of the river. These bridgeheads had a depth of three to five miles and were interconnected by a trench linking their most forward points. Numerous switch positions were built between the individual trenches and fortified lines so that, in case one sector was lost, contact between units would not be disrupted. Contrary to customary German technique, these switch positions connected the successive trenches diagonally and not vertically. Another position extending north beyond Orsha was built along the west bank of the Dnepr. During the winter the Germans also constructed a strong position farther to the rear along the Beresina.

The antiaircraft artillery, as well as the few available planes, were held in reserve to be committed in sectors under attack. The flexibility of the mobile antiaircraft guns greatly strengthened the defense system. Effective reconnaissance was of great importance. Information obtained from ground reconnaissance, sound ranging, and air observation usually provided the Germans with sufficient intelligence to determine the scope and time of Russian attacks with exactitude. Thus, the army was able to introduce effective countermeasures even before the beginning of an attack.

The Russians launched altogether eight major thrusts against the German defense system. Their last attempt to break through was warded off at the beginning of April 1944. The Dnepr defenses were still intact after six months of bitter struggle. The Russians failed to force a break-through in the direction of Orsha and Mogilev despite a series of frontal, flanking, and enveloping attacks. An analysis of this German success shows that the Fourth Army was able to compensate for a one-to-ten inferiority in manpower and matériel only by exploiting all possibilities for defense and co-ordinating all its forces. For this purpose the army had to interfere in details of the command functions of its subordinate corps and divisions, a procedure altogether contrary to German doctrine, but one which proved necessary in this instance. Orders for the formation of reserves, the purpose of which could be understood only from the perspective of the over-all situation, frequently did not make sense to lower echelon commanders. The same may be said for some of the orders pertaining to improving positions, constructing roads, transferring stocks of ammunition, and similar demands.

The unusually good communications made it possible to shift reserves freely. When Russian attacks were at their heaviest, the rate of transfer was stepped up to two battalions per day. The withdrawal of an entire division from the front and its subsequent movement to another sector usually required several consecutive nights. During the first night one or two battalions were pulled out, and adjacent sectors extended. During the following night the width of the adjacent sectors was equalized and one or two more battalions were withdrawn in the same manner. This was continued at the same rate until the movement was completed. The transfer of forces would have been accomplished much faster had single battalions been withdrawn from different divisions, but the army avoided this procedure whenever possible since it attempted to maintain the organizational integrity of its divisions.

Before the first Russian thrust, the corps sector where the enemy onslaught was expected was widened by the inclusion of two additional divisional sectors. This was contrary to the established procedure of narrowing that defense sector where an attack was expected. The purpose of this measure was to enable the corps to form strong reserves from its own forces and shift them to the points where they were most needed. In this case, the widening of the defense sector proved effective since all Russian attacks were halted.

In another instance a motorized infantry division, which had but five organic battalions in line at the beginning of the fifth Russian thrust, was subjected to particularly heavy attacks. By the time the fighting abated on the fifth day, fifteen additional battalions had been brought into the divisional sector, and the front was held. At the same time, the German lines in quiet sectors were so overextended that one mile of frontage was occupied by only thirty men. The slightest attack would have penetrated the line in these sectors, but the Russians did not attempt to launch one.

To command and troops alike, the construction of reserve positions gave a sense of security which they ordinarily lacked in the Russian theater. At no time did their existence lower the resistance of the troops or induce them to withdraw before it became absolutely necessary. The infantry felt reassured by the effective tactics the army employed in massing its artillery. The army artillery commander held far-reaching authority over all organic artillery, giving full support to whichever corps was under attack and withdrawing units not needed in quiet sectors. He made all arrangements to provide an adequate supply of ammunition by diverting supplies slated for quiet sectors and using them where they were most needed. Supply movements were facilitated by the availability of the main highway and railroad leading from Minsk which, however, were frequently cut by partisan attacks. During lulls in the fighting, ammunition was saved for impending enemy thrusts.

The mass employment of supporting units such as assault gun, panzer, tactical air support, antiaircraft, and antitank elements was stressed by the army commander. These units were pulled out wherever they were not absolutely essential and shifted to sectors under attack.

The Russian offensive tactics during these operations varied little from those used earlier in the campaign. The infantry fought bravely, launching attack upon attack, often with only a few hours' interval. Manpower was no problem to the Russians. In seemingly never-ending waves, they came out of their trenches, advanced, withdrew, and returned to the attack. During the five thrusts along the Minsk–Smolensk highway, the Russians usually renewed their attacks at the identical spot where they had tried before. They persisted in their efforts to force a break-through at a particular point and entirely disregarded the cost. A more flexible command might have considered other solutions.

The Russian was capable of concentrating tremendous fire power and employing artillery effectively. During the first day of an operation, artillery fire was well coordinated, but thereafter its unity of effort gradually disintegrated and its effectiveness decreased. During the second thrust he assembled approximately 800 pieces along a six-mile front and fired a quantity of ammunition which was hitherto unsurpassed in the Russian theater of operations. The number of German guns available for counterfire was approximately 250. On the first day of the thrust the Russians achieved a deep penetration between the Dnepr and the Minsk highway. An attempt to straighten out the salient was unsuccessful. The next day the Russians penetrated the German lines north of the highway and isolated an entire artillery battalion-group. In spite of the commitment of additional reserves, the German line had become so fragile that the army decided to withdraw to the second line of the Panther position. When the Russians renewed their attack, it seemed that their artillery lacked unity of effort and co-ordination. The Germans repelled all further assaults and prevented a break-through.

Russian camouflage and concealment were excellent. The enemy moved at night and disappeared from sight during daylight, hiding in villages and wooded areas. Although the Russians often regrouped their forces, their movements could rarely be observed.

The Soviet lower command echelons often lacked initiative. After having succeeded in pushing back the German line, for instance, the Russians had difficulty in sustaining the momentum of the attack and in assembling their infantry and artillery forces for an attack on the next objective. On the other hand, the enemy showed extraordinary skill in exploiting even the smallest penetration with amazing speed. Because of these infiltration tactics, the Germans were forced to make every possible effort to immediately seal off penetrations, however small their own counterattack force. Otherwise, it would have been impossible or would have involved heavy casualties to ferret the Russian out of the break-through area. Once they had sufficient time to organize positions, even planned attacks by fresh units often failed to overcome the stubborn resistance offered by the Russians.

The enemy's zone of attack was usually strictly limited, almost as if it had been cut to measure. The German supporting weapons outside the attack zone proper were not neutralized. For instance, the flanking fire delivered by a German artillery battalion-group from an adjacent sector straight into the Russian attack waves was not interfered with in any way.

The Russian rarely launched diversionary attacks at points outside the main zone of attack. Considering the extent to which the Germans had weakened the quiet sectors of their front, such diversionary attacks would probably have caused some very critical situations.

The Russian proved once again that he was practically immune to unfavorable weather conditions. Snow, rain, cold, and ice affected him but little. His winter clothing was of excellent quality.

Except for attacks against German infantry in the front line, the enemy air force was almost inactive, although German antiaircraft defenses were inadequate. Since the Russians never undertook strategic air operations, the Germans were able to move supplies without enemy interference.

CHAPTER 24

Position Defense in Strong Points and Improvised Fortresses

The defender who decides to hold out in places in strong points and improvised fortresses usually employs emergency measures rather than defense tactics. The Germans were forced to resort to such measures because of the acute manpower and matériel shortages from which they suffered once the war had spread all over Europe and to North Africa. In Russia, the overextended front lines, the bitter struggle against a superior enemy, and the elements of nature led to an expenditure of forces for which German manpower resources and industrial potential were insufficient. The long duration of the war accentuated these deficiencies with the result that position defense in improvised strong points and fortresses became ever more frequent. Excessive losses, difficult terrain, and bad weather forced the Germans to anchor their defense system on inhabited localities along wide sectors and to use these defense areas as substitutes for a continuous front line. These tactics often proved effective because they helped to gain time and overcome critical situations. During the winter or during the muddy seasons, for instance, holding villages and towns was the only way to escape annihilation. Then, it was the weather and terrain that imposed the adoption of these emergency measures. During the summer and dry weather many an enemy break-through attempt was delayed and whittled down by the same tactics until the Germans were capable of containing the Russians along a continuous line prepared in the rear.

Service troops took a major part in the defense of inhabited localities. In most instances they built and improved fortifications in areas where they were stationed and made strong points of them. Frequently, supply elements were organized into alert units and committed as replacements in the most forward fortified areas. The system of mutually supporting strong points provided for defense in depth and maximum utilization of all available forces for combat purposes. Every soldier in a headquarters or service unit and in rear installations received combat training with emphasis on proficiency in the use of antitank weapons in close combat. Whenever the training schedule was rigidly adhered to, the results were favorable. In 1943, for instance, in Zolochev (near Kharkov) a divisional bakery company stopped Russian

162

tank units which had broken through, destroyed several tanks, and forced the remaining ones to turn about.

The practice of defending strong points should, however, not be overdone or adopted as a standing operating procedure. It would be wrong to order all unit trains and supply trucks to stop in the midst of a withdrawal and make their service personnel fight to the last man. If such an order was obeyed to the letter, it would lead to the loss of all transportation facilities and disrupt traffic. This, in turn, would jeopardize the supply of the combat forces, greatly impair freedom of maneuver, and result in disaster.

During the battle for Lithuania in October 1944, the German defense based on fortified inhabited localities did not actually stop or even delay the Russians for long, but it achieved a certain continuity in the defense and checked the enemy advance by causing many delays and inflicting casualties. Since no new reserves could be formed or provided by army group, a number of service schools and headquarters units, all available trains and supply troops, as well as all other auxiliary units, had to be employed in the defense. They strengthened the resistance at crucial defiles and potential points of penetration. A tightly knit defensive network was built up which even strong enemy forces could penetrate or bypass only by a time-consuming process. The strongly defended towns usually withstood the enemy's daylight attacks. During the evening hours, however, the Russians bypassed or attacked these towns from all sides, and the German elements had to be withdrawn under cover of darkness to escape encirclement and annihilation. In the meantime, renewed resistance was organized along another line, which the German forces occupied by dawn and the process was repeated. The Russians did not advance more than five to six miles a day, even in the sector where they placed their main effort. They did not achieve a break-through or open a gap in the front. Once they reached the Memel River, the German forces, reinforced by other improvised units, brought the enemy offensive to a halt.

CHAPTER 25

Improvised Zone Defense

A variant of zone defense was improvised by the Germans during the battles for the city of Lvov and for East Prussia in the final phase of World War II. Though similar to the doctrine of elastic defense in depth and the evacuation of forward positions introduced during the First World War, these defensive tactics are not identical with any others employed before 1944. The characteristics of this improvisation, as applied during the battle for Lvov, have been explained in Part One, pp. 27 ff. Since the prerequisites for their successful application rarely existed, and since most German commanders in the field doubted their practicability and utility, these tactics were not employed on any other front. Besides, the over-all situation was so critical that there was a general reluctance to introduce experiments. By the second half of 1944 the Germans rarely had sufficient time for the construction of numerous positions or for the thorough indoctrination and training of troops. Only the most ardent faith in this improvisation could overcome all handicaps and achieve final success. During both battles improvised zone defense tactics helped to keep intact the combat strength of the German divisions subjected to terrific concentrations and to prevent the enemy from breaking through. On both occasions the Russians suffered heavy casualties and were forced to shift their main effort to other sectors.

In East Prussia the Third Panzer Army, with its 9 weak divisions, 50 tanks, 400 artillery pieces, and insignificant air support was opposed to 44 Russian divisions, 800 tanks, 3,000 guns, and strong air forces. The use of improvised zone defense tactics enabled the army to stop the Russian onslaught for one month, after which the collapse of the adjacent armies forced a withdrawal from this sector. During December 1944 special training in zone defense was introduced with the active participation of both command and troops. Army engineer and construction units supervised the paramilitary and civilian labor forces building position after position. Antitank obstacles, mine fields, and a system of local strong points and nests of resistance, fifty miles in depth, were built (map 14). The foremost fifteen-mile belt was fortified on the basis of the lessons learned at Lvov. Everyone, from corps commander to private, made strenuous efforts to improve the defense system. Strong points and pillboxes were to afford maximum protection and defensive power by the construction of perimeter defenses. At the same time precautions were taken to prevent pillboxes or nests of resistance from becoming traps for their defenders. Tactical details and technical improvisations were carefully planned to preclude disagreeable surprises. All of East Prussia became one fortress with the zone defense area its strongest outpost. The morale of the troops was excellent, and they faced coming events with confidence.

The Russians attempted a war of nerves by announcing the start of their offensive at three different times and by telegraphing their punches in advance. The Germans did not take these announcements too seriously and refused to be intimidated by the Russian show of armored strength in front of their lines. They were more concerned about Russian preparations along a railroad embankment, a few hundred yards in front of the German lines, where the enemy brought up antitank guns and dug eight passages through a dam which his tanks were unable to surmount. These preparations were too close to remain unobserved, although the Russians tried to cover the noise of the nightly demolitions by heavy mortar fire and camouflaged the passages with boards and foliage. This was the line on which the Russians emplaced their most forward heavy weapons which were to eliminate any German interference by direct fire and cover the tanks advancing through the gaps in the embankment. Other indications of an imminent major offensive were the trenches dug by the Russians to facilitate the approach of infantry spearheads and the construction of positions connected by communication trenches to provide cover for the assembly of the first-wave infantry. Changes in the daily aerial photographs provided information on newly constructed emplacements and showed fresh tracks in the snow leading to ammunition dumps and battery positions. Reports from agents gave information on the arrival of new divisions, and a few radio signals, intercepted despite the enforcement of strict radio silence by the Russians, uncovered the location of forward command posts. These indications made it clear where the Russians intended to place their main effort and at what time and with which forces they planned to start the attack. The Russian attack preparations were methodical: enemy artillery observers occupied newly constructed observation posts; medium guns registered cautiously; enemy fighters suddenly swept the sky to stop German aerial reconnaissance; and dive bombers plastered approach routes, command posts, and towns behind the German front with machine gun fire and bombs. Together with heavy Russian troop movements toward the front, particularly during the nights of 9 and 10 January, these indications were closely observed and studied to enable the army commander to give the code word for the withdrawal to the main battle position at the right moment. It required steady nerves and expert evaluation of combat intelligence not to exhaust the troops by repeated premature withdrawals or to suffer heavy casualties from the enemy's barrage because delayed withdrawal orders had jeopardized the defensive maneuver.

On 11 January there was a noticeable reduction in enemy combat activity and movements. The German troops were nervously waiting for the orders which were to spare them from the enemy's deadly fire, but they failed to receive any such order at the front line. Instead, the graduating class of the Luftwaffe Academy was to be conducted on a tour of the army sector. The young officer candidates watched demonstrations by the newly arrived 5th Panzer Division and inspected the fortifications of the battle position. Since the front was calm, it was possible to fulfill their request to visit some outposts and observe the enemy's positions and movements. Here and there an enemy machine gun fired a few rounds, breaking the silence of a sunny afternoon. Suddenly, some projectiles whizzed through the air and dug up the earth near a crossroads. Several mortar shells exploded near the outposts, and the platoon leader shouted the command: 'Take cover.' Detected by the enemy, the visitors quickly took cover in a deep dugout. After a few more rounds registered in the vicinity, two German artillery salvos hit back at the enemy observation posts and silence was restored. Proud of their front-line experience, the officer candidates returned unharmed to the rear.

The following day was even more peaceful. No new clues regarding the probable H Hour of the enemy attack were observed by the outposts. On the other hand, radio intercepts as well as the latest observations of night reconnaissance planes left no doubt that strong Russian columns were moving into their assembly areas, that the artillery emplacements were fully occupied, and that the armed units had moved up into the depth of the concentration area. The Germany army commander therefore decided to give the code word at 2200 on 12 January. The evacuation of the two forward lines went smoothly and the units moved into the battle position. Three hours later the movement was completed, the new command posts were occupied, and the signal communications functioned normally.

As usual before a major Russian offensive, several deserters arrived at German outposts; their statements agreed – a heavy artillery preparation at 0600 was to precede the launching of the attack on 13 January. The army commander immediately issued orders that the German artillery deliver at 0530 a concentration on the assembly areas of the enemy infantry and use the two basic loads set aside for this purpose. Thus, a heavy German preparation led off the second battle for East Prussia. At 0600 the enemy unleashed a hail of fire with more than 3,000 pieces pouring shells of all calibers on the two forward German positions evacuated only a few hours earlier. By then the German infantry and artillery occupied the battle position which had its forward boundary in the third position. The area fire, covering up to three miles in depth, was scattered and damaged only evacuated towns and former command posts, the obvious targets of the Russian artillery. The German reserves were hidden in the woods and remained unharmed by the preparation fire. By 0800, after pulverizing the first position, the Russian fire concentrated on the second one, but with less intensity. Half an hour later the shells were scattered in the depth of the battle position, gradually diminishing to area or harassing fire without definite targets.

Following the first salvos of artillery fire, the Russian infantry had gone into action, carefully advancing through thick fog which covered the terrain until 1100. Only slightly delayed by the fire of German rear points left behind in the first position, the Russians soon rushed beyond this obstacle. But even before they reached the evacuated second position, they were pinned down by artillery and rocket fire. Their reports, announcing the capture of the first and second German positions to higher headquarters, failed to mention that they had taken no prisoners or booty. It was not until 1000 that they reached the forward line of the battle position. Pinned down by the fire of all German guns and the ladder fire of the rocket projector brigade, their advance came to a sudden halt. The Russian infantry sent out distress signals for immediate tank support. Poor visibility prevented the enemy from taking advantage of his superiority in fire power and in the air. Nevertheless, the Russian infantry succeeded in penetrating between individual strong points. When the fog lifted, these spearheads were cut off and annihilated.

The Russians directed their main thrust against the only elevation in this area, near Kussen, which they captured around noon after a strong armored attack. Their infantry, attempting to follow the tanks, was repelled with heavy casualties along the forward line of the main battle position. The Russian armored units, however, continued their thrust from the Kussen area because the German antitank guns were unable to cope with such masses of tanks. This threat was all the more serious since enemy planes appeared in great number and were initially unopposed. They bombed towns, roads, evacuated command posts, and artillery emplacements and attacked everything that moved on the ground. German planes, called to the rescue, attacked the low-flying Russian formations, shot down several planes, and dispersed the rest. This was the cue for the German counterattack. Leading the attack, 5th Panzer Division columns emerged from the protective cover of the forests and launched simultaneous thrusts against the flank and rear of the Russian armor in the Kussen area. The clash, in which the panzer division was supported by an assault gun brigade and rocket-firing planes, raged for several hours. After the Germans recaptured Kussen, Russian tank reserves made a counterattack, but were turned back by assault guns and fighter planes.

The German infantry, supported by assault guns, tore gaps into the Russian attack columns which had been weakened by heavy artillery and rocket fire. Before long the entire enemy attack force wavered and fell back in confusion. During the evening the former main line of resistance was reoccupied by the German infantry. The booty was rich, aside from 122 burned-out tanks piled up on the slopes near Kussen. Improvised zone defense had saved the German forces from being annihilated and had stopped all enemy break-through attempts.

The Russians continued their assaults during the following days, feeding them with a constant flow of men and matériel. They were unable, however, to repeat the deadly preparation of the first day because they lacked the necessary ammunition. Despite tenfold superiority and extreme sacrifices, they made little headway and were unable to overcome the zone defense belt. The high ground near Kussen changed hands several times, and 200 additional enemy tanks met with destruction in that area. The enemy finally succeeded in penetrating some marshy woods to the south of the zone defense area and forced the panzer army to withdraw in order to escape envelopment.

CHAPTER 26

Isthmus Defense –
The Sea as Flank Protection

Military history offers many examples of the defense of an isthmus. This terrain feature affords a multitude of opportunities to deny the attacker access to large and usually important areas with a minimum expenditure of forces. The short frontage of an isthmus defense can be anchored on bodies of water, and the line can be quickly fortified and easily defended. Although the adjacent shore line has to be secured, this can often be achieved with small forces. An isthmus separating two oceans is an unsurmountable obstacle if the defender's flanks are protected by superior air and naval forces. Even with inadequate naval forces, the defender will be able to repel enemy landings with the help of artillery and air power or to destroy a beachhead with mobile ground forces. During World War I the British were unable to break through the Turkish lines on the Gallipoli Peninsula, despite their overwhelming superiority on the sea and in the air.

An isthmus between lakes can also be of great tactical value. The Battle of Tannenberg in 1914 offers a valid example. In this battle the Germans took advantage of the fortified isthmus near Loetzen, in the East Prussian lake district, to delay the Russian First Army until the German Eighth Army had completed the encirclement and annihilation of the Russian Fourth Army.

Both during the Russian withdrawal in 1942 and that of the Germans in 1943, the swampy isthmus between Lake Peipus and the Baltic Sea proved a formidable obstacle. The German thrust on Leningrad was blocked along the isthmus near Narva until an envelopment from the south across the Luga forced the Russians to abandon their positions. The Russian offensive in 1943 encountered similar difficulties when it was stalled at the same isthmus.

In 1941–42 weak Russian forces delayed the German advance for a long time on the strongly fortified isthmus of Kerch in the Crimea. With the reversal of the tide in 1943, two German corps, blocking the Perekop and Kerch Isthmuses, succeeded in delaying the many-times superior Russian armies for six months. The story of the defense of the two Crimean isthmuses by the Germans shows how effectively break-through attempts can be frustrated by taking advantage of this geographic feature. The subsequent withdrawal to Sevastopol indicates the importance of the sea as flank protection. At the beginning of October 1943 the mission of defending the Crimea was assigned to the German Seventeenth Army. The forces available for this mission were constantly dwindling since one division after another was transferred to the Sixth Army which was trying to stem the Russian onslaught north of the Crimea. By mid-October Seventeenth Army had two corps with two German and four Romanian divisions at its disposal. One Romanian corps guarded the south coast of the Crimea (map 15).

The V Infantry Corps was to prevent an enemy landing on the Kerch Peninsula or throw the Russians back into the sea wherever they landed. If possible, the corps was to form mobile reserves. The area under the jurisdiction of the V Corps included the city of Feodosiya which, during the winter 1941–42, had been the target of an amphibious operation conducted by the Russian Black Sea Fleet, resulting in an extremely critical situation. The port of Feodosiya and the surrounding territory was held by Task Force Krieger, a motley unit composed of two weak battalions of limited service and over-age German personnel and one Azerbaijan and one Turkoman battalion. Three divisions – the German 98th Infantry Division and the Romanian 6th Cavalry and 10th Infantry Divisions – were available for the defense of the approximately 200-mile coast line of the Kerch Peninsula. The 6th Romanian Cavalry Division was good but numerically weak, whereas the Romanian infantry division was militarily and politically unreliable. Although there were many instances of individual bravery in the performance of these Romanian troops, they were subject to panic when faced by tanks and lacked stamina under heavy, continuous artillery fire. Under these circumstances it was obvious that the German 98th Infantry Division had to be committed in the most vulnerable sector around the city of Kerch, with Eltigen as boundary in the south and Cape Tarkhan in the north. Since the combat strength of the 98th Infantry Division had dropped to approximately 40 to 50 men per company, a continuous line of defense along the entire coast was out of the question. After one regiment had been designated as sector reserve, the remaining forces were just about sufficient to man strong points in the port areas and at the extreme end of the peninsula at Zhukovka, with security detachments patrolling the other parts of the coast.

The 6th Romanian Cavalry Division was responsible for guarding the south coast of the peninsula and the 10th Romanian Infantry Division covered the north coast from Cape Tarkhan to Ak-Monay. The Luftwaffe was extremely weak, with the shortage of reconnaissance planes a matter of real concern to the German command. At times only one reconnaissance plane was expected to cover the entire Crimea. As a result, the V Corps lacked information about the size of the Russian landing preparations, which doubtless were in progress on the other side of the Straits of Kerch. Any plan to delay these preparations by air attacks was frustrated by the lack of intelligence on Russian concentrations on the Taman Peninsula. Obviously, the Germans had no clue as to the probable Russian landing points.

During the night of 19–20 October 1943, one Russian division landed at Eltigen which was defended by a company from the 98th Division numbering forty-six men. Immediately alerted, the German reserves were able to narrow down the Russian beachhead but were not sufficiently strong to eliminate it. While this fighting was under way, the Russians attempted to land in force near the city of Kerch during the night of 31 October–1 November. The landing parties in the port of Kerch proper and along the coast between Kerch and Zhukovka were repulsed. But immediately north of Zhukovka the Russians overcame the security detachment and moved in reserves, widening the beachhead in the course of a bayonet engagement. Soon the Russian pressure from the newly won beachhead increased so that a German counterattack was out of the question. After overcoming some critical situations, the German forces in this sector were barely able to hold the important heights northeast of the city of Kerch. Thus began a fierce struggle which was to seesaw in the immediate vicinity of the city for five long months.

The area which the Russians had chosen for their main landing had one great disadvantage. They had gained a toehold on the easternmost part of the peninsula on a comparatively narrow isthmus which protruded beyond the city of Kerch. The Russians were unable to deploy their forces to expand their beachhead until they had captured the city and the high ground north of it. The German defense could succeed only if the Russians remained hemmed in on the small isthmus. German defense tactics therefore called for blocking the Russians on Mount Mitridates, overlooking Kerch, and along the mountain range north of the city, denying them access to the rest of the peninsula.

This German plan succeeded although the Russians gradually built up their beachhead until it contained twelve divisions including many tanks. The 98th Division bore the brunt of the fighting against this superior force during the months of November, December, and January. It was assisted by one German infantry regiment which Seventeenth Army had moved across the Crimea from the Perekop area and by some Romanian battalions which were held in reserve and committed in emergencies. Elements of the only assault gun battalion in the Crimea repeatedly intervened at danger points. Toward the end of January 1944, when the weakened line of the 98th Division was at the point of breaking, the 73d Infantry Division was brought in by air without its artillery components.

On 7 December 1943 the 6th Romanian Cavalry Division, concentrating all its forces and assisted by the assault gun battalion, eliminated the Eltigen beachhead which menaced the German flank and was close to the main landing. Although the operation was successful and resulted in the capture of 2,000 Russian prisoners, it led to an unexpected crisis. During the night, elements of the Eltigen force broke through the Romanian line and moved north to link up with the Kerch beachhead. This force overran several batteries which were zeroed in on the main Russian beachhead and before dawn attacked German artillery outposts on Mount Mitridates from the rear. From there some Russian elements infiltrated into the southwestern part of the city of Kerch. The Russian commander of the Kerch beachhead, who had launched an attack as soon as he knew about the German assault on Eltigen, recognized the favorable opportunity and redoubled his efforts to link up with the Eltigen force. Since there were no readily available German reserves, this critical situation had to be overcome by the forces on hand. Three assault detachments were formed by pulling combat-seasoned troops out of the line. They recaptured Mount Mitridates in one swoop and held on to it. Later on, elements of the 3d Romanian Mountain Division, moving up from the north coast of the Kerch Peninsula, annihilated the remnants of the Eltigen force.

The 98th and 73d Divisions, reinforced by Romanian troops, withstood four major Russian attacks launched from the Kerch beachhead. Individual heights and key trenches constantly changed hands during the weeks of bitter fighting. German counterattacks alternated with minor local withdrawals and corrections in the front line in order to save manpower and reduce casualties. All these actions were dominated by the primary consideration of holding the key position on Mount Mitridates and the area to its north. Another landing gave the Russians control over the northern mole of the port of Kerch and the eastern part of the city, but the Germans kept their hold on the western portion and the crucial mountain. The Russians also landed along the coast of the Sea of Azov near Cape Tarkhan, where they captured an important hill. German counterattacks restored the situation somewhat.

Two outside threats hovered over the fighting around Kerch: the Russian Black Sea Fleet and the impending defeat of the German Sixth Army defending the land communications with the Crimea. A large-scale landing, for instance at Feodosiya or Sevastopol, in co-operation with the Russian Black Sea Fleet, would have put the German forces in the Crimea in an untenable position because they were powerless to prevent any such attack. Actually, the Russians did not commit their fleet, not even for a deceptive maneuver. They seemed to attach more importance to keeping their fleet intact than to achieving a quick success in the Crimea. This was easily comprehensible since the offensive north of the Sea of Azov proceeded so well that there was every reason to expect that the Crimea would fall sooner or later. While the Eltigen beachhead was being reduced by the Romanians, the badly shattered divisions of the German Sixth Army were driven back to Melitopol. At the time of the main enemy landing near Kerch, the Russian armies in the north crossed the Dnepr and achieved a break-through toward Krivoi Rog. By the beginning of November 1943, the Russian forces north of the Crimea were attacking the Perekop Isthmus which connects the Crimea with the mainland. The German forces in the Crimea were cut off and hemmed in. The Russians continued their advance on the mainland

and by mid-December had reached the Kherson and Nikopol bridgeheads and the Kirovograd area. With the continuation of the Russian offensive in January 1944, all hope for a German counterattack from the Nikopol bridgehead had definitely vanished. Nikopol was evacuated on 8 February, Kherson on 13 March, and Odessa fell on 8 April 1944. The German units in the Crimea were isolated far behind the Russian lines without hope for relief.

By the end of March, the fourth major attack on Kerch was repelled by the Germans. On the morning of 5 April, a heavy artillery preparation preceded another attack, resulting in an insignificant penetration north of Kerch. This was sealed off by a German counterattack on the next day. For the first time the Russian attack was co-ordinated with simultaneous assaults against the XLIX Mountain Corps on the Perekop Isthmus. There, the situation was similar to that at Kerch. So long as the weak and gradually tiring German forces were able to contain the Russians on the narrow isthmus, they had a chance of putting up a successful defense. Once the Russians got through this bottleneck and penetrated into the open terrain of the northern Crimea, the Germans had no means of stopping them. The so-called Gneisenau position had been constructed in an arc around Simferopol, but this position was incomplete and could serve only as immediate protection for the city proper. The Russians were free to bypass it to the west or east. The distance from Krasnoperekopsk to Simferopol is 60 miles by air, that from Kerch to Simferopol 110 miles. In the event that the Russians should break through at the Perekop Isthmus, Seventeenth Army planned that the XLIX and V Corps join forces in the Simferopol area. In view of the disparity in the distance to be covered, it seemed questionable whether V Corps, withdrawing on foot, would be able to reach Simferopol in time.

If the Crimea was to be evacuated, Sevastopol was the only possible port of embarkation for crossing the Black Sea to Romania. The port of Yalta was much too small, inaccessible, and surrounded by mountains. The Russians knew this only too well and there was every reason to believe that, once they had broken through the Perekop Isthmus, they would bypass the Gneisenau position with their armored and motorized units and thrust straight toward Sevastopol.

Although there was a close similarity between the situations at Kerch and Krasnoperekopsk, the latter had one peculiarity. This was the flat, shallow, muddy island and lagoon region of the Sivash east of the isthmus. The Russians had built some causeways over this almost impassable area; German planes occasionally succeeded in damaging the causeways, but were unable to destroy them. Shortage of ammunition prevented their destruction by artillery fire, as in general the scarcity of ammunition had become an ever-present problem after the separation of the Crimea from the mainland. On 8 April the Russians launched an all-out offensive in the XLIX Corps area and achieved major penetrations in the Sivash region and on the isthmus. The next day V Corps was warned that the situation in the XLIX Corps sector was tense and that the withdrawal to Simferopol might be ordered for the following day. Several plans for the withdrawal had been studied and prepared for the event of a voluntary or forced German evacuation of the Crimea. As one of the first measures, the assault gun battalion, some of the artillery, and all the Luftwaffe elements in the V Corps area were to be transferred to XLIX Corps. On the morning of 10 April, V Corps received orders to start its withdrawal to Sevastopol via Simferopol by 1900.

During the winter the so-called Parpach position had been constructed across the narrowest isthmus of the Kerch Peninsula and strengthened by a continuous wire obstacle, an antitank ditch, and emergency shelters. But the infantry could not possibly reach this defense line in a one-night march from Kerch. An intermediate position was therefore to be established between Kerch and Parpach on either side of Murfovka and this line was to be reached before dawn and held during the day. The withdrawal to the Parpach line was to be completed during the following night. The first units to be withdrawn from the front were to secure the most important roads and terrain features ahead of the intermediate position and cover the withdrawal of the main body. Upon completion of this mission, the security detachments were to fight a rear guard action, withdraw behind the intermediate position, and form a reserve force. This plan could not be carried out because the critical situation in the Perekop Isthmus necessitated the immediate transfer of these elements. As a result, the covering positions were inadequately manned and the corps was without reserves.

Except for a reconnaissance in force, the Russians in the Kerch beachhead were inactive on 10 April. After the V Corps had transferred all its fighter planes to the XLIV Corps area, the Russian air force reigned supreme and became extremely active. Since the Russian forces in the north crossed most of the Perekop Isthmus and the Sivash flats, the enemy command at Kerch felt certain that the withdrawal of the V Corps was imminent. Any attempt at deceiving them as to the German intentions was futile.

Nevertheless, the disengagement carried out during the night of 10–11 April proceeded without unforseen incident. Just before midnight the Russians entered the German positions, held by rear guards. A few Russian tanks, followed by motorized infantry, took up the pursuit of the German units moving toward the intermediate position. This line was not fortified and followed the so-called Tartar Wall, an ancient wall leading from Lake Uzunlarskoye via Murfovka to the Kasantipskiy Bay on the Sea of Azov. The 6th Romanian Cavalry occupied the sector between the lake and Murfovka, the 73d Division the central one on both sides of the Kerch–Feodosiya highway, and the 98th Division the northern sector up to Kasantipskiy Bay. The average strength of the German companies varied between 30 and 40 men. Despite the fact that the Crimea had been cut off from the mainland since November 1943, fourteen-day furloughs were granted to all soldiers who had not been on leave for a year or more. Although this was an excellent way of boosting morale, the German units in the Crimea gradually lost their battle-tested cadre because few of the men returned to their outfits. Upon returning from furlough, Army Group A intercepted them at Odessa while they were waiting for transportation, organized them into battalions, and committed them on the mainland.

The Kerch Peninsula is a rolling treeless steppe. Trees are so rare that the four high ones standing west of the village of Libknekhtovka were a landmark which served as a point of orientation for the entire area. Outside the inhabited places there is no cover or concealment in the open terrain. The forests of the Yaila mountains began at Stary Krym, west of Feodosiya. There, too, began the territory of the partisans. Firmly entrenched, strong partisan forces had intercepted the traffic along the Feodosiya–Simferopol highway for many months, forcing the Germans to travel in armed convoys.

Shortly after 0700 on 11 April, even before front-line reports could be evaluated, the Russians launched a powerful thrust in the 73d Division sector north of the Kerch–Feodosiya highway. After suffering heavy casualties, the Germans succeeded in stopping the Russian tanks and supporting infantry about one mile behind the intermediate position. While the Germans were struggling to get this situation under control, a fierce Russian attack hit the 6th Romanian Division sector. The lack of reserves made itself felt. During the early afternoon, Russian tanks broke through at Murfovka, thrust deep into the rear area, wrought havoc with the Romanian trains, and reached Arma-Eli, twenty-five miles behind the intermediate position. Russian infantry poured through the gap opened by the armor.

This was a full-fledged break-through with no German reserves to stop it. The original intention to hold the intermediate position till dusk and withdraw to the Parpach position under cover of darkness could no longer be carried out under the prevailing circumstances. It was altogether doubtful whether the German infantry and the horse-drawn artillery would reach the Parpach position before the Russians. If the Russians exploited the break-through and moved up strong motorized forces behind their armored spearheads at Arma-Eli, they could easily penetrate and outflank the position held by weak security detachments. Once the Russians captured the Parpach position, the V Corps faced certain encirclement and destruction on the Kerch Peninsula.

The Russians recognized this possibility and moved up motorized forces behind their armored force at Arma-Eli. In addition, they went over to the attack along the entire front. Nevertheless, they did not overrun the Parpach position although some individual tanks succeeded in crossing the antitank ditch along the Feodosiya road where the Germans had delayed the demolitions too long. It is difficult to determine in retrospect exactly how the Germans were able to hold the Parpach position. The weak security detachments were reinforced by troops shifted from one danger spot to another, and the Russians also seemed to show some reluctance to throw their full weight against the line they had themselves so successfully defended during the winter 1941–42. Undoubtedly, the lower echelon commanders of the Russian spearhead units were diverted from their objective by the extraordinary spectacle which unfolded in front of their eyes: fleeing supply columns, rows of vehicles in the distance, horse-drawn artillery, long lines of trucks, and small detachments of troops stumbling northwestward in wild disorder. The Russians could not resist the temptation to attack such easy prey and, destroying many columns of vehicles, forgot about the more important objective – the Parpach position.

The daylight retreat from the intermediate to the Parpach position over a distance of thirty miles led to bitter fighting on 11 April, causing more casualties than any one of the long defensive engagements around Kerch. Russian fighter and fighter-bomber formations met with no opposition in the air and could lend their full support to the Russian ground forces. The steppe, with its lack of cover, provided the Russian fliers with a variety of targets. The Russian fighters seemed to concentrate on prime movers and draft horses pulling heavy weapons and artillery as well as on infantry units on the march, while the fighter-bombers attacked horse-drawn and motorized convoys. As a result the Germans lost most of their horse-drawn artillery in the steppe since they had to blow up the pieces after the horses had been killed from the air. Light and medium howitzers and antitank guns fared only slightly better. The retreating infantry forces faced many difficulties in the steppe. Subjected to continuous air attacks, their plight was worsened by frontal and flank attacks on the ground while individual Russian tanks blocked their route of withdrawal. The approach of darkness brought some relief, although the Russians continued their air attacks on roads, towns, and communication centers.

The V Corps had suffered a major defeat on 11 April. The 6th Romanian Cavalry Division was wiped out except for small remnants which reached the Parpach position and were assigned to a small sector on the right wing. The last elements of the 73d and 98th Divisions did not arrived in the position until the morning of 12 April, after fighting their way back step by step. The casualties were heavy – one regiment of the 73d Division was reduced to 200 men, its reconnaissance battalion to 50. Available forces were no longer sufficient to man the Parpach position in its entire fifteen-mile length. Artillery and antiaircraft personnel had to be used as infantry in order to occupy the most important points. Despite their exhaustion and the enemy's numerical superiority, the German troops repelled all attacks throughout the day and eliminated minor penetrations in hand-to-hand fighting.

Nevertheless, there was no doubt this weak defense force would have to give way to the mounting Russian pressure before long. Since the German artillery which had escaped the carnage was too weak to counteract, let alone crush, Russian attack preparations and armored concentrations, the Germans had to defend the Parpach line with small arms and machine guns.

There were other reasons for a change in the planned withdrawal schedule. Signal communications between V Corps and Seventeenth Army were disrupted on 12 April. No reliable information regarding the situation on the XLIX Corps front was available but, according to rumours, Russian tanks had captured the railroad junction at Dzhankoy, twelve miles south of the Perekop Isthmus. Around noon the first reliable reports received from service units traveling from Feodosiya to Simferopol were anything but reassuring. At Zuya, twelve miles northeast of Simferopol, they had encountered Russian tanks and had also been intercepted by partisan units emerging from the forests. A motorcycle messenger returning from Karasubazar reported that another column was fired on by Russian tanks in the same vicinity.

The significance of this information was that armored Russian elements had broken through or bypassed the Gneisenau position The distance from the Parpach position to Zuya was sixty miles by air. The question was whether the V Corps would be able to reach Simferopol in time to join forces with the XLIX Mountain Corps. In any event, it seemed certain that the corps would have to fight its way back while holding off the Russian divisions fanning out of the Kerch beachhead. If the Russian tanks at Zuya and Karasubazar were not just advance detachments but elements of a strong force thrusting from the Perekop Isthmus, the continuation of the V Corps withdrawal toward Simferopol was no longer feasible. In this event, the only way out of the trap was to turn south at Saly, six miles west of Stary Krym, and to reach Sevastopol by the coastal road across the Yaila and Yalta Mountains. The distance from Simferopol to Sevastopol is 40 miles by air, that from the Parpach position to Sevastopol 105 miles. If the Russians had actually reached Zuya or the area west of Simferopol in force, the V Corps would probably arrive in front of Sevastopol after its capture by the Russians.

No matter whether the V Corps withdrew via Simferopol or along the coastal road via Sudak, it had to take immediate steps to secure and hold the area around Saly where the road branches off the main Simferopol highway to the south. If the Russians got there first they would deprive the corps of both routes of withdrawal. Since the corps had no reserves, it could only use the troops fighting in the Parpach position. This meant that the position would have to be evacuated immediately after dusk on 12 April and that the troops withdraw to the Saly area in one night. The remnants of the 6th Romanian Cavalry Division and the 73d Division received orders to move to the Sudak area and the 98th Division was to occupy the high ground north and west of Saly.

The events which took place on the afternoon of 12 April complicated the implementation of these orders but, instead of changing their scope, speeded up their execution. During the early afternoon a strong Russian armored column drove past the northern anchor of the Parpach position near the Sea of Azov and penetrated into Ak-Monay, but was stopped in that town. Immediately afterward, at 1530, Russian motorized units broke through at the boundary between the 6th Romanian Cavalry Division and the 73d Division along the road to Feodosiya.

At 1615, when the fighting for the Parpach position reached a decisive stage, telephone communications with army were re-established for a short period. Army confirmed that the Gneisenau position was lost and that the Russians exercised strong pressure in the Simferopol area. A link-up with the XLIX Corps at Simferopol was no longer feasible. The V Corps was to attempt to reach Sevastopol via the coastal road. This decision did not modify the orders issued by the corps. Once again the Germans had to evacuate their positions during the daylight hours. The withdrawal of the 98th Division was further complicated by the fact that it had to take place over open terrain, between Ak-Monay, and Vladislavovka, where there is no cover. The exact location of the XLIX Corps was still unknown. Moreover, here were conflicting reports about a Russian advance from Karasubazar toward Saly. Stary Krym, a town in the foothills of the Yaila Mountains situated along the route of withdrawal of the 73d Division, was suddenly attacked by partisans who descended from the surrounding woods disguised as peaceful civilians. The 73d division was faced with a difficult situation since it had to ward off the pursuing enemy forces on its front while partisans blocked its route of withdrawal at Stary Krym. The division tried to clear a path in hard house-to-house fighting, gained temporary possession of a few city blocks, and was thus able to detour the vehicular traffic which had to pass through the town. Except for brief intervals, the fighting in Stary Krym continued all through the night of 12–13 April.

On the morning of 13 April the 73d Division, its line facing east, held the high ground on either side of Stary Krym. Enemy forces in hot pursuit attacked the German positions and linked up with the partisans in the town. The 73d Division, joined by the remnants of the 6th Romanian Cavalry Division, was ordered to hold the high ground west of Stary Krym until the 98th Division had passed through Saly on the march to Sudak. Upon completion of this mission, the 73d Division was to withdraw immediately to the wooded heights south of Saly and block the enemy advance toward Sudak.

These movements went according to plan because the corps concentrated all its remaining forces within a narrow area despite continuous Russian air attacks. This was contrary to established doctrine but the heavily wooded mountainous terrain provided good cover for the corps troops and hid their sudden pivoting movement to the south. The Russians were deceived by German reconnaissance in force west of Saly which led them to believe that the bulk of the V Corps was retreating toward Karasubazar. The Russian reaction was to throw all available forces into a westward drive from Stary Krym. The 98th Division reached the Sudak area without meeting resistance and the 73d Division had no particular difficulty in warding off the unco-ordinated Russian attacks against its blocking position on the high ground two miles south of Saly.

Romanian demolition parties along the winding road between Feodosiya and Sudak had prepared a number of charges to be blown up after the last vehicles from Feodosiya had passed the demolition points, closing the road to a Russian advance. While the successful pivoting maneuver to the south constituted a minor success, the objective of reaching Sevastopol by the coastal route through the Yaila Mountains before its capture by the Russians was much more difficult to attain. Russian news broadcasts announced the capture of Simferopol and reported fighting southwest of the city. A quick glance at the map indicated only too clearly the difficulties the V Corps would have to face. The obstacles presented by the terrain of the long mountainous route were considerable. The I Romanian Corps had been unsuccessful in dislodging the partisans from the Yaila Mountains. If the partisans blew up one single turn in the road, they could jeopardize the entire withdrawal. A Russian landing at Alushta or Yalta would have the same effect. Aside from the Saly–Sudak road, firmly held by the Germans, no less than seven usable roads branch off to the south across the mountains from the Saly–Karasubazar–Zuya–Simferopol–Bakhchisaray highway, and most were in Russian hands. At least three of these are improved roads, suitable for all types of troop movements. The Russians therefore had a variety of possibilities to block the V Corps withdrawal and they also had the necessary forces at their disposal. Twelve divisions with many tanks advanced from the Kerch Peninsula with an equal number thrusting across the Crimea from Krasnoperekopsk. A joint drive of these powerful forces in the direction of Sevastopol would crush the weak German forces. On the other hand, most of the Russian divisions were infantry units marching on foot and their link-up was bound to take some time. If the V Corps plan was to succeed, it could only be achieved by outrunning the Russians. The only possible solution was to provide motor transportation for the weak German units which had suffered such heavy losses during the withdrawal from the Kerch Peninsula. The corps and GHQ troops as well as the flak artillery had organic truck transportation and it was therefore a matter of providing motor transportation for the infantry units, horse-drawn artillery, and horse-drawn supply columns. Most of the trucks needed were taken from army motor pools and supply depots. They were commandeered, unloaded, and used for the movement of troops. The naval coast artillery which had to blow up its fixed batteries near Feodosiya and along the coast, supplied a certain number of trucks. The tractors belonging to German agricultural organizations in the Crimea and the normally untouchable trucks of the well-equipped Organization Todt [paramilitary construction organization of the Nazi Party, auxiliary to the Wehrmacht] units were also put into service.

In Sudak, the corps suddenly ran into several Romanian battalions without any transportation. Although this addition to the corps strength was welcome, the presence of the Romanians was bound to slow down the withdrawal of the now motorized V Corps. Despite unrelenting Russian air attacks, the bulk of the Romanian units was loaded on Navy landing craft in the small harbor of Sudak and taken to Sevastopol by sea. The rest rode along the coastal road to Alushta on German trucks with their horse-drawn service units following.

The simplest and quickest way to reach Sevastopol was to drive from Sudak during the following night, from 13 to 14 April. It turned out that this was impossible, not because of enemy interference, but because more Romanian units were encountered between Sudak and Alushta. Some of them were withdrawing to Alushta to embark in that port, while others blocked the roads against a Russian advance through the mountains. The withdrawal of the German forces slowed down until all the Romanian units along the coast were embarked in Alushta and Yalta.

Russian pressure on the 73d Division front increased during the afternoon of 13 April. Fighting a delaying action, the division withdrew step by step southward from Saly. It was planned that the 98th Division move to Alushta at dusk. The 73d Division was to follow at a one-hour interval and, acting as rear guard, occupy the high ground west of Uskut. But the enemy cancelled all these plans. As soon as dusk set in, firing began east and north, and very shortly thereafter, also southeast of Sudak. At first it was small arms fire, but then heavy machine guns and antitank guns opened up, and finally there were sharp reports of tank fire. Since the V Corps had no tanks, these could only be Russian. It was never determined how these tanks suddenly appeared in the Sudak area, but it was believed that they might have come from Feodosiya along side roads.

This surprise attack was particularly inopportune because it separated the 98th Division from the 73d. Moreover, it cut the only highway along the coast leading to Uskut. No detours for motor vehicles were available. A counterattack conducted by the 98th Division during the night established that the opposing forces were mainly partisans. No sooner was contact re-established between the two German divisions, than a second enemy raid began and Russian tanks penetrated into the center of Sudak. This new threat was finally eliminated by another German counterattack.

The withdrawal of the 98th Division was thereby delayed until after midnight. Direct enemy interference was negligible during the night march which, however, turned out to be full of adventures because most of the drivers were inexperienced. The road leading through the Yaila Mountains was very poor and many steep turns were without guard rails. At several steep gradients the roadbed was as slippery as soap. Artillery pieces with long barrels had to back up several times before they could negotiate some of the narrow turns. There were endless traffic jams all along the road. Since the drivers were not allowed to use headlights, a number of vehicles plunged into the abyss. Fire signals on the mountain tops and burning farm houses along the road revealed that the partisans were never far off.

During 14 April the 98th Division reached the area northeast of Alushta, while the rear guards of the 73d Division covered the withdrawal west of Uskut. The demolitions were set off according to plan and no Romanians were left behind. The over-all situation continued to be uncertain all through the day since wire communications with army were interrupted most of the time. Atmospheric conditions made it impossible to establish radio contact. The V Corps commander believed that, after the capture of Simferopol, the Russian command would drive straight to Sevastopol. If the Russians entered the city on the heels of the XLIX Corps, the Seventeenth Army was doomed. The V Corps commander was therefore not surprised to find that there was no strong enemy pressure along the roads leading across the mountains toward the south coast. He expected the Russians to block the seven mountain roads and attack via Bakhchisaray toward Yalta or Foros.

Reports from German reconnaissance patrols confirmed these suspicions. Some Russian units advanced along the Bakhchisaray–Yalta road which had been mined and was blocked by a Romanian battalion, while stronger forces thrust southward in the direction of Foros. Midway between Bakhchisaray and Foros some hastily assembled German units were digging in, but it was difficult to predict how long they would be able to withstand the Russian pressure. Every possible step had to be taken to move the V Corps troops into Sevastopol before the escape route was closed.

During the night of 14–15 April, the V Corps established telephone communications with Seventeenth Army at its new command post in Sevastopol. The XLIX Mountain Corps had succeeded in stalling the Russian advance at the ramparts of Sevastopol, but army doubted whether the weak German units on the Bakhchisaray–Foros road could hold out throughout 15 April. The arrival of the V Corps was essential for the defense of Sevastopol which was indefensible without immediate reinforcement. If the V Corps was unable to reach the city, Seventeenth Army had no other choice but to form a beachhead at some favorable point along the coast and wait for evacuation by the sea.

A rough estimate by the corps commander indicated that the corps could not possibly arrive in Sevastopol on 15 April unless it started its withdrawal from Alushta no later than 1000, since this was not just a drive over normal terrain but over a rugged mountain road across partisan-infested territory. The chances of reaching Sevastopol before regular Russian troops or partisans cut the road were slight. Was this sufficient reason to give up trying to reach the city? After all, the corps was strong enough to fight its way back to Sevastopol. If it stayed put and formed a beachhead at Alushta or Yalta, the corps would lose all heavy weapons and trucks should the troops be evacuated by sea. In addition, this desperate expedient could still be tried after all efforts to reach Sevastopol had failed.

The corps commander therefore issued orders that all German units move out of Alushta during the morning of 15 April immediately after the Romanians had completed the embarkation of their forces. The 98th Division, acting as advance guard, was to be ready at 1000. The 73d Division was to follow at a one-mile interval. The town commander of Alushta was instructed to hold a position north of Alushta with two Romanian infantry battalions until the evening of 15 April and to embark under cover of darkness. He was allotted the necessary landing craft and a German staff was put in charge of the final loading operations.

While the corps commander issued these orders during the early morning hours, the Russians suddenly attacked the two Romanian infantry battalions blocking the road to Alushta. German liaison officers attached to the two battalions reported that some of the companies were falling back. Soon afterward, individual soldiers were seen running through the streets of Alushta toward the boats. It was not without difficulty that these stragglers were returned to their outfits which had continued to resist and had meanwhile repelled the Russians.

The 98th Division started moving out of Alushta by 1100 and the other troop movements took place according to plan. At Yalta, the Germans were joined by Romanian troops which had secured the road to Bakhchisaray. The Russian air force was ineffective because thick fog rose from the Black Sea and hid the coast line around Yalta, forcing the planes to drop their loads at random. The coastal road out of Yalta is modern and of excellent construction. Interference by partisans was broken up by immediate countermeasures and none of the many road turns were blown up by them. One such demolition, placed at the right point, might have blocked the entire mountain road and cut off the corps.

After the last truck had gone through, the extensive demolitions prepared by the Germans were set off. The rocky defile at Foros collapsed in a cloud of dust and a short distance from there a steep turn, including the buttress, rolled down the mountain slope. None too soon, the V Corps marched into Fortress Sevastopol. Two hours later the Russians cut off the last approaches by land.

CHAPTER 27

Delaying and Blocking Actions

One of the frequently tried and always effective methods of defense against break-throughs consist of delaying and blocking a main enemy thrust with the help of strong reserves. Like most others, these defense tactics presuppose the existence or early availability of adequate reserves. Compared to the enemy attack forces these reserves may be much weaker without necessarily being at a disadvantage. During the Russian Christmas offensive in 1943, for instance, the enemy wedge had a five-to-one superiority over the German blocking forces. In such a case the block must be sufficiently resilient to withstand the terrific impact of hostile tank forces and must be absolutely shockproof. The block should be placed in favorable terrain if it is to prevent the enemy advance or divert its axis.

Whenever a blocking force fails in its mission, its must be withdrawn to another line farther to the rear. Its essential task is to disable as many hostile tanks as possible in order to weaken the enemy's striking power and re-establish the balance of forces. An attack by infantry without the assistance of armor will rarely constitute a threat to tank-supported units.

Eventually, the block will form the nucleus of the new defense line that is to be built up. The line must be extended on both wings as soon as possible and be strengthened by forces moved up from other sectors which are not under attack. Tactical expedients, dictated by momentary needs, often lead to confusion in the disposition of units. The command must attempt to eliminate these deficiencies at the earliest possible moment. The methods used and sequence observed in closing any remaining gaps will depend upon the situation and local conditions. Overextended frontages and shortage of manpower will often prevent a further extension of sectors. Along the German front in Russia in 1944, quite a few gaps remained open for weeks or even months – for instance the so-called Wehrmacht Gap in the Pripyat marshes. Ground and air reconnaissance had to be constantly on the alert since the Russians rarely failed to take advantage of such gaps by some surprise move.

It is extremely important to recognize the exact time at which the enemy finally abandons his attacks against a blocking force, only to renew them with fresh troops on the flank, at some other gap, or in a different sector. Often the destruction of his last remaining tanks and the fading of his infantry assaults will indicate the change in the enemy's intentions. Whenever the Germans observed any such indications, they immediately withdrew all their tanks from the blocking force in order to build up strong reserves. This was all the more necessary since they could not count on the arrival of reinforcements, except in rare instances.

Whenever towns or major natural obstacles such as rivers are situated within the break-through area, it will prove advantageous to integrate them into the defense system. Towns should be organized for all-around defense and, in accordance with their characteristics, obstacles should be used to strengthen the block. If extensive marshes or other impassable areas are close behind the front line, the routes for bypassing them in case of a withdrawal must be determined in advance. Efficient guides, road repairs, bridges, corduroy roads, secure defiles, and timely orders for withdrawal are some of the numerous elements for the success of such difficult retrograde movements.

The duration of each delaying action by a blocking force, the number of successive withdrawals, and the depth of a retrograde movement depend upon the over-all situation, the terrain conditions, and the distribution of forces, and therefore vary in each instance. Three co-ordinated withdrawals to a total depth of sixty miles were necessary during the Russian Christmas offensive in 1943. Additional intermediate movements of minor significance were performed by individual units whenever they were under particularly heavy pressure. Strong resistance in every position was essential to accomplish the delaying mission. Partial withdrawals were permitted only with the approval of the army commander. The retrograde movement of the entire blocking force was contingent upon his personal orders.

The Russian offensive followed the operations described in Chapter 19. Even during the fighting in the Teterev–Irsha triangle, German aerial reconnaissance reported increasing rail traffic from the north-west in the direction of Kiev (map 16). Day and night, enemy troop transports including hundreds of tanks moved across the Dnepr bridges toward the west. Doubtless the Russians transferred strong armored and infantry units into the Kiev area. They either intended to commit them in an effort to regain the terrain they had lost northeast of Zhitomir, or they planned a new operation. Since no new units were identified along the Teterev front, everything seemed to indicate that preparations for a new major offensive were under way. It was not until the last days before Christmas that the Russians started local probing attacks along and to the south of the Kiev–Zhitomir highway in order to find some weak points in the German dispositions and to acquire advantageous jump-off positions. Air photographs, taken daily, indicated a steady increase in the number of enemy artillery emplacements which at first remained unoccupied. New batteries moved into the emplacements and adjusted their fire. These were clear indications of an impending enemy offensive. Russian tank movements, conducted simultaneously on the right army wing near Kanev along the Dnepr, did not fit into the general picture and were carried out so clumsily that they were immediately recognized as feints. Even though radio intercepts indicated no change, the heavy truck traffic which started to roll toward the front every night after 20 December left no doubt that the Russian attack was imminent. German reconnaissance planes sighted between two and three thousand loaded trucks rolling from Kiev to the front during several successive nights with just as many returning empty. This was the best indication that the enemy would soon launch his attack in this sector. The sudden calm descending upon the front on 23 December deceived nobody. On the contrary, it indicated that the Russian offensive could start at any moment, especially since the Russians liked to launch large-scale operations on Christmas Eve, believing that the German soldiers could be caught off guard on this important religious festival.

The Germans took a number of precautionary steps to absorb the initial shock of the first enemy assaults and to add to the depth of their defense. The fully motorized artillery division, which had arrived only two weeks earlier and had been committed on a quiet sector in accordance with specific orders issued by Hitler, was now moved to Zhitomir. This division was equipped with 60 light and 40 medium pieces and 24 assault guns, and was therefore particularly capable of shattering mass attacks. In addition, the XLVIII Panzer Corps was pulled out and assembled in the vicinity of Korosten. A motorized infantry division, undergoing rehabilitation in rest areas west of Berdichev, was to form a regimental combat team with all those elements which were ready for commitment. This combat team actually consisted of two motorized infantry battalions, one light artillery battalion, and one signal company. The weak local reserves near the Kiev–Zhitomir highway were reinforced with forty tanks. Although the formation of reserves was of vital importance, army was unable to relieve any other units because its front was so greatly overextended. Army group could not help at this time, and the Fourth Panzer Army therefore had to face the Russian onslaught with very meager reserves.

An antitank ditch was dug approximately ten miles behind the main line of resistance. Its eastern section lay behind an unfordable stream. The important railroad junctions at Zhitomir, Berdichev, and Kazatin were protected by fortifications for the defense of which, however, only alert units formed by service troops were available. All nonessential rolling stock and supplies were evacuated to the west.

As expected, the Russian offensive began on 24 December south of the Kiev–Zhitomir highway. After a heavy one-hour preparation, the enemy succeeded in breaching the positions held by two under-strength panzer divisions. But the two divisions continued to defend their main line of resistance although they were completely encircled. By noon this Russian force reached the antitank ditch and crossed it at some points. A second powerful armored thrust penetrated the overextended front in the central sector during the morning. Only slightly delayed by local resistance, several hundred enemy tanks rolled in an endless stream toward Berdichev. Here, too, the antitank ditch caused little delay because the Germans lacked sufficient manpower for its effective defense. By the end of the first day the enemy force forming the main effort reached the Kiev–Zhitomir railroad line.

Another enemy thrust, carried out farther north in the direction of Zhitomir proper, initially made slow progress in the swampy forests south of the highway because of the strong German antitank fronts. During the night the two encircled panzer divisions, ordered to break out to the west, attacked the enemy from the rear and disorganized him so completely that he was incapable of continuing the attack on the next day.

In an effort to stem the Russian advance, the XLVIII Panzer Corps was withdrawn from the Korosten area and committed in a counterattack south of the Teterev. The corps commander had orders to block the hostile advance behind the undulating terrain between Kazatin and Berdichev and to delay the Russians as long as possible. Up to this time some 800 enemy tanks had appeared in this area. When the panzer corps arrived south of the Teterev at dawn, enemy tank columns, many miles long, suddenly came into view. The corps commander could not resist the temptation and, instead of following his instructions, he decided to make an immediate surprise attack against the open enemy flank. But this flank attack had no chance of succeeding because 150 German tanks could not combat or even deflect the axis of the mass of Russian armor which had meanwhile grown to 1,000 tanks. As expected, the enemy quickly recovered from his initial surprise and held off the panzer corps with one-fourth of his armor and some antitank weapons. Although the panzer corps disabled seventy-eight tanks, it was unable to overcome this obstacle. The bulk of two Russian tank armies rolled on to the area north of Kazatin which was defended by a regimental combat team of 20th Panzer Division, the twenty-four assault guns of the artillery division, and the alert units stationed within the city limits. If this unforeseen threat was to be met and a break-through in depth to be prevented, the other elements of the artillery division which had just moved into the Zhitomir area had to be pulled out immediately and transferred to Kazatin. Traffic bottlenecks, created by the simultaneous use of the Zhitomir–Kazatin road by units of the panzer corps traveling in the same direction, was unavoidable. The excellent condition of the asphalt road made it possible to pour enough reinforcements into Kazatin at the last moment, enabling the Germans to withstand the impact of the Russian onslaught.

The other enemy thrusts in the Berdichev area and east of Zhitomir were also brought to a halt. Thus, the XLVIII Panzer Corps was afforded sufficient time to comply with its original orders and take up positions between Kazatin and Berdichev. The corps arrived on 26 December, just in time to see the Russians streaming into Kazatin. Their next objective was to cut the Zhitomir–Vinnitsa highway. The German tanks repelled the enemy spearheads and retook the ridge east of the highway. The Russians then split their attack forces and attempted to find a weak point for a break-through to the west, but the panzer units took advantage of the good road net and always reached the critical point in time to block the advance of the hostile armor. Well concealed by terrain and brush, they let the Russian tanks approach and scored direct hits before they were discovered. On one day alone, 26 December, more than 200 enemy tanks succumbed to these tactics. By the third day of the thrust the break-through area of the attacking Russian tank armies was blocked by the panzer corps which constantly received infantry reinforcements. For five days the Russians tried to break through this blocking force. The only visible result they achieved was their mounting losses of armor. When the enemy realized the futility of his efforts, he changed the direction of his thrust and attempted to unhinge both flanks of the blocking force by outflanking Zhitomir in the north and bypassing Kazatin on the south. To counteract this move, the LIX Corps was withdrawn from Korosten to Novograd–Volynskiy and the XIII Corps evacuated Zhitomir in order to take up new positions south of the swampy forests along the Teterev. In addition, all available elements of two divisions were moved closer to Kazatin to extend the front of the blocking force. A local withdrawal of the XLVIII Panzer Corps completed these measures and helped to build up a new, integrated defense system. On the other hand, Hitler refused to permit the withdrawal of the two right wing corps in position along the Dnepr bend although these forces were in imminent danger of being cut off. A light screening force maintained contact between these two corps and the rest of the heavily engaged Fourth Panzer Army. For the time being the Russians probed this screening force without realizing their opportunity. Before long, however, the pressure on the VII Infantry Corps front increased, the salient was over-extended, and the front line was breached. The enemy poured more and more troops into the gap north of Uman without meeting any opposition. There was still a possibility of extricating the two corps from the tightening noose, although they were seriously threatened from the rear. Had they been allowed to use detours or to break through, they could have re-established contact with the Fourth Panzer Army and would have been integrated into the second blocking line put up by the army. But the two corps were ordered to stay in place despite increasingly emphatic requests addressed to Hitler. By the time the German command fully realized the danger, the enemy had assembled one army north of Uman with a second one following close behind. The staff of First Panzer Army – and two battle-weary panzer divisions – was quickly relieved in another sector, shifted to Uman, and put in charge of the two corps cut off in the north.

In the meantime, heavy fighting continued for weeks along the Fourth

Panzer Army front. In the center, the XIII Corps was weakened by the heavy losses of equipment it had suffered during its withdrawal across the swampy woods south of Zhitomir. Realizing this weakness, the Russians concentrated their armor opposite the sector held by this corps. They anticipated that the break-through they had hitherto been denied could be achieved by attacking the sector. During this phase of the fighting they attained several small penetrations. These were quickly eliminated with the assistance of XLVIII Panzer Corps units, but the divisions of XIII Corps were gradually reduced and crushed. Their remnants held out among the panzer units and, to unify the command, they were subordinated to the panzer corps and the staff of XIII Corps was withdrawn. In a last desperate attempt to break through, the Russians massed all available tanks and penetrated the German lines. But in the subsequent melee all seventy tanks that had gone through were put out of action. Thus ended the attacks along this sector during the last days of January.

The Russian armored thrust on Vinnitsa failed at about the same time after enemy spearheads had come within reach of Zhmerinka, the important railroad junction from which the double-track lines branch off to Odessa. The XXVIII Infantry Corps, recently transferred from the northern front, launched a powerful counterattack with one panzer and three strong infantry divisions, repelled the hostile tank army, and cut off those elements which had advanced as far as Zhmerinka.

The last major enemy thrust against the extreme west wing of Fourth Panzer Army was directed against the Shepetovka railroad station. One weak infantry division held Shepetovka against vastly superior enemy forces, but this Russian attack also failed. A subsequent attempt to cut off the LIX from the XLVIII Panzer Corps by an enveloping thrust via Polonnoye was equally unsuccessful. An additional infantry division transferred from the northern front was detrained in Shepetovka in time to launch a counterattack. The division recaptured Polonnoye, sealed the gap, and re-established contact with the adjacent panzer corps.

This brought the Russian Christmas offensive to its end. After five weeks of hard struggle, Fourth Panzer Army with its four corps and some 200 tanks had scored a major defensive success against six enemy armies with 1,200 tanks. Although the Russians forced the Germans to withdraw their front lines by about sixty miles, they did not achieve a strategic break-through with far-reaching objectives. Their plan had been to crush Fourth Panzer Army, unhinge the two army groups in the Ukraine, and nail them against the Black Sea or push them into Romania. This plan failed and, in view of its proportions, the territorial gains obtained by the Russians were really insignificant. The Fourth Panzer Army remained intact and held a continuous front line. This defensive success was achieved because, after the third day of the Russian offensive, a strong panzer corps was employed as blocking force. At that time the center of the army sector had been broken through and gaps up to ninety miles in width extended on its flanks. But the blocking force formed the steel clamp that held together the isolated infantry corps and preserved the army from disintegration. The Russians were unable to split this solid army front of twelve divisions. By fighting three successive delaying actions, the blocking force had prevented a break-through and stabilized the situation sufficiently to permit the formation of a continuous front.

CHAPTER 28

Delay on Successive Positions

In a situation where enemy infantry attempts to break through without much armored support, a delaying action in successive positions may be the most promising defensive tactic. The underlying principle of this maneuver is to inflict casualties upon the enemy without becoming too closely engaged. By offering limited resistance on successive positions, the defender attempts to weaken the enemy until his forces are too disorganized to mount a sustained offensive. After the hostile attacks have lost their momentum, strong resistance may be offered on a permanent position or a counteroffensive may be launched. Delaying actions are therefore temporary expedients to prevent a break-through by trading a minimum of space for a maximum amount of time to allow the defender to move up new forces.

Complications arise when the flanks of a weak delaying force are open to attacks by strong hostile armor supported by ample reserves. In August 1943, during the delaying action south of Belgorod, the Germans reached Kharkov after co-ordinated withdrawals from eight successive positions which they held during daylight and evacuated under cover of darkness (map 17). The distance covered by each withdrawal varied between five and six miles. Kharkov was held for a week and then the delaying operation was continued by a withdrawal via Poltava toward the Dnepr. During this phase, however, the unfavorable situation in the Kiev area compelled the German commander to accelerate the withdrawal, forcing him to abandon 120 miles of terrain within twelve days. During the retrograde movement from Belgorod to Kremenchug on the Dnepr, the enemy was never able to break through or push by the flanks. The entire delaying force, consisting of twelve divisions, crossed the Dnepr and established a permanent defense line on the west bank of the river.

The auspices for this delaying action were not favorable. After the failure of Operation ZITADELLE, the German pincers attack on Kursk in July 1943, the Russians held the initiative. They launched the pursuit with powerful reserves, while the Germans withdrew to the positions they had held before the ill-fated offensive. The XI Infantry Corps moved into the heavily fortified defensive system anchored on Belgorod and repelled all enemy attacks across the Donets River. The Fourth Panzer Army, adjacent to the northwest, tried to offer resistance in open terrain and was overrun by strong Russian armored forces.

Remnants of one of its infantry divisions sought refuge behind the left wing of the XI Corps. An attempt by Fourth Panzer Army to close the gap by an armored counterattack was unsuccessful. The Russian tanks advanced without much interference and reached Bogodukhov on 6 August. This enemy thrust endangered the XI Corps north of Belgorod. Russian armored spearheads advanced towards Poltava and Akhtyrka fifty miles to the rear, while other enemy forces attacked the front and flank of the corps to encircle and annihilate it. The corps front formed a deep salient into enemy territory which might have disintegrated with complete encirclement its final destiny. This would have meant a widening of the gap from 15 to 50 miles and the immediate loss of 5 divisions. To prevent such a disaster the corps had to withdraw from Belgorod, but the retrograde movement was to be gradual in order to gain time for the preparation of countermeasures. In view of the limited strength of the corps, it would have been a mistake to attempt to close the gap by widening the corps sector nor was any such plan feasible since the enemy kept up his pressure on the entire front. On the contrary, the corps had to keep its forces together and form a solid block against the superior enemy forces.

These considerations determined the conduct of operations. The corps commander decided to fight a delaying action in successive positions until the corps reached Kharkov and then to hold the city. The corps had to build up a front facing north and protect its left flank against an enemy envelopment, while the right flank was anchored on the Donets River. Elements of two infantry divisions were reinforced by an assault gun battalion, an antitank battalion, and twelve Tiger tanks to provide cover for the left flank.

During the night from 5 to 6 August, Belgorod was evacuated after heavy street fighting and the next position, prepared on the high ground immediately south of the city, was occupied. Luftwaffe and service troops defended the road crossings in the swampy lowlands along the Lopan River against enemy spearheads threatening the deep flank. The greatest danger, however, loomed along the Belgorod–Kharkov *Rollbahn*, where the enemy massed his forces in an attempt to break through to Kharkov. A full-strength assault gun battalion, with forty-two self-propelled guns, moving up from Kharkov, was to protect the highway. Its mobility and fire power were to enable the battalion to stop any possible armored break-through.

The position south of Belgorod was held for one day and abandoned after the enemy had deployed his forces. Continued resistance in one position would have led to heavy casualties and the annihilation of the isolated corps. Constant enemy attempts to outflank the left wing submitted the command to a severe nervous strain and made extreme demands on the physical endurance of the troops. However great the sacrifices, they had to be made if worse disaster was to be averted. On 9 August the limits of endurance seemed to have been exceeded when, after an all-night evacuation, the Germans failed to reach the new phase line by dawn. Enemy spearheads broke through along the *Rollbahn* and the whereabouts of an entire division, the 168th Infantry Division, was uncertain. News from the Donets and Lopan sectors was no less alarming. Enemy armor had broken out of the Donets bridgehead, other Russian forces had crossed the Lopan, and the assault gun battalion from Kharkov had failed to arrive. Low-flying hostile planes in great numbers dropped fragmentation bombs and machine gunned troops on the march. Suffering heavy casualties, the German forces grew restless. A few division commanders came over to the corps command post, which by then was situated close to the front line, and requested authorization for an immediate speedy withdrawal to Kharkov in view of the critical situation and the low morale of their forces. Suddenly several trucks loaded with stragglers came tearing down the highway, ignoring all stop signals. When the trucks were finally brought to a halt, the stragglers explained that they had become separated from their 168th Division unit and had been seized by panic when they were subjected to an armored assault farther up the road. Their intention was to drive straight through to Kharkov, at that time forty miles behind the German front. They reported that their division had been wiped out and added that the 88-mm. antiaircraft batteries, detailed to block the highway, were no longer in place.

Every experienced combat commander is familiar with this sort of panic which, in a critical situation, may seize an entire body of troops. Mass hysteria of this type can be overcome only by energetic actions and a display of perfect composure. The example set by a true leader can have miraculous effects. He must stay with his troops, remain cool, issue price orders, and inspire confidence by his behavior. Good soldiers never desert such a leader. News of the presence of high ranking commanders up front travels like wildfire along the entire front line, bolstering everyone's morale. It means a sudden change from gloom to hope, from imminent defeat to victory.

This is exactly what happened. The corps commander stood at a crucial point along the *Rollbahn*, orienting unit commanders and assigning them a mission in the new defense system which he attempted to build up. Self-propelled antitank guns arriving at this instant were immediately committed to block the highway against an armored break-through which seemed imminent as the fire from approaching tanks came ever closer. The corps commander quickly drove past the newly established line toward the din of battle to find out for himself whether the antiaircraft guns were holding out. Driving around a corner, he suddenly witnessed the destruction of a Russian tank by the improvised anti-tank front. He counted eleven more disabled tanks and saw the remaining enemy armor withdraw straight into an extensive mine field where one tank after another was blown up.

Shortly afterward, German fighter planes appeared, and shot down more than a dozen enemy aircraft, clearing the air over the corps front. German heavy weapons and artillery pinned the enemy infantry to the ground when they advanced on a broad front. The threat of a break-through along the *Rollbahn* was eliminated and the German lines held.

The 6th Panzer Division on the left flank faced a difficult situation when, in addition to its own sector, it had to take over the one previously held by the missing 168th Division. The enemy exerted heavy pressure and the panzer division requested immediate antitank support. The corps commander dispatched twelve antitank guns and arranged for an air strike on the Russian tank column advancing east of the Lopan River. These combined efforts prevented the immediate collapse of the German flank cover.

Delayed by traffic jams, the long-awaited assault gun battalion did not arrive until noon. After refueling in some gullies covered with underbrush, it was committed in a counterattack against the enemy tanks threatening the left flank. The massed attack of the forty-two guns surprised the enemy and hit him hard. The assault guns destroyed all enemy tanks and antitank guns on the east bank of the Lopan, shattered the Russian bridgehead, and drove the remaining enemy forces across the river. By early afternoon the situation was under control. Reports from the Donets sector indicated that the enemy was unable to enlarge his bridgehead in the face of stubborn resistance from German infantry units supported by assault guns.

Even though an entire division was missing, the corps had scored an initial defensive success. The enemy's intention to annihilate the German forces by a concentric attack from three sides had failed. Heavy Russian losses in personnel and matériel, including sixty disabled tanks, resulted from the day's operations.

During the night to 10 August, the corps made an unobserved withdrawal to a hastily prepared position about six miles to the south, the salient points of which were occupied by advance detachments. Weak rear guards, left behind in the former position, led the enemy to believe that the line was fully occupied. The next morning, when Russian infantry attacked the position after a heavy concentration, they found only the rear party maintaining contact. The German troops, exhausted by the previous day's fighting and the night march, were able to recuperate during the morning hours. By noon the first enemy patrols cautiously approached the new position. Its gun emplacements and strong points were well camouflaged, and enemy ground and air reconnaissance therefore failed to locate them. Three divisions held the line; one of them had left its positions along the Donets to join the corps.

The Russian attacks resumed during the afternoon with increasing violence. The most dangerous Russian arm was not the badly mauled armor or the tactical air support, but the powerful artillery. In this instance, the effect of the heavy artillery fire was not so devastating since the excellent camouflage of potential German targets forced the Russians to deliver flat trajectory fire. But whenever German machine guns or heavy weapons fired from open terrain, they were spotted by hostile observers and quickly neutralized. If they were to escape destruction, they had to use well-concealed and readily accessible alternate and dummy positions.

By the evening of 10 August, the enemy attacks had lost some of their sting. In view of the experience of the last few days, the Russians made probing thrusts after dusk to maintain contact with the corps in case of another German night withdrawal. The enemy infantry was given a hot reception and, after all attacks had been repulsed, the corps withdrew to the next prepared position. By the time the infantry occupied the new line, the bulk of the artillery and antitank guns were ready to fire. Forming a solid block, the corps was unshaken by renewed enemy onslaughts.

The same delaying tactics were employed during the following days. The withdrawal to successive positions was exhausting, but the casualty rate remained low. The enemy suffered disproportionately high losses, which forced him to gradually relax the pressure on the German lines. The corps front was shortened and strengthened by units no longer needed for flank protection, and reserves were formed. The 168th Division, missing for several days, was found in a well-concealed area when the corps commander made a reconnaissance trip north of Kharkov. The division commander explained that he had understood his unit was to act as corps reserve and that he had therefore withdrawn to the forests twenty-five miles behind the front. After his conduct had been casti-gated in no uncertain terms, he was told to commit his division as covering force in the next position to be occupied. This made it possible to pull out the 6th Panzer Division, designate it corps reserve, and move it to the forest area for a well-deserved rest.

The XLII Infantry Corps, adjacent to the right, was forced to join the XI Corps withdrawal during the night of 11–12 August because its defense line along the Donets formed a deep salient in Russian-held territory. The infantry division on the left wing of this corps had not previously been engaged in a tank battle; it offered little resistance to strong Russian armored forces, which broke through without difficulty and suddenly appeared in the rear of the XI Corps front outside Kharkov. The situation became even more critical when the recruits of a newly arrived regiment, overcome by fear of the approaching Russian tanks, ran for their lives until they were stopped at the bridges in the suburbs of Kharkov. Strong enemy infantry poured through the wide gap to exploit the initial break-through achieved by the tanks. The 6th Panzer Division was immediately alerted and its spearheads intercepted the enemy in the southeastern outskirts of Kharkov where he had occupied the big tractor plant. The division counterattacked, dislodged the enemy from the factory after fierce fighting, destroyed many tanks, dispersed the Russian infantry, and closed the gap. The danger was eliminated for the time being.

Tank fright is frequent among newly activated infantry divisions when training in antimechanized defense has been neglected. Combined arms training with armored or assault gun units is essential in order to give each soldier the experience of being overrun by a tank while in his foxhole and to acquaint him with the use of antitank weapons.

A recently arrived panzer division strengthened the corps flank and blocked the approach routes to Kharkov. The battles for Kharkov proper have been analyzed in Department of the Army Pamphlet No. 20-230, pages 53–56. The evacuation of Kharkov by the Germans became necessary because of unfavorable developments on the southern front. It was carried out without difficulty on 18 August, and a previously prepared position a few miles to the west was occupied by the corps. The new position was situated on high ground protected by a swampy valley cutting across the approach roads. It was considerably shorter than the position skirting Kharkov and could therefore be held very effectively.

During the withdrawal of the German rear guard, the only bridge across the marshes which had been left intact collapsed under the weight of some Hornets (88-mm. tank destroyers). One infantry battalion reinforced by eight Hornets was thereby cut off on the east bank. The enemy attempts to annihilate this small rear guard were frustrated by German units supporting the bridgehead from the west bank. The rear guard held out for twenty-four hours until the bridge was repaired and it could cross under cover of darkness.

In its new position, the corps had to ward off some fierce attacks by enemy forces trying to envelop both flanks. Several local penetrations were sealed off by armored counterattacks. But even this strong position had to be evacuated after a short while since it formed a dangerous salient to the east after the adjacent units were forced to pull out. The next withdrawal led the corps into exposed, flat terrain where it had to extend its wings until the sector covered the forty-mile stretch between the Kolomak and the Berestova Rivers.

In the meantime the over-all situation forced general withdrawal behind the Dnepr River. The XI Corps was given the mission of organizing and covering the withdrawal of twelve divisions across the highway and railroad bridges at Kremenchug (see Part One, pp. 103 ff). During this retrograde movement, the same delaying tactics were employed which had been so successful during the withdrawal from Belgorod to Kharkov. Again and again, delay on successive positions forced the enemy to make time-consuming preparations for battle and to suffer heavy casualties, leading to the gradual exhaustion of his forces. The Russians recognized these intentions and tried every day to force the issue by achieving an armored break-through. Above all, the enemy wanted to capture major cities commanding the road net needed for speedy maneuver. In view of the rainy weather, the possession of hard-surface highways became a decisive factor to both sides since the mud prevented any movement off the roads. The Germans took this factor into account and concentrated their antitank defenses in and around important towns. During this phase, cities were therefore far more important than during the fighting in the area north of Kharkov. The enemy achieved only one armored break-through when he blocked the German withdrawal across the Orchik River near Karlovka. A critical situation developed because of additional delays in the river crossing caused by floods, mud, and the steepness of the west bank. There was a grave danger that enemy tanks might reach the weakly held west bank before the arrival of the German units which were forced to take devious routes. The densely populated suburban area of Karlovka near the river was set ablaze by enemy artillery fire, which meant a further delay in the crossing. Demolitions of factories, railroad installations, depots, and supplies, ordered by higher headquarters in line with a German scorched earth policy, caused still more delays. A major enemy break-through at this point seemed certain, when suddenly the Russian tanks were forced to slow down because of mud, and the danger subsided.

With a change in the weather the ground dried; the infantry divisions were able to move faster and the daily rate of withdrawal was stepped up to twenty to thirty miles. The Russian tanks did not renew their pressure until the corps halted for several days at the Kremenchug bridgehead. Russian striking power was impaired by several weeks of German delaying actions on successive positions. The enemy counteroffensive had spent itself.

CHAPTER 29

Defense against Break-throughs – a Combination of Defense Tactics

Every protracted defensive engagement requires the application of a combination of tactics which correspond to the changes in the situation. During the Russian campaign several defensive methods were employed simultaneously or successively with no single one exercising a predominant or, even less, a decisive influence on the outcome of the operation. Even within one action, subordinate units sometimes applied tactics differing from those used by the main body. At the beginning of August 1944, for instance, during the fighting along the foothills of the Carpathian Mountains, six infantry battalions blocked the enemy advance while the two divisions to which they belonged carried out a simultaneous flank attack. As a rule, defensive actions are designated by the tactical measure which predominates. During the battle for East Prussia, for instance, the Germans at first used improvised zone defense tactics. Subsequent Russian break-through attempts were frustrated by defensive pincers, flank attacks, delaying and blocking maneuvers, and attacks with reversed fronts, but the outcome of the battle was determined by the employment of zone defense tactics.

On the other hand, a combination of defense tactics stopped the major offensive in which the Russians drove from the Volga to the Dnepr in the winter of 1942–43. Delaying and blocking maneuvers by panzer and infantry units, combined with pincers, flank thrusts, and the encirclement of an armored corps prevented a Russian break-through to Rostov in December 1942. This would have endangered the German troops in the Caucasus and south of Stalingrad. In another instance, rigid defense by infantry combined with mobile maneuvers of armored units stopped a Russian break-through attempt toward the Sea of Azov during January and February 1943. Delay on successive positions during the withdrawal toward the Dnepr in the summer of 1943 slowed down the enemy's thrust to the west and made it possible to move up German reinforcements. The pincers attack following that retrograde movement crushed the Russian armored wedge in the Dnepr bend and broke the backbone of the offensive.

During the fighting near Kirovograd in January 1944, the Germans employed delaying and blocking tactics, defensive pincers, flank attacks, envelopments, and break-through maneuvers which were of equal importance and followed each other in quick succession. For this reason the Kirovograd operation is a typical example of the application of combined defense tactics.

Toward the end of 1943, the Russian operations in the south seemed to indicate that the Soviet command planned to break through the German front in several places, split the forces of Army Groups A and South, and drive them into the Black Sea and toward the Romanian border. In line with these plans the Second Ukrainian Front launched a major offensive in December 1943 in order to break through in the Kirovograd area. The Russians opened a breach in the Eighth Army front, but this initial attempt was frustrated by swift counter-attacks of German motorized units. During the first days of January 1944, German ground and air reconnaissance as well as radio intercepts indicated Russian concentrations and attack preparations. Strong artillery forces were assembling in the rear of the Russian lines. While only about sixty Russian tanks were discovered in the concentration areas close to the German front, intelligence estimates assumed that strong armored forces were located in rest areas farther to the rear.

The Eighth Army front was overextended and few reserves were available to conduct an active defense. It seemed unlikely that any sizable units could be shifted from sectors not under attack because all the divisions were under-strength and the enemy exercised pressure along the entire front. The armored elements of two panzer divisions committed along the front line were held back as corps reserves. Eight GHQ artillery battalions were available to strengthen the two potential centers of gravity. Artillery ammunition on hand was abundant, a fact which partly compensated for the German inferiority in number of guns.

The Russians launched their attack at 0600 on 5 January, jumping off from their two principal concentration areas. Preceded by half an hour's artillery preparation and several air strikes, massed infantry poured through the gaps in the German front in an attempt to break through to the Kirovograd area. Following closely, additional infantry and some antitank units widened the areas of penetration and secured the interior flanks for the advancing Russian armor. In conjunction with the two main thrusts the Russians conducted holding attacks in varying strength along the entire army front. By the time the infantry assault got under way, the heavy preparation, in which two-thirds of the enemy's batteries participated, had neutralized most of the German artillery and inflicted extremely heavy casualties. The combat strength of some divisions dropped even lower – even before the start of the offensive the 2d Parachute Division held a twelve-mile sector with 3,200 men and the 10th Panzer Grenadier Division covered eleven miles of frontage with 3,700 men. The

Russian infantry forces, six to seven divisions strong and supported by armored groups of varying strength, achieved deep penetrations during the morning hours. At the southern point of main effort they advanced 6 miles on a 4-mile front, and in the XLVII Panzer Corps sector 13 miles on a 10-mile front (map 18).

When the Russian armored forces attempted to exploit the initial break-through, the German corps reserves launched small-scale flank attacks. Supported by antitank units, they destroyed altogether ninety-three enemy tanks, mainly in the southern sector. Nevertheless, it became evident that the Eighth Army forces alone would be unable to seal the gaps in the front. As requested by army, the 3d Panzer Division was transferred during the late morning and committed in the XLVII Panzer Corps sector. In the southern break-through area, approximately 200 Russian tanks were held up by diversionary flank attacks before they could reach the Ingul River. In the northern area of penetration, however, the counterthrusts carried out by elements of 11th Panzer Division failed to stop the armored forces driving toward the southwest. There, the enemy threatened to envelop Kirovograd from the north and west and cause its fall by cutting the German lifelines.

On this first day of the Russian offensive the Germans destroyed 153 enemy tanks and caused heavy casualties, but their own losses were proportionately high. The 10th Panzer Grenadier Division, for instance, lost 620 men in one day. By the end of the day the situation was confused since, despite a German withdrawal to Adzhamka and a corresponding shortening of the line, the Russian penetrations were not adequately sealed off.

During the night the enemy moved strong infantry forces into the newly captured terrain. Approximately twenty-two infantry divisions were equally divided between the two areas of penetration. These divisions had been hastily reorganized and their replacements consisted of inadequately trained troops; nevertheless, the over-all ratio of infantry strength was eight to one in favor of the Russians.

The Russian infantry protected the interior flanks of the penetration by a quick build-up of antitank gun fronts echeloned in depth. Lacking centralized fire direction and flexibility in forming points of main effort, the Russian artillery did not make its overwhelming superiority properly felt. This was partly due to transportation and supply difficulties which delayed the arrival of many Russian artillery units. Not until the capture of Kirovograd was the enemy able to mass his artillery effectively. The German artillery played an important part in the defense, delivering well-co-ordinated concentrations with high expenditure of ammunition. During the first day of the offensive the Germans expended six to seven times more ammunition than the enemy, firing approximately 177,000 rounds against 29,000. This enabled them to inflict extremely heavy casualties and break up Russian attack preparations. In view of the high casualty rate suffered by the German infantry, the artillery was in some sectors, especially along the shoulders of the gaps, the sole obstacle confronting the Russians.

Statements by prisoners of war and captured documents permitted the Germans to estimate the Russian armor at 620 tanks. Against these forces the Germans could assemble only 56 tanks and 109 assault guns. The enemy regrouped and reinforced his armor in the northern penetration area during the night of 5 January. His mobile units were deployed in accordance with German doctrine but lacked concentration of effort in one direction and paid too much attention to flank cover. The latter fact was probably due to the relentless local flank attacks which the Germans conducted even when they only had a few tanks on hand. During these small-scale actions the German tank crews proved their superiority over and over again. Moreover, this type of active defense deceived the enemy as to German strength.

When the enemy renewed his attack on the morning of 6 January, the Germans were able to tie down strong forces by active defense and to delay the advance of some Russian armored units by hit-and-run tactics. In the north, however, the 3d Panzer Division counterattacks failed to close the gap and in the south the enemy tanks thrust toward Kirovograd without much obstruction, reaching the southern suburbs of the city by evening. The other jaw of the Russian pincer crossed the Ingul River at Severinka, cut the Kirovograd–Novomirgorod highway, and threatened Kirovograd from the north.

Since German resistance east of the Ingul had crumbled, the army commander intended to block any further break-through attempts to the west by moving up new forces which were to annihilate the enemy spearheads west of the river. For this reason he urgently requested reinforcements from army group. Even a further withdrawal and shortening of lines would not have led to the formation of counterattack forces since every man was needed up front. The army group replied that advance units of Panzer Division Grossdeutschland were to arrive in the area southwest of Kirovograd during the evening of 7 January in order to close the gap south of the city. Until then the German forces had to gain time and contain the enemy in a series of quickly changing seesaw actions. East of the Ingul, a reinforced panzer battalion made an enveloping thrust, attempting to cut the enemy's rear communications. After initial success the attack bogged down against strong resistance by antitank guns. When the three divisions holding out in the sector between the two areas of penetration were pulled back to defend the perimeter of Kirovograd, one of them – the 14th Panzer Division – was given the mission of closing the southern gap. But during the night, while the preparatory movement took place, strong Russian infantry and armored forces penetrated into Kirovograd from the south and hit the assembly of 14th Panzer Division. In stiff house-to-house fighting the enemy advanced to the railroad tracks and breached the perimeter defense. The two other divisions were fighting their way back north of the tracks when they were suddenly attacked by enemy forces from three sides, squeezed into Lelekovka, and isolated. In its withdrawal from Kirovograd, the 14th Panzer Division succeeded in establishing contact with the Lelekovka force after some bitter fighting. After withdrawing to the west bank of the Ingul, the 3d Panzer Division attacked the Russian armored concentrations but met with little resistance when the enemy sidestepped the attack (map 19).

Southwest of Kirovograd, the newly arrived units of the Grossdeutschland Division were thrown piecemeal against strong Russian forces advancing unobstructed toward the southwest and succeeded in delaying the enemy advance.

The attempt to block the Russian advance in front of Kirovograd had failed. The isolated force at Lelekovka, forming the last anchor of the German position in this area, held out and tied down strong enemy forces, thereby preventing a junction between the two areas of penetration. But on each side the enemy's motorized and armored forces poured through the gaps, crossed the Ingul, and assembled on the west bank for a major break-through. During the night of 8–9 January, a strong armored force advanced as far as Malyye Viski, overran the command post of the XLVII Panzer Corps, and threatened rear communications.

In this situation it was imperative that the army stabilize the front wherever possible and then close the gaps. Since the available forces were inadequate for a co-ordinated effort, it was necessary to resort to local expedients. Above all, the blocking forces had to pin down strong enemy units by vigorous resistance. Then, those Russian forces that had broken through had to be weakened by limited objective attacks and armored thrusts so that they would be incapable of breaking through to the west in strength. This was achieved by a series of local actions. By the evening of 9 January, the Grossdeutschland Division pounced on the flanks of the enemy forces advancing south-west of Kirovograd and turned them back. The gap in the sector adjacent to the right was temporarily closed by a frontal counterattack of newly arrived improvised units.

The closing of the gap to the left of the Grossdeutschland Division was accomplished by a pincers attack which cut off two Russian infantry divisions and some armored units. After their annihilation the Germans recaptured the high ground near Karlovka and restored the front line southwest of Kirovograd by a frontal counterattack.

In the northern sector, elements of the 3d Panzer Division were given the mission of restoring the situation at Malyye Viski. After heavy fighting the enemy's tank losses were so high that he was forced to withdraw his troops from this area. The isolated German forces holding out at Lelekovka were in a precarious situation. Unrelenting Russian ground attacks, supported by waves of fighter bombers, left no doubt about the outcome of this unequal struggle.

The shortage of ammunition was only partly relieved by air drops. A relief thrust by the 11th Panzer Division did not materialize because the division was unable to free itself from a holding attack by superior Russian forces. As a last resort, a motorized infantry battalion was reinforced with a few tanks and assembled in the Bolshay Vyska area. After overcoming stiff resistance, the task force advanced across enemy-held territory via Gruznoye to Oboznovka. During the night of 9 January, the pocket force in Lelekovka broke out, linked up with the relief force, and withdrew to Gruznoye. The defense in place at Lelekovka had delayed and finally prevented an enemy break-through to the west. The XLVII Panzer Corps front was consolidated along the line Karlovka–west of Gruznoye–Vladimirovka and the XI Corps, adjacent to the north, was aligned with the panzer corps. This withdrawal permitted the transfer of the 282d Infantry Division to the panzer corps, which held the division in reserve against any further Russian break-through attempts in its sector. Despite the heavy tank losses they had suffered, the Russians were expected to renew their attacks after regrouping their forces.

By 11 January the enemy launched a new attack in the Gruznoye–Vladimirovka area after an artillery preparation lasting half an hour (map 20). His armor was organized into several strong attack formations which were to pave the way for the infantry. The German blocking forces were unable to hold the line which was breached in several places. During the following day the penetrations were partly sealed off by local counterattacks. After the arrival of several infantry divisions from other sectors, the enemy, on 15 January, resumed his attacks with a heavy artillery preparation. Eleven infantry divisions, supported by tanks, breached the German line between Gruznoye and Vladimirovka, opening a seven-mile gap to a depth of three miles. The three German divisions holding this sector were split up and isolated. Resisting stubbornly, they fought their way to the shoulders of the area of penetration and, by clinging to their positions, made it possible to close the gap on the next day.

On 16 January, while the Russians concentrated all available ground forces and air support for an all-out attack, the newly arrived 3d SS Panzer Division made a spoiling attack into the enemy's offensive preparations. The three German divisions holding the shoulders joined the panzer forces and closed the gap.

The Russian break-through attempts had failed after twelve days of bitter fighting in the Kirovograd area. The thirty-one Russian infantry divisions used during this operation were weakened to such an extent that many regiments were reduced to 300–400 men. By 17 January only about 120 Russian tanks were available for commitment. Throughout the entire operation the German army commander was handicapped by the low strength of his units which dropped at an alarming rate under the pressure of the Russian offensive. Unable to echelon his forces in depth, he had no means of preventing the enemy from exploiting local penetrations in the German front. Intermediate and lower commands were rarely in a position to form reserves. The weak corps reserves, usually consisting of small armored units, succeeded in delaying the enemy and inflicting slight losses, but were incapable of turning the tide. The complete lack of general reserves forced the army commander to resort to improvised tactics. During the entire struggle in the Kirovograd area, the army commander was under strict orders prohibiting retirement to shorter lines, otherwise he might have regained his freedom of maneuver and would have been able to form reserves in divisional strength. Finally, after having received reinforcements, the German Eighth Army frustrated all further Russian breakthrough attempts. During this ten-day period the Germans had demonstrated extraordinary flexibility in the use of different defense tactics.

CHAPTER 30

Conclusions

The dynamic offensives executed by the German Army during the first part of the Russian campaign ground to a halt in front of Moscow and at Stalingrad. During the following months of bitter struggle against a tenacious enemy who cleverly exploited the vast space and climatic conditions of his homeland, German strength declined so much that the subsequent Russian counteroffensive could no longer be repulsed. It was Hitler's worst mistake not to have recognized the impending disaster in time or, if he did realize it, to have dismissed it in his peremptory manner. This obstinate denial of obvious facts forced the German Army to fight a series of defensive actions against breakthroughs along overextended front lines during the second part of the Russian campaign. Every time the Germans succeeded after extreme sacrifices in closing one gap, the line gave way at another point. Resolutely they went to their doom in a long succession of exhausting battles and withdrawals. The disintegration of the German forces was speeded up when corps, and even entire armies, under orders to hold critical cities and areas, were cut off from the main force. The perfection of defense tactics and the superhuman efforts of the field forces were insufficient to turn the tide so long as the Germans were unable to restore a balance of strength essential to an eventual victory over the Russians. Under the prevailing circumstances an equilibrium in the fields of manpower and matériel was beyond expectation. But it was within the realm of possibility that the German military performance in the field would first equal and later outdistance the Russian. As a prerequisite, the German potential should have been brought into the proper relationship with the elements of time and space to compensate for the Russian superiority in manpower and matériel so that victory could eventually have been achieved through the application of superior strategy. At no time should the German Army have expended its strength as recklessly as it was required to do in front of Moscow and at Stalingrad. The Russians thereby gained a superiority which enabled them to hold the initiative. Contrary to Hitler's concepts, a timely halt in the offensive or a temporary withdrawal would not have undermined the confidence of the field forces, but would have led to additional successes, the sum total of which might have brought the war with Russia to a favorable conclusion.

After the Stalingrad disaster the Germans fought delaying actions along a 1,000-mile front for a four-month period. Even then they succeeded in sealing off the wide gaps and stabilizing the front and achieved a defensive victory by

March 1943. However, the German lines were overextended and the panzer forces, reconstituted during a lull lasting three months, were still too weak to withstand the renewed onslaught of the forces which the Russians had meanwhile moved up. Once again the enemy broke through the German front, but this time the eleven best, fully reorganized panzer divisions which were assembled in the Kharkov–Poltava area were able to frustrate the Russian intentions by a determined counterattack. Even so, the time had not yet come to seize the initiative. The Russians still had to suffer heavier casualties. If necessary, the Germans should have abandoned more terrain and shortened their lines to establish a balance of strength which would have prevented other break-throughs. Only then could a decisive German counteroffensive have assured a German victory in Russia before the Allies landed in France. Defeat of the western powers was contingent upon Russia's being driven out of the war.

The German defense against Russian break-throughs, as presented in this study, was only a means toward attaining this over-all objective. In 1943 the German Army in Russia almost succeeded in putting an end to enemy break-throughs by adroitly combining various defense tactics. Victory was once again in the offing, but it turned out to be a Russian one. Before the eleven panzer divisions could come to grip with Russian reserves and annihilate them, the German armor was thrown into Operation ZITADELLE in July 1943 and bled white when it ran into a fortified system of hitherto unknown strength and depth. Hitler thereby fulfilled the enemy's keenest hopes and presented him with the palm of victory. The subsequent Russian counteroffensive, conducted with powerful reserves which were fully intact, broke through the German line. The enemy break-throughs started anew not only in this sector but also in others, where no adequate reserves were available.

At best, skillful defense tactics and supreme personal sacrifices were instrumental in producing local, temporary relief. The German strategy of self-sacrifice precluded the possibility of stabilizing the front along a line which by then had been shortened by the course of events. Finally, a suggestion to shift all German forces from the West to the East in order to stop the Red Army's invasion of Germany and prevent the territorial expansion of communism was turned down by Hitler. While he believed his principal enemies to be in the West, the German military leaders, for all their antagonism toward the western powers, considered Russia their irreconcilable enemy.

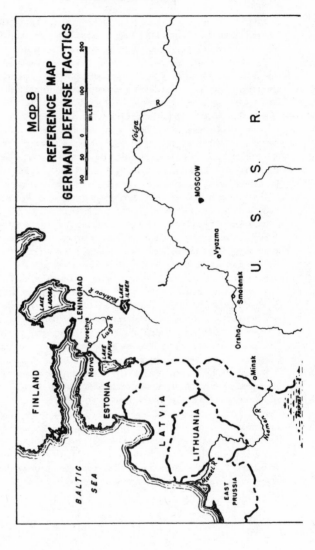

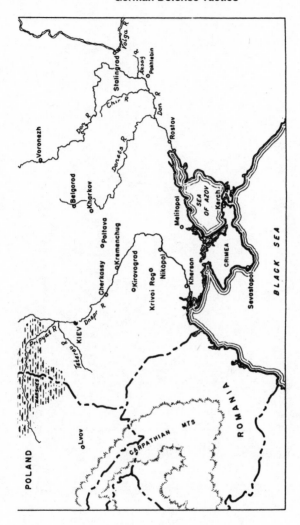

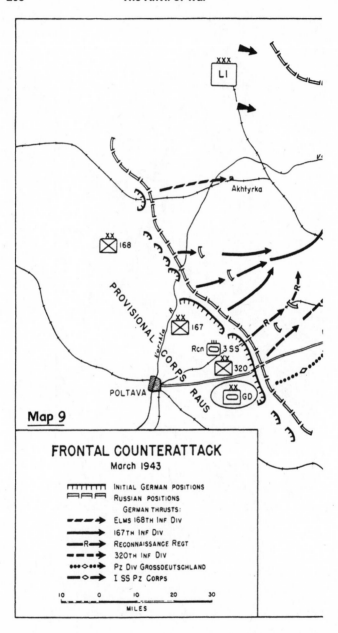

Akhtyrka

168

PROVISIONAL CORPS RAUS

167

Rcn 3 SS

320

GD

POLTAVA

Map 9

FRONTAL COUNTERATTACK
March 1943

⊓⊓⊓⊓⊓	INITIAL GERMAN POSITIONS
⌐⌐⌐	RUSSIAN POSITIONS
	GERMAN THRUSTS:
➡	ELMS 168TH INF DIV
➡	167TH INF DIV
R➡	RECONNAISSANCE REGT
➡	320TH INF DIV
●●●◇◇●●	PZ DIV GROSSDEUTSCHLAND
➡◇➡	I SS PZ CORPS

10   0   10   20   30

MILES

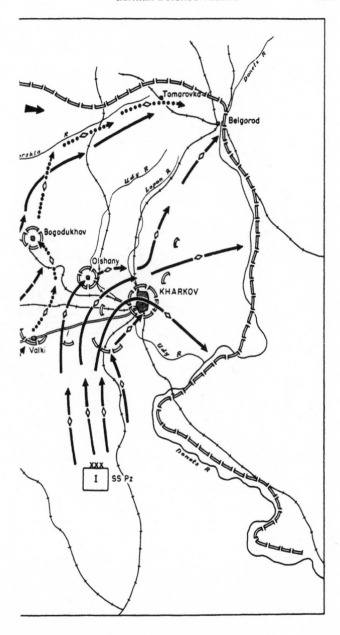

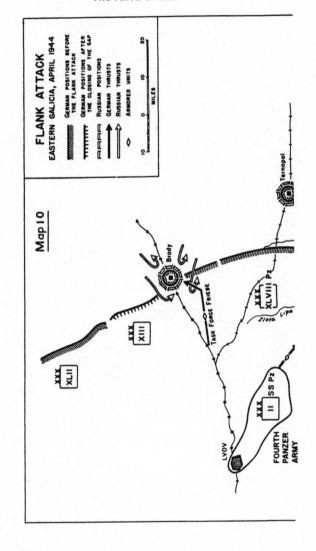

Map 10

FLANK ATTACK
EASTERN GALICIA, APRIL 1944

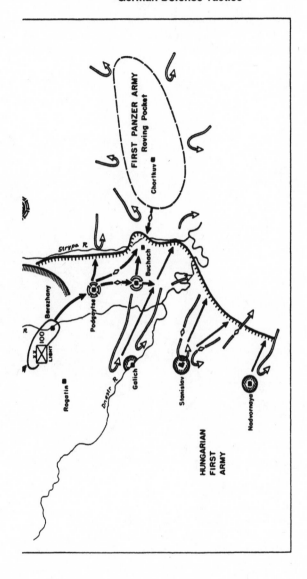

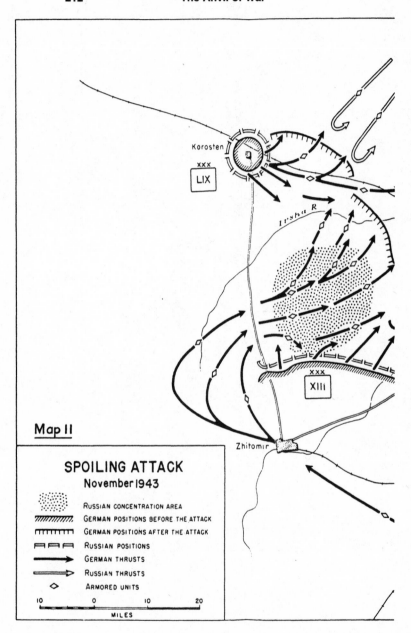

Korosten

xxx
LIX

Irsha R

xxx
XIII

Zhitomir

Map II

SPOILING ATTACK
November 1943

Russian concentration area
German positions before the attack
German positions after the attack
Russian positions
German thrusts
Russian thrusts
Armored units

10   0   10   20
MILES

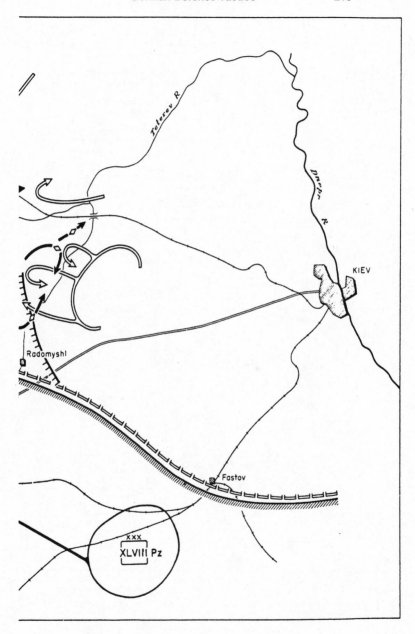

Teterev R.

Dnepr R.

KIEV

Radomyshl

Fastov

xxx
XLVIII Pz

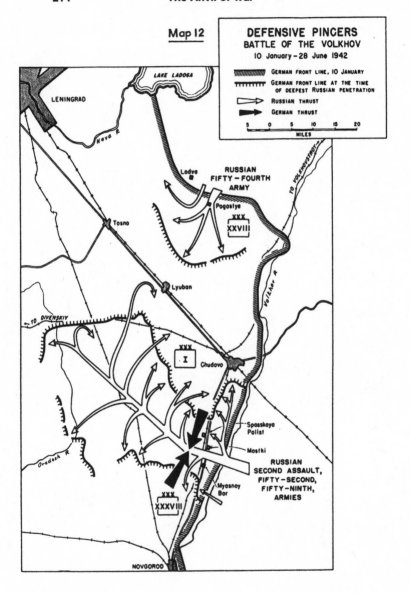

Map 12

DEFENSIVE PINCERS
BATTLE OF THE VOLKHOV
10 January – 28 June 1942

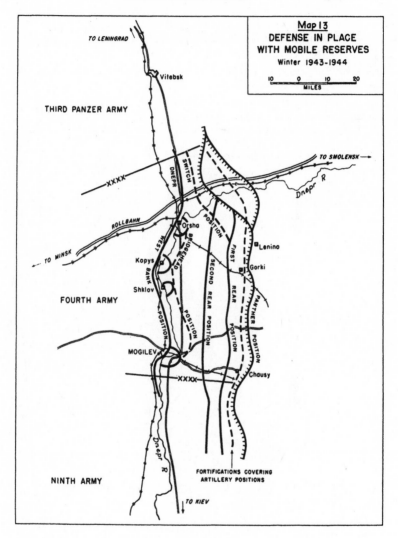

Map 13
DEFENSE IN PLACE
WITH MOBILE RESERVES
Winter 1943-1944

10   0   10   20
MILES

TO LENINGRAD

Vitebsk

THIRD PANZER ARMY

XXXX

DNEPR

SWITCH

TO SMOLENSK →

Dnepr R

ROLLBAHN

POSITION

FIRST

Orsha

← TO MINSK

Lenino

Kopys

BRIDGEHEAD

WEST BANK

Gorki

Shklov

SECOND REAR POSITION

REAR POSITION

PANTHER POSITION

FOURTH ARMY

POSITION

POSITION

MOGILEV

Chausy

XXXX

FORTIFICATIONS COVERING
ARTILLERY POSITIONS

Dnepr R

NINTH ARMY

↓ TO KIEV

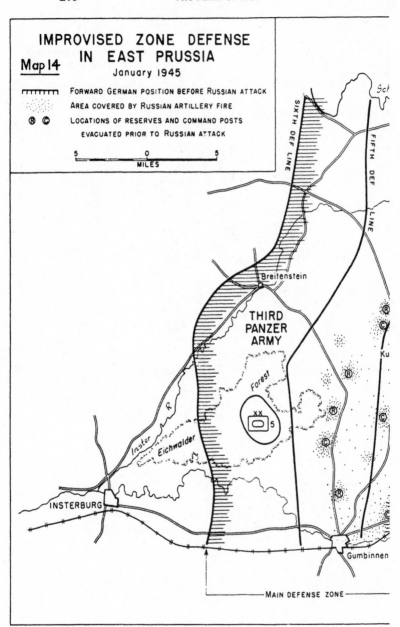

IMPROVISED ZONE DEFENSE
IN EAST PRUSSIA
January 1945

Map 14

⊓⊓⊓⊓⊓ Forward German position before Russian attack
∴∴∴   Area covered by Russian artillery fire
Ⓡ Ⓒ   Locations of reserves and command posts
          evacuated prior to Russian attack

5   0   5
          MILES

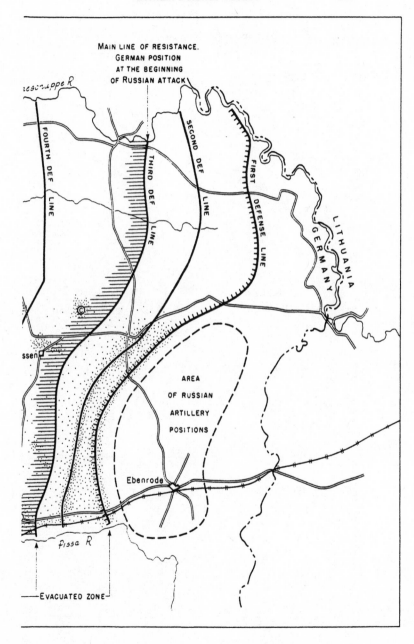

MAIN LINE OF RESISTANCE.
GERMAN POSITION
AT THE BEGINNING
OF RUSSIAN ATTACK

FOURTH DEF LINE

THIRD DEF LINE

SECOND DEF LINE

FIRST DEFENSE LINE

LITHUANIA

GERMANY

ssen

AREA
OF RUSSIAN
ARTILLERY
POSITIONS

Ebenrode

Pissa R

EVACUATED ZONE

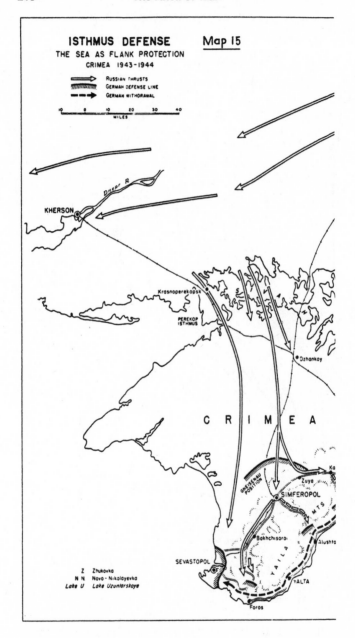

ISTHMUS DEFENSE   Map 15
THE SEA AS FLANK PROTECTION
CRIMEA 1943-1944

RUSSIAN THRUSTS
GERMAN DEFENSE LINE
GERMAN WITHDRAWAL

10   0   10   20   30   40
MILES

Dnepr R

KHERSON

Krasnoperekopsk

PEREKOP
ISTHMUS

Dzhankoy

C R I M E A

GNEISENAU POSITION

Zuya
SIMFEROPOL
Ka

Bakhchisarai
Alushta

SEVASTOPOL

Y A I L A
M T S

YALTA

Foros

Z   Zhukovka
N N   Novo - Nikolayevka
Lake U   Lake Uzunlarskaye

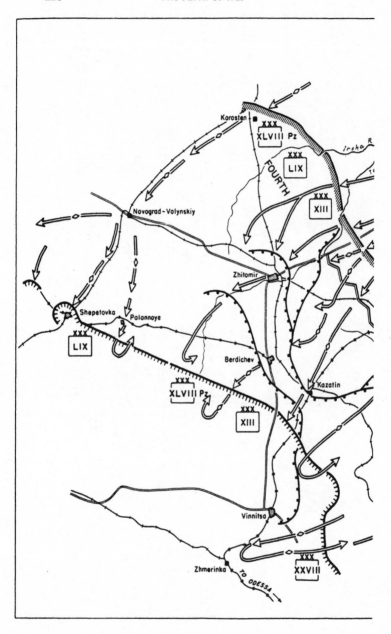

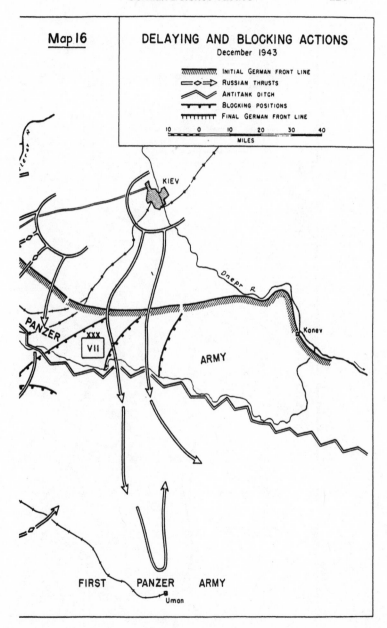

Map 16

DELAYING AND BLOCKING ACTIONS
December 1943

///////// INITIAL GERMAN FRONT LINE
▭◇⇒ RUSSIAN THRUSTS
ANTITANK DITCH
BLOCKING POSITIONS
FINAL GERMAN FRONT LINE

10   0   10   20   30   40
MILES

KIEV

Dnepr R.

PANZER

xxx
VII

ARMY

Kanev

FIRST   PANZER   ARMY

Uman

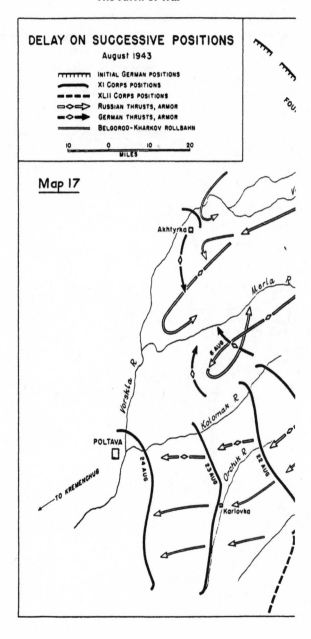

DELAY ON SUCCESSIVE POSITIONS
August 1943

INITIAL GERMAN POSITIONS
XI CORPS POSITIONS
XLII CORPS POSITIONS
RUSSIAN THRUSTS, ARMOR
GERMAN THRUSTS, ARMOR
BELGOROD-KHARKOV ROLLBAHN

10   0   10   20
MILES

Map 17

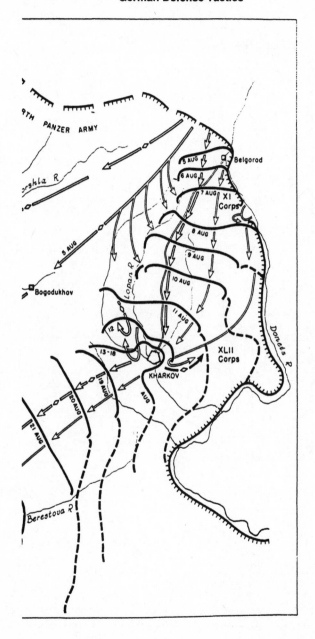

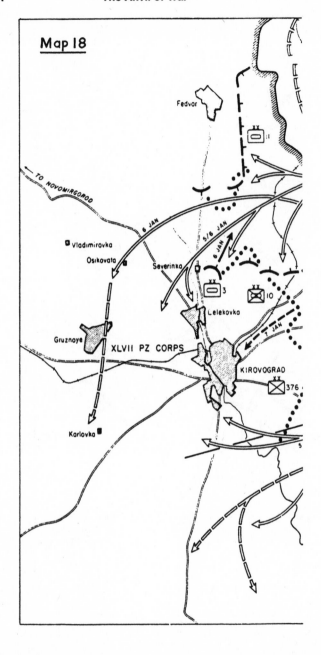

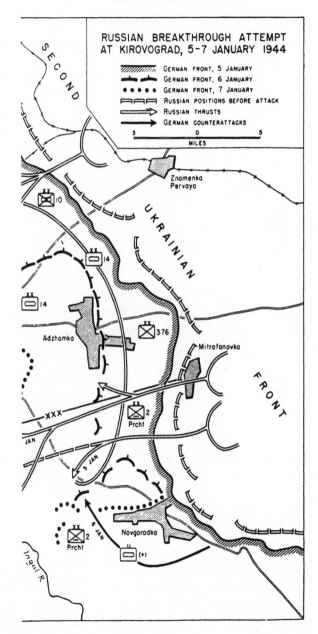

RUSSIAN BREAKTHROUGH ATTEMPT
AT KIROVOGRAD, 5–7 JANUARY 1944

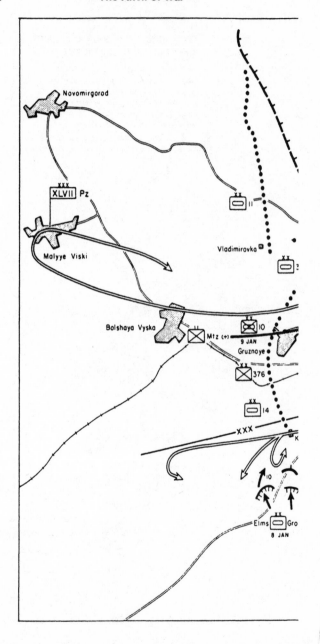

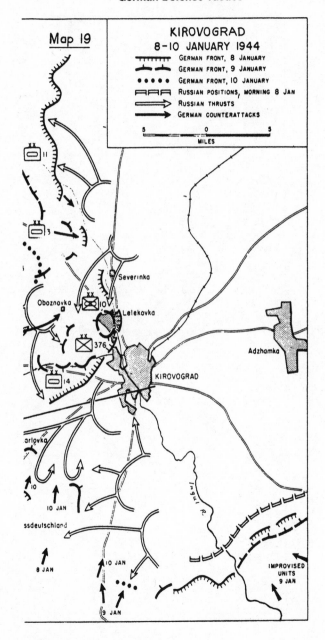

Map 19

KIROVOGRAD
8-10 JANUARY 1944

GERMAN FRONT, 8 JANUARY
GERMAN FRONT, 9 JANUARY
GERMAN FRONT, 10 JANUARY
RUSSIAN POSITIONS, MORNING 8 JAN
RUSSIAN THRUSTS
GERMAN COUNTERATTACKS

5   0   5
MILES

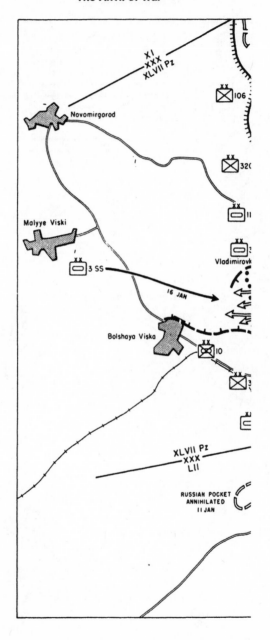

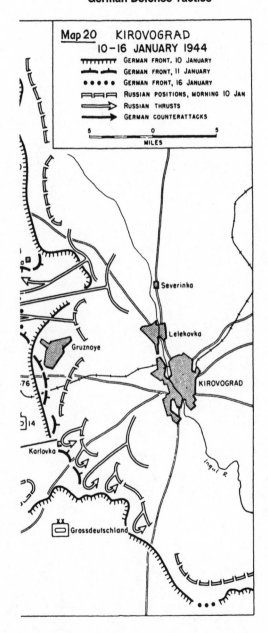

Map 20 KIROVOGRAD
10-16 JANUARY 1944

GERMAN FRONT, 10 JANUARY
GERMAN FRONT, 11 JANUARY
GERMAN FRONT, 16 JANUARY
RUSSIAN POSITIONS, MORNING 10 JAN
RUSSIAN THRUSTS
GERMAN COUNTERATTACKS

5   0   5
MILES

Part Three

Operations of Encircled Forces: German Experiences in Russia

BY GENERALLEUTNANT OLDWIG VON NATZMER
Chief of Staff, Army Groups North and Center

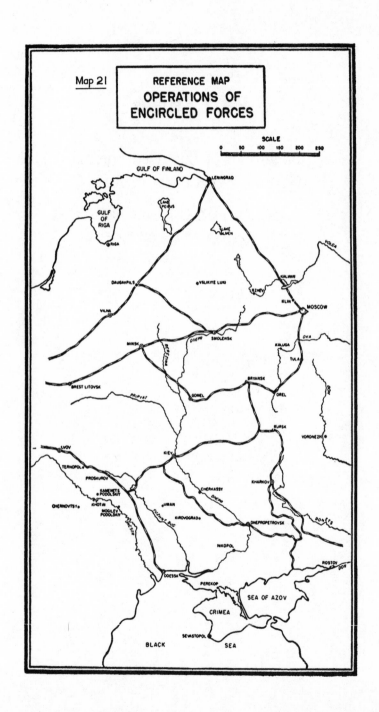

Introduction

Pockets are formed as the result of operations in which the attacker entirely surrounds a large number of the opposing forces. Such encirclement is usually followed by a battle of annihilation, the classic goal of all types of ground combat. The principles involved in carrying out penetrations and envelopments, and in closing the ring around an enemy force are well established in tactical doctrine. In the following study, however, the problem is approached exclusively from the defender's point of view. German pockets in Russia – often the result of peremptory orders to hold out in the face of certain encirclement – are used as examples to illustrate the tactical principles applied by the encircled units and the measures taken in each instance to permit a breakout in the direction of the German lines.

The experiences of World War II demonstrate that under conditions of modern, mobile warfare such pockets are more easily created than in military operations of the past. Their tactical significance has changed considerably. The encirclement of military forces by the enemy no longer signals the end of their usefulness. Pockets have become frequent occurrences in modern combat and must be countered by appropriate tactical measures designed to tie down large numbers of the enemy and, eventually, to rescue the encircled troops.

Generally, encirclements are effected by an opponent with considerable superiority in men and matériel. Without these prerequisites, only superior planning can lead to the entrapment of substantial military forces. Such cases are extremely rare.

The maneuver of deliberately allowing one's forces to be encircled by the enemy so as to tie up his troops in sufficient numbers to even the odds, rarely achieves the desired result. Should the total opposing forces be approximately equal, such a maneuver can be of value, but only if the number of enemy troops engaged in maintaining the encirclement is large enough to affect the outcome of other operations. Even in this case, however, the deliberate creation of a pocket is a costly enterprise which will hardly justify the probable loss of the entire encircled force.

Success or failure of the encircled troops in fighting their way back to the German lines depended almost entirely on the tactical situation in and around the pocket. Whereas a discussion of strategic decisions is normally outside the scope of tactical studies, the situations described in the following chapters are the direct result of decisions by higher headquarters and can only be understood agains the background of these decisions.

In addition to minor German pockets in Russia, the battles of encirclement near Cherkassy and Kamenets–Podolskiy (chapters 33 and 34) have been selected as typical examples of large-scale pocket engagements and breakout attempts. In chapter 33, furthermore, the report on developments inside the pocket is contrasted with impressions gained of the same operation by an officer at a higher headquarters outside the ring of encirclement. Excerpts from the diary of a German pocket commander show the increasing psychological pressure exerted by the enemy on encircled troops, especially the attempt at persuasion by the so-called Committee for a Free Germany, which was organized by the Russians and composed of captured German officers.

CHAPTER 31

The Pocket of Klin –
Breakout of a
Panzer Division

When the German offensive against Moscow came to a halt on 6 December 1941, the 1st Panzer Division was located at a point fifteen miles north of the Russian capital. It was immediately ordered back to Klin (map 22) with the mission of keeping that town open for the withdrawal of other German armored forces. Deep snow obstructed every movement, and the highway running through Klin was the only route over which the withdrawal of mechanized and motorized columns could be effected.

The division reached Klin, after fighting the elements as well as the enemy, and succeeded in holding that important junction against persistent Russian attacks until the retrograde movements of other German units through the town were completed. At that point, however, as the division was ready to break contact and withdraw in the direction of Nekrasino, it found itself completely surrounded by strong enemy forces. The division was ordered by higher headquarters to abandon its vehicles if necessary, and to break through to Nekrasino where it would be able to link up with other German forces.

During the days of heavy fighting that preceded the entry of the division into Klin, the road to Nekrasino had been cut by the enemy on several occasions. In these engagements other German units lost numerous vehicles by enemy action and collisions. Wrecks had piled up all along the road and left no more than a narrow lane between them.

By reconnaissance in force, the encircled division discovered that enemy resistance was weakest southeast of Klin, and that a breakout in this direction would be most likely to succeed. The terrain, however, was such that practically all vehicles would have to be left behind. There were from 800 to 1,000 wounded in Klin who could not be evacuated without transportation. Furthermore, despite considerable loss of equipment, the encircled force was still well provided with vehicles and not inclined to give them up, if that could possibly be avoided.

After short deliberation it was agreed that the division, in order to retain its mobility, would have to break out along the road to Nekrasino, although that road itself was held by enemy forces in considerable strength. Chiefly

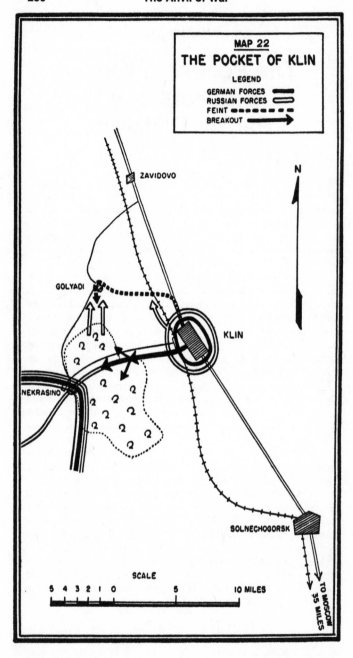

MAP 22
THE POCKET OF KLIN

LEGEND
GERMAN FORCES
RUSSIAN FORCES
FEINT
BREAKOUT

N

ZAVIDOVO

GOLYADI

KLIN

NEKRASINO

SOLNECHOGORSK

TO MOSCOW
35 MILES

SCALE

5 4 3 2 1 0   5   10 MILES

responsible for this decision was the large number of casualties that were to be evacuated at any cost.

In preparing for the breakout, the division made use of its experiences during a previous encirclement at Kalinin. There, after executing a feint in a different direction which diverted some of the hostile forces, the division had succeeded in making a surprise breakout, losing no equipment and suffering few casualties. The great flexibility of the artillery had been of decisive importance. Shifting their fire rapidly from one target to the other, all pieces were able to support the diversionary attack as well as the actual breakout. Equally important had been the possibility of throwing all the tanks that survived the diversionary maneuver into the main effort.

After a careful survey of the situation around Klin, a plan was adopted. All available tanks, one company of armored infantry, and one rifle battalion were to conduct a diversionary break-through north of Klin, and then to proceed in a westerly direction toward the town of Golyadi. Turning sharply south after reaching Golyadi, these forces were to initiate an attack in the direction of the main road. The artillery was to remain in position around the railroad station of Klin. The main breakout toward Nekrasino was to take place as soon as the Russians reacted to the threat near Golyadi and began to divert their forces from the main road. The Germans calculated that the turning movement at Golyadi would force the enemy to shift his front toward the north in order to avoid envelopment from that direction. Initially, the entire German artillery and all available antiaircraft weapons were to support the forces carrying out the feint.

While all remained quiet in the area designated for the main effort, the German units were assembled in proper order inside the encircled city. H Hour for the diversionary maneuver – actually an attack with limited objective – was set for dawn. The time of the main break-through depended on the development of the situation.

The intended deception of the enemy was accomplished with full success. A well-organized German task force fell upon the Russians at Golyadi and caught them by surprise. At the appearance of German tanks the Russians immediately shifted their reserves to meet the diversionary attack which they assumed to be the main German breakout. The attacking German troops, incidentally, had not been informed that their effort at Golyadi was no more than a feint. It was felt that they would not fight with quite the same zeal if they knew that they were merely trying to deceive the enemy. Only the division artillery commander was entrusted with the full details of the plan, including the code word for shifting fire to his new targets on either side of the Klin–Nekrasino road. The German task force took Golyadi and pivoted south. As expected, the enemy began to pull out from the area of the main road and to move north across the railroad line, determined to counter the threat of envelopment.

This was the appropriate time – about noon of the same day – to launch the main breakout along the road to Nekrasino. Upon prearranged signal, artillery and antiaircraft weapons shifted their fire. Only one artillery battalion continued to fire on the old target so as to cover the withdrawal of the diversionary force from Golyadi. Simultaneously, on the road leading out of Klin toward the west, the main attack got under way. The division's armored infantry battalion drove the first gap into the lines of an enemy taken completely by surprise. Dismounted armored infantry and motorcycle troops followed and widened the penetration. Some of the tanks initially engaged in the diversionary maneuver had made their way back to Klin and were now committed on both sides of the road. Under their protection, the wounded on trucks and sleds and accompanied by armored personnel carriers were moved out of the town. By now the artillery was covering the flanks of the break-through column. In the eastern part of the city combat engineers held off the enemy while the evacuation took its course. With the rate of progress determined by the movement of numerous vehicles, and by the need for gradual displacement of the artillery north and south of the road, the entire force fought its way through to Nekrasino, where it was received by other German units.

Undoubtedly the division owed much of its success to the proper employment of its combat elements, but it was primarily the maintenance of strict traffic control that permitted the evacuation of an unusually large number of vehicles and thus determined the outcome of the entire operation. All vehicles that broke down were immediately pushed off the road to keep the column moving without interruption. A large number of officers and noncommissioned officers with minor combat injuries had been added to the military police to assist in the strict enforcement of traffic discipline. The division staff, at first located at the western edge of Klin and later with the main body of the division, directed the initial break-through and the subsequent movements of individual elements with the use of radio and messengers, but without telephone communications.

Substantially intact, the division emerged from the pocket of Klin, taking along its casualties and nearly all of its equipment. Twenty-four hours later, on a different sector of the front, it was again in action against the enemy.

CHAPTER 32

Encirclement at Velikiye Luki – Failure of a Rescue Operation

By mid-November 1942 the northernmost corps sector of Army Group Center extended seventy miles, from the town of Velizh north to the army group boundary. Inadequately covered by LIX Corps, the line contained two large gaps, each about ten miles wide and partly swampy but not entirely impassable. There, only reconnaissance and combat patrols provided a minimum of security. Despite persistent requests by the army group commander, no reinforcements arrived to strengthen the precarious German defenses on that sector.

Late in November the Russians attacked north and south of Velikiye Luki (map 23) and succeeded in encircling the city which was held by a strong regimental combat team of the 83d Division. A few miles farther south two additional German combat teams suffered the same fate. Thus three separate German pockets completely cut off from the main force were created in the same general area.

By that time all available reserves of Army Group Center had been thrown into the fierce battle at Rzhev and could not be extricated for the relief of the encircled units in the Velikiye Luki area. The army group commander therefore requested authority from Army High Command to order breakouts of the encircled forces toward the west. If carried out at once, these could have been accomplished without great difficulty or excessive casualties, but it would have meant pulling the German line back about ten to fifteen miles. The new defense positions, as proposed by army group, would still assure the undisturbed operation of the Nevel–Novosokolniki–Nasva railroad, and the resulting Russian salient was then to be reduced, as soon as possible, by a German flank attack from the south.

Hitler, who in December 1941 had assumed direct control of all military operations in Russia, flatly rejected this proposal. Instead, he ordered that the pockets be held at all costs, that other German forces, by attacking from the west, re-establish contact with the encircled units, and that the front be pushed even farther to the east. He referred to a recent German success in a similar situation at Kholm by the same officer who now commanded the

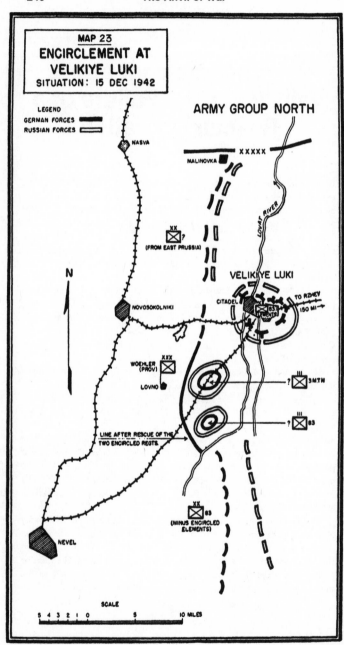

MAP 23

ENCIRCLEMENT AT VELIKIYE LUKI
SITUATION: 15 DEC 1942

LEGEND
GERMAN FORCES
RUSSIAN FORCES

NASVA

ARMY GROUP NORTH

MALINOVKA   XXXXX

LOVAT RIVER

XX
? (FROM EAST PRUSSIA)

VELIKIYE LUKI

CITADEL

TO RZHEV
150 MI

N

NOVOSOKOLNIKI

WOEMLER (PROV) XXX

LOVNO

? III 3 MT.N

? III 83

LINE AFTER RESCUE OF THE
TWO ENCIRCLED REGTS.

XX 83
(MINUS ENCIRCLED ELEMENTS)

NEVEL

SCALE
5 4 3 2 1 0   5   10 MILES

83d Division in the area of Velikiye Luki. Army group tried in vain to call Hitler's attention to the lack of reserves and the extreme hardships imposed by winter weather and difficult terrain. All such representations were impatiently brushed aside.

The two German combat teams surrounded in the area south of Velikiye Luki meanwhile conducted a fighting withdrawal toward the west. With the assistance of other German forces, they broke out of encirclement and succeeded in establishing a new front.

At Velikiye Luki the Germans had previously constructed a perimeter of hasty field fortifications around the town. Advance positions, located several hundred yards from the edge of the city, proved of considerable value during the initial stages of the siege. The encircled garrison consisted of a strong infantry regiment of the 83d Division, two artillery battalions, one observation battalion, one engineer company, two construction battalions, and strong service and supply units. The pocket commander, a lieutenant colonel, had assumed command of his regiment only a few days earlier, and accordingly did not know his troops.

The enemy had so disposed his forces that at the beginning of December only two Russian brigades were deployed in a wide arc west of Velikiye Luki. As late as two weeks after the pocket was closed, a breakout in that direction would still have been possible, but despite the personal intervention of the army group commander, Hitler did not change his mind. The pocket was to be held, and should only be relieved by a push from the west.

With no reinforcements in sight, the troops required for this relief thrust could only be taken from other sectors of Army Group Center, all of which had been severely drained in an attempt at strengthening Ninth Army at Rzhev. The direction for the attack was to be from southwest to northeast with the so-called citadel – a part of Velikiye Luki west of the Lovat River – designated as the primary objective (map 24).

It was obvious that LIX Corps, already responsible for an excessively wide sector of the front, could not be expected to take on the additional task of conducting this attack. The situation not only called for the use of fresh combat units but also for the establishment of a new tactical headquarters to direct the proposed relief operation. Unable to pull out a corps headquarters from any other sector, army group had to resort to an improvisation. A provisional corps headquarters, Corps Woehler, was formed under the command of the army group chief of staff assisted by the army group training officer, the chief artillery officer, and another young staff officer. Subordinate to LIX Corps which remained responsible for supply and administration, the newly formed command group was ready to take charge of the front sector opposite Velikiye Luki by mid-December. Its command post, established on 15 December at Lovno, was no less improvised than the staff by which it was occupied. A one-room peasant hut had to serve as living and working headquarters for six officers, three clerks, three drivers, and two orderlies.

The terrain designated for the attack was desolate, rolling country, virtually without forests. Here Stalin's scorched earth policy had been fully effective in the Russian retreat of 1941. Subsequent partisan operations completed the work of destruction. Most of the formerly inhabited places had vanished and even their last traces were now blanketed by heavy layers of snow. No roads or recognizable terrain features broke the monotony. Orientation was extremely difficult and at night a matter of pure chance. The entire area gave the impression of a landscape on the moon.

The German units initially available for the attack were a division from East Prussia, the 83d Division minus elements inside Velikiye Luki, the mountain regiment that had escaped encirclement south of the city, and two construction battalions. They had been weakened by considerable losses in men and matériel and were suffering from the effects of heavy frosts alternating with sudden thaws. Although their morale appeared unbroken, their combat value was definitely limited. Fortunately, their new commander, because of his experience as army group chief of staff, had no difficulty in finding out at what depots in the army group area ammunition and equipment could still be obtained. With railroads and transport planes doing their part, it took only a few days for the troops to be resupplied and re-equipped with new winter clothing. This brought about a rapid decline in the number of cold weather casualties.

Reinforced by a motorized division, a battalion of light infantry, two batteries of 105-mm. guns, and a rocket projector brigade, the improvised corps continued its preparations for the attack. They had to be cut short, however, since Hitler advanced the attack date by several days despite all objections by army group. The attack was launched shortly before Christmas but, after making good progress at first, bogged down at the half-way mark.

By now it had become clear that additional forces of considerable strength would have to be brought up in order to achieve success. The reinforcements finally made available consisted of two divisions and one tank battalion. At least one of these divisions, however, proved wholly inadequate for the type of operation in which it was to participate. Originally used as an occupation unit in western Europe, it had recently been transferred east and employed as a security force on a quiet sector of the Russian front. Two of its regimental commanders were considerably over-age and incapable of leading their units in combat. The third regimental commander, who was still in good physical condition, actually had to command each of the three regiments in turn as they were successfully committed in the attack.

Army group had requested the approval of the Air Force for the employment of a parachute division which was then in a quiet position southeast of Velizh. [In the German system of organization, parachute units were part of the

Luftwaffe.] Goering refused, insisting that the division remain intact in its present position. Undoubtedly this refusal was one of the chief reasons why the liberation of Velikiye Luki failed.

The second German relief thrust was launched early in January 1943. Leading elements advanced to less than five miles from the northwestern outskirts of the beleaguered city (map 24). At that stage, however, enemy pressure against the long flanks of the penetration forced the Germans to assume the defensive.

Inside the pocket, the citadel on the left bank of the Lovat River had meanwhile become the refuge for some 500 wounded from all parts of the city. On 5 January the Russians attacked from the north and succeeded in cutting through the town and severing the citadel from the main part of Velikiye Luki. Thus two separate pockets came into existence, each one precariously defended after the loss of all positions beyond the edge of the town, and particularly threatened by enemy attempts at infiltrating from block to block.

Liberating the main German force encircled in the eastern part of Velikiye Luki had become even more difficult. In any event, the immediate objective was to cut through the ring of encirclement that surrounded the smaller pocket west of the river. A general advance of the corps front, however, as demanded by Hitler, was by now definitely out of the question.

After lengthy negotiations the Air Force finally released one battalion of its parachute division for commitment at Velikiye Luki. It was too little and too late, but a last attempt had to be made to open a rescue corridor to the citadel. In order to bolster the fighting strength of the encircled garrison, a reinforced company of light infantry riding on trucks and tank destroyers was to ram its way through the enemy into the surrounded citadel. On 10 January, in a daring daylight attack, this force took the Russians by surprise and succeeded in joining the German defenders inside the pocket.

During the night of 14–15 January, the parachute battalion was to advance in a surprise attack to the southwest side of the citadel. There, by 0100, the fresh troops recently arrived in the pocket were to attempt a breakout, taking with them all wounded who were still able to march. Although initially led by a regimental commander familiar with the area, the parachute battalion lost its way in the featureless terrain and failed to reach its objective. The citadel force broke out nevertheless, and in the early morning hours, reduced by casualties to about 150 men, appeared at the corps' advance command post on the Novosokolniki–Velikiye Luki railroad line.

By now, irreplaceable losses in the ranks of the German relief force made it impossible to repeat the rescue attempt. Also, no more radio signals were coming from the eastern part of Velikiye Luki – a clear indication that in six weeks of relentless fighting, despite the most determined resistance, the German force in the eastern pocket had been wiped out to the last man. The pocket

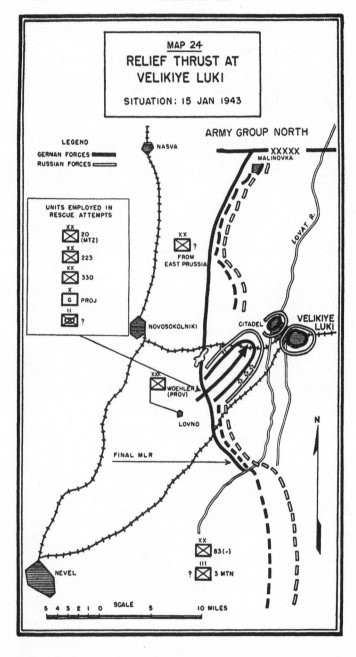

MAP 24

RELIEF THRUST AT
VELIKIYE LUKI

SITUATION: 15 JAN 1943

commander's final radio message, received on 14 January, was 'With last strength and ammunition still holding two bunkers in center of city. Enemy outside my command post.'

The struggle for Velikiye Luki was over. While it had the effect of tying down a greatly superior and constantly growing enemy force for six weeks, it also resulted in the annihilation of the German garrison, exorbitant casualties among the relief forces, and a loss of terrain along the entire corps sector (map 24). The important Nevel–Novosokolniki–Nasva railroad line still remained in German hands, free from enemy interference. However, the plan proposed by army group would have assured the same result without necessitating the futile struggle for Velikiye Luki. At the end of this ill-fated operation German casualties amounted to 17,000 officers and men, 5,000 of whom perished in the beleaguered city, while 12,000 were lost in rescue attempts from outside. Even if the relief thrust had eventually succeeded, the cost was far too high.

The experiences gained at Velikiye Luki might be summarized as follows:

1. Wherever a pocket comes into existence, it is usually the result of the attacker's numerical superiority over the encircled force. The deliberate adoption of a pocket-type defense can only be justified when early relief is assured; otherwise it will lead to the loss of the entire pocket force, and thus to a further decrease in the over-all fighting strength of the forces in the field.

2. The enemy's effective military strength, his combat troops, is his principal means of waging war. It must be destroyed. To fight constantly for terrain features, industrial installations, or simply for propagandistic purposes is to violate the basic principles of warfare.

3. It was Hitler who originally pronounced: 'I must hold all pockets to the last in order to tie up superior enemy forces as long as possible.' This may be correct in exceptional cases, but can never be elevated to the level of a general principle.

4. If an encircled force must be liberated by a relief thrust from the outside, only the best troops should be used in that operation. The more rapidly such a mission is completed, the fewer will be the casualties, and the greater the success. The maintenance for any length of time of a long, narrow salient obviously pointing at the pocket will involve murderous casualties. In the end such tactics are almost certain to fail because of the pressure exerted by the enemy on both flanks of the salient.

5. Speed is an absolute requirement, but should not be gained at the cost of hasty and inadequate preparations. The selection and assembly of the relief forces involves careful deliberation and considerable effort. In the situation described, the supreme commander, on whose specific order the date for the attack had been moved up, was far away from the fighting front, and the effect of this intervention proved disastrous. There was nothing to justify such lack of

confidence in the judgment of the local commander or in the recommendations of army group.

6. Constant communication with the encircled forces was maintained via radio which functioned smoothly and met all requirements. On several occasions the artillery fire of the relief force was actually directed by observers inside the pocket. Shuttle flights by liaison aircraft were possible only in the beginning, and then only at night.

7. Having the light infantry unit break out of the citadel at night proved to be a wise decision. Direction toward the forward elements of the rescue force was maintained with the aid of prismatic compasses. Advancing in several single files, the men succeeded in inching their way forward through the hollows and silently overpowering the Russian sentries.

8. Supply of the German pocket was at first effected from reserve stocks available at Velikiye Luki. Soon, however, airdrops became necessary, marking the first occurrence of a situation that was later so characteristic of all German pockets in Russia – the plight of encircled forces, inadequately supplied with ammunition, rations, and equipment, who were expected to do their utmost in a hopeless situation. If Hitler himself had ever been an eyewitness to such developments, Goering's arrogant promises of adequate air supply for German pockets might have been discounted once and for all. The Luftwaffe units concerned were not in any way to blame. The missions assigned to them proved impossible of fulfilment, but they did their duty again and again in a superior manner, at Velikiye Luki, as well as at Stalingrad, and in all subsequent cases where German ground troops found themselves in hopeless encirclement.

CHAPTER 33

The Pocket West of Cherkassy – The Inside View

Events Leading to the Formation of the Pocket

By the end of December 1943 – with Kiev (map 21) retaken by the enemy and a Russian bulge extending as far west as Zhitomir – the German forces in the Dnepr bend were ordered to hold their positions at all costs. XLII Corps (map 25), on the right flank of First Panzer Army, had been under persistent enemy attack since 26 December when some of the Russian forces recently engaged in the battle for Kiev were shifted south and renewed their pressure against the corps sector. To the right, Eighth Army's XI Corps, the 5th SS Panzer Division *Wiking* as its left flank, was likewise engaged in heavy defensive fighting along its entire front. Both corps had the specific mission of continuing to hold their front lines against superior Russian forces in order to assure a favorable base for a projected German counteroffensive. To the left of XLII Corps, VII Corps had been operating against the flank of the Russian bulge. Since about 20 December the corps had been attacking in a westerly direction, but without achieving any significant results.

The situation of XLII and XI Corps, their most advanced elements fighting along the Dnepr and their long exterior flanks inadequately secured, was certain to invite attempts by the enemy to encircle and annihilate both corps. As early as mid-December the commander of XLII Corps had requested authority to fall back behind the Ross River. This would have meant that, instead of having to defend a frontage of seventy-five miles with two divisions, the corps would have been able to occupy a shortened defensive position behind a natural obstacle. However, that request was turned down.

Nevertheless, XLII Corps had taken a few precautionary measures during December. Two rear positions had been prepared north of the Ross River, east of Boguslav, which were to prove very useful later on in the withdrawal of the corps toward the south. Also, all food stocks of the former German civil administration in the corps area had been evacuated south of the Ross River, a move that turned out to be of decisive importance as these provisions soon became the sole source of supply for the German pocket forces.

Day after day, from the end of December 1943 until 24 January 1944, Russian infantry, often supported by tanks, attacked the positions of XLII Corps. From mid-January on the enemy's main effort was clearly directed

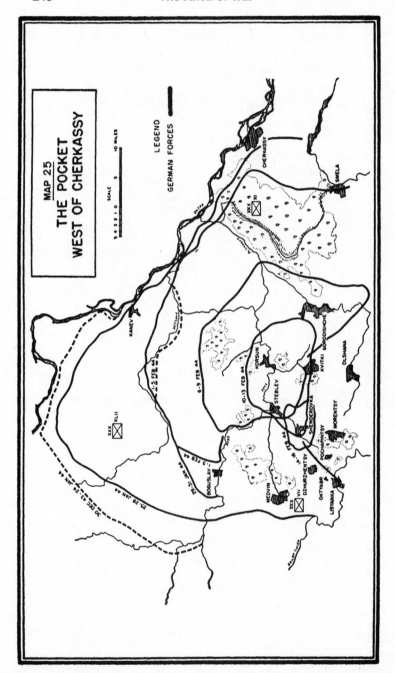

against the left flank of the corps. On 25 January Soviet forces launched a large-scale attack against the adjacent VII Corps whose right flank division fell back toward the south-east and south, so that by the end of the same day the roads leading to the flank and rear of XLII Corps were open to the enemy. Over these roads the pursuing Russians pressed forward via Medvin toward Boguslav and Steblev.

Simultaneously, XI Corps had suffered enemy penetrations on the right boundary and at the center of its sector. To escape the danger of envelopment and keep its front intact, the corps withdrew its right wing and center toward the west and northwest where it was eventually to form the eastern front of the German pocket.

Before 24 January most enemy attacks against XLII Corps were blocked or repelled. These engagements, both in terms of battle casualties and lowered physical resistance of individuals, drained the fighting strength of the German forces. Their commanders were under constant pressure, trying to seal off the daily penetrations by virtually uncovering other sectors which were not under heavy attack and by using all available trucks, horses, and horse-drawn carts to shift their units to the threatened points. Initially, each of the two divisions on line with a troop strength of six battalions had to defend a frontage of 35 to 40 miles, with weak artillery support and without tanks. Except for the Ross River sector, the area in which they were committed was almost completely flat and offered few terrain features favoring the defense.

From mid-December 1943 until its breakout from the pocket on 16 February 1944, XLII Corps was actually never in a position to offer effective resistance to a far superior enemy who attacked with numerous tanks; if it could not dodge enemy attacks by timely withdrawal, it was constantly threatened by Russian penetrations of its lines. Authority for any withdrawal, however, could only be granted by Adolf Hitler in person, and no such decision could be obtained in less than twenty-four hours. One can easily visualize the difficulties, mounting from day to day, which the corps had to face under these circumstances.

The Russian attacks on 25 January and the following days had produced a deep penetration separating XLII and VII Corps. With its left flank and rear threatened by the enemy, XLII Corps was forced to establish a new front along the general line Boguslav–Steblev. For a short time it appeared that VII Corps would be able to close the gap and restore the situation, but after a few days, as the Russians succeeded in widening their penetration, it became evident that VII Corps was rapidly withdrawing toward the southwest. At this stage the German forces east of the Russian salient were ordered for the first time to make preparations for fighting their way out of the encirclement that was now taking shape. A breakout toward the west was clearly out of the question, thus southeast or due south were the only possible directions. During the first few days of February, however, another Russian penetration turned the right flank of XI Corps and made its position untenable. With its center withdrawing west and its right wing northwest the entire corps was rapidly moving away from its neighboring units adjacent to the southeast. In that area, too, a continuous German front had ceased to exist, and a breakout in that direction was no longer possible.

Moreover, since 28 January the sole supply roads leading to XLII and XI Corps (via Shpola and Zvenigorodka) had been cut. Supply by air was requested and furnished. By 6 February, XLII and XI Corps were completely encircled.

In shifting its main effort toward the south, XLII Corps had been forced to weaken its northern and western fronts which were now slowly giving ground. This development, together with the withdrawal movements of XI Corps on the right, led to a gradual shrinking of the pocket, which in turn resulted in greater concentration – an important prerequisite for the eventual breakout from encirclement.

At the same time, it had become evident that the surrounded German units could escape annihilation only if they succeeded in breaking through the enemy lines on the southern front of the pocket. In weeks of defensive fighting, however, they had suffered excessive casualties, and the forces that would have to be used for such an operation were obviously incapable of getting through the Russian encirclement on their own; it was clear that the breakout attempt would have to be supported by a relief thrust from the outside. Accordingly, the encircled units were informed that III Panzer Corps, located about twenty-five miles southwest of the pocket, would launch an attack toward Morentsy in order to establish a forward rescue position. Simultaneously, another panzer corps at about the same distance due south of the pocket was to thrust north in the direction of Olshana.

On 6 February, in a radio message from Eighth Army, D Day for the breakout and rescue operation was set for 10 February. Because of the sudden start of the muddy season, however, the date had to be postponed for nearly a week. In order to establish unity of command inside the pocket, the two encircled corps were placed under the control of General Stemmermann, the commander of XI Corps, and designated Force Stemmermann.

Meanwhile, repeated Russian attacks – from the southeast against Korsun and Shenderovka, and from the west against Steblev – had threatened to split up the German pocket. Although all of these enemy thrusts were repelled, they further reduced the forces available for the breakout and had a detrimental effect on the morale of the encircled troops.

On 14 February elements of XLII Corps succeeded in taking Khilki and Komarovka (map 26), two to three miles west of Shenderovka, and thus reached a favorable jump-off line for the final break-through. It was high time indeed: the gradual restricting of the pocket had resulted in a dangerous massing of troops. The entire German-held area was now within range of the Soviet artillery; volume and intensity of enemy fire seemed to be merely a question of how much ammunition the Russians were willing to expend. It was feared that at any moment German casualties might amount to an unbearable level. The Russians themselves, however, were hampered by snowstorms and poor road conditions and could not use their artillery to full advantage. Thus the German troops inside the pocket were able to rally for their last effort.

The breakout began, as ordered, on 16 February at 2300. Jumping off from the line Khilki–Komarovka, three divisional columns struck in a southwesterly direction; their mission was to reach the forward rescue position established by the leading elements of III Panzer Corps at Lisyanka and Oktyabr, and to join forces with First Panzer Army.

The Units Inside the German Pocket

The composition of the two German corps encircled in the pocket west of Cherkassy was as follows:

XI Corps consisted of three infantry divisions, the 57th, 72d, and 389th Divisions, each without tanks, assault guns, or adequate antitank weapons. Of these only the 72d Division was capable of aggressive combat. The two other divisions, with the exception of one good regiment of the 57th, were unfit for use in the attack. The 5th SS Panzer Division *Wiking* was part of XI Corps until the end of January. Corps troops comprised one assault gun brigade of two battalions totaling six batteries, and one battalion of light GHQ artillery.

XLII Corps included Task Force B, the 88th Infantry Division, and, from the end of January, the SS Panzer Division *Wiking*. Task Force B was a cover name given to the 112th Infantry Division to hide its identity. Although the unit carried a corps standard, it was an ordinary infantry division consisting of three regiments, the normal complement of artillery, a strong antitank battalion, but no tanks or assault guns. Now at about four-fifths of its authorized strength, Task Force B had the combat value of one good infantry division. The 88th Division had been badly mauled during the preceding engagements. It consisted of two regiments totaling five battalions and its artillery was seriously depleted.

In terms of personnel, weapons, and equipment the 5th SS Panzer Division *Wiking* was by far the strongest division of XLII Corps. It was fully equipped as an armored division and consisted of two armored infantry regiments, one tank regiment with a total of 90 tanks, the Belgian volunteer brigade *Wallonien* organized in three battalions, and one replacement regiment of about 2,000 men. Accurate strength reports from that division could not be obtained; its effective strength before the breakout was estimated at about 12,000 men.

Diary of the Commander of XLII Corps

The tactical situation between 28 January and 16 February, as described above, was modified by a number of developments inside the pocket. A record of these events is found in excerpts from the diary kept by the commander of XLII Corps up to the time of the breakout:

28 January

Communications to the rear along the road Shpola–Zvenigorodka have been cut. We are encircled. First Panzer Army to restore communication routes. Our defensive mission remains unchanged. Telephone request to Eighth Army: 'Mission requires maintaining northeast front against strong enemy pressure. Russian advance against Steblev necessitates main effort on southern sector. Request authority for immediate withdrawal of northern and eastern fronts. This will permit offensive action toward southwest and prevent further encirclement and separation from XI Corps.'

29 January

Radio message from Eighth Army: 'Prepare withdrawal in direction Rossava up to Mironovka–Boguslav. Be ready to move by 1200 on 29 January upon prearranged signal. Authority for further withdrawal likely within twenty-four hours. Report new situation.'

Requested additional ammunition for artillery and small arms. Food supplies in the pocket are adequate. XI Corps under attack by strong Russian tank forces. Several of its regiments reduced to 100 men. Air supply beginning to arrive. Evacuation of casualties too slow. More than 2,000 wounded have to be removed.

31 January

Message from Eighth Army: XLVIII Panzer Corps will attack on 1 February toward Lozovatka [three miles northwest of Shpola] to relieve enemy pressure against XI Corps.

1 February

Daily losses 300 men. Fighter protection inadequate. Ammunition and fuel running low.

2 February

Air supply improving. Radio message from Eighth Army: 'Withdrawal of north front approved. Prepare for main effort on eastern flank of south front. Vormann [general commanding XLVIII Panzer Corps] is continuing the relief attack from the south. Breith [general commanding III Panzer Corps] will attack 3 February from southwest.'

3 February

Air supply continues to improve. Unfortunately several transport aircraft with wounded abroad were shot down on the return flight. Have requested that air evacuations be made at night only unless adequate fighter protection can be provided. Message from Army: 'To strengthen southern sector, occupy proposed line without further delaying action at intermediate positions.'

4 February

Made a determined effort to take Boguslav. Commander of Task Force B seriously wounded. Now all the division commanders are artillerymen, including the present SS big shot. The north front is tottering. Russian tanks today captured a medium battery of Task Force B that was firing from every barrel without being able to score a single hit. Evidently we have too few experienced gunners. By nightfall our line is restored. Daily ammunition expenditure of the corps 200 tons. Casualties still 300 per day. This cannot go on much longer. Have requested 2,000 replacements, also 120 tons additional ammunition per day.

5 February

Radio message from Eighth Army: 'Prepare breakout for 10 February. Further instructions follow.'

7 February

Radio message to Eighth Army: 'Roads deeply mired. Will require more time for breakout preparations.' Message from Eighth Army: 'At time of breakout the following units will attack from the outside: XLVIII Panzer Corps toward Olshana, III Panzer Corps toward Morentsy. Pocket force will effect initial break-through and, covering its flanks and rear, concentrate its entire strength in attack across the line Shenderovka–Kvitki toward Morentsy, to link up with armored wedge of relief forces. Regrouping must be completed in time to permit breakout on 10 February. Final decision will depend on progress of armored spearheads. Situation does not permit further delay.'

Stemmermann [general commanding XI Corps] assumes command of both corps in the pocket. Report to Army that because of road conditions attack impossible before 12 February.

Had a look at the 110th Grenadier Regiment and Task Force B. Morale of troops very good. Rations plentiful. Enough sugar, sausage, cigarettes, and bread to last for another ten days. Army Group Commander radios that everything is being done to help us.

8 February

Radio message to Eighth Army: 'Artillery, heavy weapons, and horse-drawn vehicles of 72d, 389th, and *Wiking* Divisions, as well as hundreds of motor vehicles of *Wiking* carrying many wounded, are stuck in the mud at Gorodishche. Withdrawal from line held today, to effect regrouping, would involve intolerable losses of men, weapons, and equipment. Line must be held at least twenty-four hours longer.'

Today I saw many casualties, including four officers; ordered more careful evacuation of wounded, and destruction of all classified documents we can possibly get rid of.

9 February

Generals Zhukov, Konev, and Vatutin have sent an emissary, a Russian lieutenant colonel, who arrived with driver, interpreter, and bugler at the position of Task Force B to present surrender terms for Stemmermann and myself. He is treated to champagne and cigarettes, receives no reply. Ultimatum remains unanswered.

Forces for breakout dwindle from day to day. Inquiry from Army High Command about Leon Degrelle, commander of Brigade *Wallonien*. He is a young man, Belgian; I saw him a few days ago among his men. They are likeable fellows, but apparently too soft for this business.

Approach of relief forces delayed by necessary regrouping. Nevertheless Army now insists we break out on 12 February. Much as we would like to, we cannot do it by then. In this mud the infantry cannot possibly cover more than a thousand yards per hour.

10 February

My old division commander of 1940, General von Seydlitz, today sent me a long letter delivered by aircraft: he thinks I should act like Yorck during the campaign of 1812 and go over to the Russians with my entire command. I did not answer. [Seydlitz was captured at Stalingrad by the Russians. Thereafter leader of the National Committee 'Free Germany' composed of German officers in Russian hands.]

Army inquires whether breakout in direction Morentsy still feasible, or whether the operation should rather be directed via Dzhurzhentsy–Pochapintsy toward Lisyanka. Reply to Army: 'Lisyanka preferable if Breith [III Panzer Corps] can reach it. Situation on east front critical. Several enemy penetrations. For the past forty-eight hours XI Corps unable to establish new defense line. Troops badly depleted and battle-weary. XLII Corps front intact. We are attacking south of Steblev. Serious danger if east front cannot be brought to a halt. XLII Corps will break through in direction Lisyanka. The troops are well in hand. Early advance of Breith toward Lisyanka decisive.'

Reply from Army: 'Thanks for comprehensive information. In full accord concerning new direction of breakout. Breith will attack 11 February in direction of Lisyanka. Will do all we can. Good luck.'

Seydlitz today sent me fifty German prisoners with letters to their commanders; in addition they are supposed to persuade their comrades to go over to the enemy. I cannot understand Seydlitz. Although the events at Stalingrad must have changed him completely, I am unable to see how he can now work as a sort of G-2 for Zhukov.

12 February

Breith has reached Lisyanka. Vormann is advancing in direction of Zvenigorodka. Our infantry has taken the northern part of Khilki [map 26]. The regimental commander leading the attack was killed in action. So goes one after another. XI Corps has taken Komarovka. The Russians, according to intercepted signals, are about to attack our left flank. Radio message to Army: 'Absolutely necessary that Breith advance to Petrovskoye as quickly as possible, in order to effect link-up. Speed is essential. Forward elements of XLII Corps now at Khilki.' Reply from Army: 'Vormann southeast of Zvenigorodka. Breith will attack 13 February with strong armored wedge in direction Dzhurzhentsy.'

Was at Khilki this afternoon. Things look bad. Our men are exhausted. Nothing gets done unless officers are constantly behind them. Am now keeping my horses inside the hut; they are in better shape than I. My orderly is burning my papers and giving away my extra uniforms.

13 February

Another message from General von Seydlitz, this time addressed to the commander of the 198th Division. Not bad: they think we are stronger than we really are. The letter was attached as usual to a black, red, and white pennant [German colors] and dropped from a plane. These people never fail to find my headquarters.

Breakout further delayed because of heavy enemy attacks against XI Corps' east front. Radio message to Army: 'Concentration for breakout prevented by heavy Russian flank attacks and final mopping up at Shenderovka. Will shorten east front, involving evacuation of Korsun, during night of 13–14 February. Forces thereby released will not be available for breakout before 15 February. Intend to continue attack throughout 14 February. Break-through of Breith's armored force toward Petrovskoye indispensable to success.'

Reply from Army: 'Breith under orders to thrust toward Petrovskoye. His forward elements now on line Lisyanka–Khichintsy.' Have requested strong fighter protection for 14 February. Russian strafing attacks are getting increasingly serious in view of the growing congestion in the pocket. I am most afraid that Army cannot comply with this oft-repeated request.

14 February

Breith will have to arrive soon. Last night the Luftwaffe dropped ammunition over the Russian lines instead of ours. Now they are trying to put the blame on us, claiming the drop point was inadequately lighted.

Stemmermann has just issued orders for the breakout. The date: 16 February. Radio message to Army: 'North front will be withdrawn during the night of

14–15 February to the south bank of Ross River. Main attack ordered for 16 February. Further advance of tank force for direct support absolutely necessary.'

We are destroying all excess motor vehicles and equipment. I have prohibited burning.

15 February

Our pocket is now so small that I can practically look over the entire front from my command post, when it is not snowing. Enemy aircraft are hard at work; lucky for us it is snowing most of the time. I was once more at Khilki to reconnoiter the terrain selected for the breakout. Then issued final order. Since this morning there is trouble at the SS Division. The Walloons and the *Germania* Regiment are getting fidgety. They must hold only until tomorrow night.

Final instructions from Stemmermann: We are to jump off on 16 February at 2300, with Task Force B, 72d Division, and SS Panzer Division *Wiking* from Khilki–Komarovka across the line Dzhurzhentsy–Hill 239 to Lisyanka; 57th and 88th Divisions will cover the flanks and the rear.

With me, at my command post, are the three division commanders with whom I am supposed to perform the miracle tomorrow. One of them is doing this for the first time, the two others are old hands.

I left no doubt in their minds that, in my opinion, this is going to be one giant snafu, and that they should not get rattled, no matter what happens. You need a guardian angel to bring you through this kind of thing.

Have given my second mount to my G–3. His *Panje* will be used by the G–2.

16 February

Ample supply of ammunition dropped in aerial delivery containers as late as last night. In this respect we are now well off – if we can take it along.

After consulting Stemmermann I decided to hand over to the Russians some 2,000 wounded together with medical personnel and one doctor from each division. This is a bitter decision, but to take them along would mean their certain death.

Saw Stemmermann once more to say good-by. My orderly takes my diary; he is a crafty fellow and will get it through somehow.

Breakout Order of XLII Corps

On the evening of 15 February, at his command post at Shenderovka, the commander of XLII Corps had issued verbal and written instructions to his division commanders. The breakout order for XLII Corps read, in part, as follows:

For days the enemy has been attacking continuously along our entire defense perimeter, with tanks and infantry, in an attempt to split up the pocket and destroy our forces.

At 2300, on 16 February, Task Force B, 72d Division, and 5th SS Panzer Division *Wiking* will attack in a southwesterly direction from the line Khilki–Komarovka, break the enemy's resistance by a bayonet assault, and throw him back in continuous attack toward the southwest, in order to reach Lisyanka and there to join forces with elements of III Panzer Corps. Compass number 22 indicates the general direction of the attack. [The magnetic compass carried by the German soldier had 32 consecutively numbered gradations. Number 22 equals an azimuth of about 236°.] This direction is to be made known to each individual soldier. The password is: 'Freedom' [*Freiheit*].

For the attack and breakout each division will be organized in five successive waves, as follows: First wave: one infantry regiment reinforced by one battery of light artillery (at least eight horses per gun, plus spare teams) and one engineer company. Second wave: antitank and assault gun units. Third wave: remainder of infantry (minus one battalion), engineers, and light artillery. Fourth wave: all our wounded that are fit to be transported, accompanied by one infantry battalion. Fifth wave: supply and service units.

The rear guard, under the direct command of General Stemmermann, will be formed by the 57th and 88th Divisions, which will protect the rear and the flanks of the forces launching the breakout attack. By 2300 on 16 February, the rear guard divisions will withdraw from their present locations to a previously determined defense line; further withdrawals will be ordered by General Stemmermann, depending on the progress of the breakout.

The entire medium artillery and certain specifically designated units of light artillery will support the attack. They will open fire at 2300 on 16 February, making effective use of their maximum range. Subsequently, all artillery pieces are to be destroyed in accordance with special instructions.

The radios of each division will be carried along on pack horses. To receive signal communications from corps, each division will, if possible, keep one set open at all times, but in any event every hour on the hour. The corps radio will be open for messages from the divisions at all times.

The corps command post will be, until 2000, 16 February, at Shenderovka; after 2000, at Khilki. From the start of the attack the corps commander will be with the leading regiment of the 72d Division.

The order was explained orally to the division commanders, and all details of the operations were carefully gone over, especially the difficult relief of the SS Division near Komarovka by the 57th Division, whose G–3 was present during the briefing conference.

The Breakout

Despite persistent enemy attacks against the pocket perimeter, constant Russian shelling of Komarovka, Khilki, and Shenderovka, churned up roads and numerous traffic bottlenecks, the German forces inside the pocket were able, by

2000 on 16 February, to report their readiness for the breakout. Determination was the prevailing mood. Apparently the large majority of the troops was not influenced by Russian propaganda, nor by the hundreds of leaflets dropped from Russian planes on behalf of the Free Germany Committee (General von Seydlitz) – they wanted to fight their way through.

Shortly after 2000, the commander of XLII Corps appeared at the command post of the 105th Grenadier Regiment which was to spearhead the attack of 72d Division. He was on horseback, accompanied by members of his staff, several aides, and radio operators with their equipment. The events that followed are illustrated by a personal account of the corps commander, written from memory at a later date, and presented here in his own words:

By 2300 the regiment – two battalions abreast – started moving ahead, silently and with bayonets fixed. One-half hour later the force broke through the first and soon thereafter the second Russian defense line. The enemy was completely caught by surprise. Prisoners were taken along. Not until the following day did it become evident that the Russians, under the protection of heavy snowfall, had pulled out most of their troops from the south front of the pocket in order to use them in an attack, on 17 February, from the area west of Steblev.

The advance toward the southwest continued. No reports from either Task Force B on the right or the 5th SS Panzer Division on the left. That they were making some progress could only be inferred from the noise of vehicles due north and south of us, and from the sounds of firing that indicated the location of their leading elements. Over roadless, broken terrain traversed by numerous gullies, our march proceeded slowly. There were frequent halts. Here and there, men and horses suddenly disappeared, having stumbled into holes filled with deep snow. Vehicles had to be dug out laboriously. The slopes were steeper than could be presumed from looking at the map. Gradually the firing decreased until it broke off entirely by 0200. About two hours later the leading elements of 72d Division were approximately abreast of Dzhurzhentsy. Still no reports from *Wiking* and Task Force B. I could not give them my position by radio because by now my headquarters signal unit was missing and could not be located.

Shortly after 0400 enemy tanks ahead opened fire. They were joined by Russian artillery and mortars operating from the direction of Dzhurzhentsy, at first without noticeable effect. The firing increased slowly but steadily, and was soon coming from the south as well. We began to suffer casualties. The advance, however, continued. By about 0600 the leading units reached a large hollow southeast of Dzhurzhentsy. Enemy fire, getting constantly heavier, was now coming from three directions. Elements of *Wiking* could be heard on the left, farther back. No message, and not a trace of Task Force B. Day was dawning. The difficult ascent out of the hollow began. The climb was steep and led up an icy slope. Tanks, guns, heavy horse-drawn vehicles, and trucks of all kinds slipped, turned over, and had to be blown up. Only a few tanks and artillery

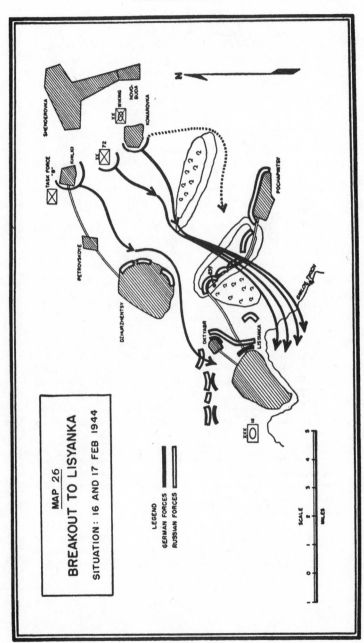

MAP 26

BREAKOUT TO LISYANKA

SITUATION: 16 AND 17 FEB 1944

LEGEND

GERMAN FORCES

RUSSIAN FORCES

pieces were able to make the grade. The units lapsed rapidly into disorder. Parts of the *Wiking* Division appeared on the left.

Between 0700 and 1000 the 72d Division made several attempts to mount a co-ordinated attack toward southwest. It did not succeed. The few guns and most of the tanks that were still firing were soon destroyed by the enemy. Armored cars and motor vehicles suffered the same fate. Except for a few tanks that had managed to keep up, there were now only soldiers on foot and on horseback, and here and there a few horse-drawn vehicles, mostly carrying wounded.

In the protection of a ravine I was able to collect a small force of about battalion size, mainly stragglers from Task Force B and the *Wiking* Division. With them I moved on toward the line Hill 239–Pochapintsy, which was visible from time to time despite the heavy snowfall, and from where the enemy was firing with great intensity. Russian ground support planes appeared, opened fire, and disappeared again. They were ineffective, and did not repeat their attack, probably because of the difficult weather conditions.

There was no longer any effective control; there were no regiments, no battalions. Now and then small units appeared alongside us. I learned that the commanding general of the 72d Division was among the missing. My corps staff still kept up with me, but the aides who had been sent on various missions did not find their way back. On the steep slope northwest of Pochapintsy, defiladed from enemy fire, I found the G-3 of the 72d Division. He reported that infantry units of his division had penetrated the enemy line along the ridge south of Hill 239. Nevertheless, enemy fire was still coming from there, maintained principally by about ten Russian tanks.

Behind and alongside me thousands of men were struggling southwest. The entire area was littered with dead horses, and with vehicles and guns that had either been knocked out by the enemy or simply abandoned by their crews. I could not distinguish the wounded; their bandages did not show, as we were all wearing white camouflage clothing. Despite the general confusion and complete lack of control one could still recognize the determination in the minds of the troops to break through toward the southwest, in the direction of III Panzer Corps.

During a lull in the firing I readied my battalion for the attack across the line Hill 239–Pochapintsy which unfortunately could not be bypassed. My staff and I were still on horseback. After leaving the draw that sheltered us against the enemy, we galloped ahead of the infantry and through the gaps between our few remaining tanks. The enemy tank commanders, observing from their turrets, quickly recognized our intention, turned their weapons in our direction, and opened fire. About one-half of our small mounted group was able to get through. The chief of staff and the G-3 were thrown, but later found their way back to us. The greater part of the infantry battalion was still following behind me. While riding through the enemy sector, I noticed a few German soldiers surrendering, but the main body was pushing southwest without letup. Soviet tanks were now firing at us from the rear and quite a few men were still being hit. From the eastern edge of the forest south of Hill 239 came intensive enemy fire. I led my battalion in an attack in that direction and threw the Russians back into the woods. Rather than pursue them into the depth of the forest, we continued advancing southwest, still harassed by fire from Russian tanks.

Gradually between 1300 and 1500, large, disorganized masses of troops piled up along the Gniloy Tikich River, east of Lisyanka. Units from all three divisions participating in the breakout were hopelessly intermingled. A few medium tanks had been able to get through to the river bank, but there were no heavy weapons and artillery pieces left. The river, below and above Lisyanka, was 30 to 50 feet wide, had a rapid current, and reached a depth of about 10 feet in most places. The banks were steep and rocky, with occasional shrubs and trees. Several tanks attempted to drive across, but the river was too deep and they failed to reach the opposite bank.

Heavy fire from Russian tanks located southeast of Oktyabr set the congested masses into forward motion. Many thousands flung themselves into the river, swam across, reached the opposite shore, and struggled on in the direction of Lisyanka. Hundreds of men and horses drowned in the icy torrent. An attempt by a small group of officers to create an emergency crossing for casualties succeeded only after several hours.

Toward 1600 the enemy fire ceased. I crossed the Gniloy Tikich swimming alongside my horse, traversed the snowy slope southeast of Lisyanka which was covered with moving men, and finally reached the town. There I found the commander of the 1st Panzer Division, the forward element of III Panzer Corps. I learned that no more than one company of armored infantry and three companies of tanks of 1st Panzer Division were now at Lisyanka, while one armored infantry battalion consisting of two weak companies was established at Oktyabr, the village immediately north of Lisyanka.

A reinforced regiment of Task Force B had made its way into Lisyanka, and I received the report that the commander of Task Force B had been killed in action. Next, the chief of staff of XI Corps appeared; he had lost contact with General Stemmermann in the morning of 17 February, while marching on foot from Khilki to Dzhurzhentsy. He reported that the rear guard of the pocket force was in the process of withdrawal and that some of its units would soon appear.

I assumed command of what was left of Force Stemmermann. By now the situation was the following: the 72d and *Wiking* Divisions were completely intermingled. No longer did they have any tanks, artillery, vehicles, or rations. Many soldiers were entirely without weapons, quite a few even without footgear. Neither division could be considered in any way able to fight. One regiment of Task Force B was intact and still had some artillery support. However, this regiment also had no vehicles and no rations left. All wounded, estimated at about 2,000, were being gradually sheltered in the houses of Lisyanka, and later were evacuated by air.

For lack of vehicles and fuel, III Panzer Corps was unable to reinforce its units in the area of Lisyanka and Oktyabr. The corps commander, with whom I conferred by telephone, informed me that he had been forced to assume the defensive against heavy Russian attacks from the northwest in the area immediately west of Lisyanka. He had no extra supplies of any kind, and his forward elements were unable to provide rations for the troops emerging from the pocket. Thus I had to order the pocket force in its miserable condition to move on westward, while I requested supply, evacuation of casualties by air, and the bringing up of vehicles and weapons from the rear.

The march toward the main rescue area continued throughout the night, despite frequent bottlenecks, and was not completed until noon on 18 February. Renewed Russian flank attacks from the north endangered the roads to the rear and necessitated further withdrawal southwest and south during the following day. In the afternoon of 20 February, having clarified the question of food supply for the pocket force and dealt with a number of other problems, I was instructed to proceed to headquarters of Army High Command in East Prussia. From that moment on I had no further connection with XLII Corps or Force Stemmermann.

Of the 35,000 men launching the breakout from the pocket about 30,000 successfully fought their way out. 5,000 were killed or captured. The force lost all of its heavy weapons, artillery, tanks, vehicles, horses, equipment, and supplies.

CHAPTER 34

The Pocket West of Cherkassy – The Outside View

The Encirclement

[This description of the encirclement west of Cherkassy was prepared by a German staff officer at army group level on the basis of his personal recollection and is presented as a supplement to the preceding narrative.]

The second Russian winter offensive of 1943–44 was launched early in January 1944 against the German Eighth Army sector in the Dnepr bend. The First and Second Ukrainian Fronts – the latter consisting of four armies, including one tank army – attempted to cut off German forces deployed from a point southeast of Kiev to the Dnepr estuary. The Soviet offensive fell short of accomplishing its purpose, but in twelve days of fighting the Russians drove a deep wedge south-westward across the Dnepr and captured the town of Kirovograd. Two large German salients remained, one to the northwest, the other to the southeast of the Kirovograd area.

Despite heavy tank losses, the Russians could be expected to reorganize their armored forces in the shortest possible time and continue their heavy attacks designed to push Army Group South farther back in the direction of the Romanian border. It was evident that the enemy would bend every effort to destroy the German bulge northwest of Kirovograd, held by elements of Eighth Army and First Panzer Army.

The commander of Eighth Army sent urgent messages to army group; he expressed grave doubts about continuing to hold the curving line of positions northwest of Kirovograd which committed an excessive number of men. Pointing out the Russian superiority in strength, he recommended withdrawal of the interior flanks of Eighth Army and First Panzer Army by retirement to successive positions, first behind the Olshanka–Ross River line, and eventually to the line Shpola–Zvenigorodka–Gorniy Tikich River. Permission for such a withdrawal, however, was denied on the grounds that the salient had to be held as a base for future operations in the direction of Kiev.

The expected attack was launched by the Second Ukrainian Front, on 24 January, against the right flank, and by the First Ukrainian Front, on 26 January, against the left flank and the rear of the German salient. By 28

January the armored spearheads of both Russian army groups met in the area of Zvenigorodka and thereby accomplished the encirclement of XI and XLII Corps. Having effected the original link-up with elements of two tank armies, the Russians rapidly committed strong infantry units from four additional armies which attacked toward the west, southwest, and south in order to widen the ring of encirclement and provide effective cover against German counterattacks from the outside.

Plans for the Breakout

In this situation the German Army High Command directed Army Group South to assemble the strongest available armored units along the boundary between Eighth Army and First Panzer Army. These forces were to execute converging counterattacks, encircle and annihilate the enemy units that had broken through, re-establish contact with the pocket force, and regain a favorable jump-off base for the projected counteroffensive.

Actually, the assembly of the German attack force presented the greatest of difficulties. Two of the panzer divisions of Eighth Army designated to take part in the operation were still in the midst of heavy fighting in the area of Kapitanovka. They had to be replaced by infantry units with frontages extended to the utmost. Two additional panzer divisions, recently engaged south-east of Kirovograd, were on the march toward the left flank of Eighth Army. Of these four armored units, only one was at full strength, while the others, after weeks of uninterrupted fighting, were actually no more than tank-supported combat teams.

The relief attack from the right flank of First Panzer Army was to be carried out by the four armored divisions of III Panzer Corps. They were still engaged in defensive operations on the left flank of the army sector, and could only be brought up after they had completed their previous missions.

The two corps inside the pocket were to attack at the appropriate time in the direction of the Eighth Army and First Panzer Army units approaching from the south and west. It was clear that any build-up on the southern front of the pocket could only be accomplished at the expense of other sectors. Still, Army High Command insisted on holding the entire pocket area, and not until the situation of the encircled forces became far more critical was permission obtained for successive withdrawals on the northern sector. Even then, the pocket had to be kept sufficiently large to afford a certain freedom of movement. Also, despite the effort on the southern sector, adequate forces had to remain available to seal off enemy penetrations elsewhere.

The plan for a two-pronged drive by III Panzer Corps of First Panzer Army from the southwest and XLVII Panzer Corps of Eighth Army from the south, to coincide with an attack launched by the pocket force, was adopted on 1 February. The units concerned were ordered to complete their assembly for the proposed operation during the following two days. Then XLVII Panzer Corps was to jump off from the area of Shpola, thrusting into the rear of the Russian forces that were threatening the southern front of XI Corps. Simultaneously, III Panzer Corps was to launch a surprise attack in the general direction of Medvin, where enemy units were operating against the southwest front of the pocket defended by XLII Corps. After destroying these Russian units, III Panzer Corps was to pivot due east to effect close co-operation with the attacking elements of XLVII Corps coming from the south.

During a commanders' conference on 3 February, the Eighth Army commander voiced serious doubts whether, in view of the limited forces available and the muddy roads, this ambitious plan was practicable. He recommended instead that the attack by III Panzer Corps be led in a more easterly direction which would assure early co-operation with the advancing elements of XLVII Panzer Corps. This recommendation was turned down.

Meanwhile, the enemy had committed strong infantry and armored units in an attack toward Novomirgorod, temporarily tying down two of the panzer divisions that were to take part in the relief operation from the south. The muddy season was rapidly taking effect and as the roads deteriorated all movements became extremely difficult.

Similar conditions prevailed in the area of III Panzer Corps. Engaged in continuous fighting on its left flank, this corps also suffered considerable delay in the assembly of its units for the projected relief thrust and could not be expected to launch its attack until 4 February.

The forces inside the pocket, in an attempt to keep the enemy from separating XI and XLII Corps, had shifted their main effort to the south front of the perimeter. Despite heavy losses in defensive engagements they could not afford to give ground in that sector, as their only remaining airfield, at Korsun, had to be kept out of range of the Russian artillery. At the high rate of casualties, however, a continued stand along the entire perimeter of positions was obviously out of the question. To conserve its strength and reduce the threat of Russian penetrations, the pocket force eventually obtained permission to execute limited withdrawals on the northern and eastern sectors while bolstering its defenses to the south.

The full impact of the muddy season soon made itself felt on all fronts and, in addition to causing losses of motor vehicles and other equipment, began to endanger German air supply operations The requirements of the encircled force called for supplies to be flown in at the rate of 150 tons daily. Despite the most determined efforts of the Luftwaffe units, this quota was never reached. Enemy antiaircraft fire from at least three flak divisions in the Russian-held strip of terrain and interception by enemy fighter planes had seriously reduced the number of available transport aircraft. To prevent further losses, strong German fighter forces had to be committed in protection of the vital air supply line instead of supporting preparations on other sectors for the impending relief operation.

With the start of the muddy season, the lack of paved runways further aggravated the situation. One airfield after another became unusable, and even the Korsun field, the only one inside the pocket, had to be partially closed. Airdropping supplies, because of a shortage of aerial delivery containers, met only a small part of the actual requirements. Eventually, because of the road conditions, the two corps approaching from the outside also became dependent in part upon airborne supply, which force a wide scattering of the air effort.

Time was obviously working against the Germans. As their difficulties continued to increase, it became clear that each day of delay further reduced their chances for success.

The Relief Operation

The assembly of an attack force on the western flank of XLVII Panzer Corps (Eighth Army) bogged down in a series of heavy local counterattacks south of Lebedin and Shpola. A small German force gained a temporary bridgehead at Izkrennoye and inflicted serious losses on the enemy. In all these engagements, however, the strength of XLVII Panzer Corps was constantly being whittled down until, by 3 February, it had only 27 tanks and 34 assault guns left. At that point it became clear that Eighth Army could do no more than to tie down enemy forces by continued holding attacks. Thus the original plan which provided for two converging relief thrusts had to be abandoned.

Nevertheless, on 4 February, First Panzer Army attacked toward the north in order to take advantage of favorable tank terrain, achieve surprise, and avoid any further loss of time. Successful during the first day, it was, however, unable to maintain this direction of attack, as terrain and road conditions grew worse by the hour.

Meanwhile, the situation inside the pocket had become more critical and made it imperative to establish contact with the encircled forces over the shortest possible route. Therefore, on 6 February, Army Group South issued new orders to First Panzer Army. After regrouping its units, III Panzer Corps was to attack due east, its right flank advancing via Lisyanka toward Morentsy. At the same time the encircled corps were ordered to prepare for an attack in the direction of III Panzer Corps, the attack to be launched as soon as the armored spearhead of the relief force had approached to within the most favorable distance from the pocket.

Planned for 8 February, the attack of III Panzer Corps, because of unfavorable weather conditions, did not get under way until three days later. It was initially successful and, by the end of the first day, led to the establishment of three bridgeheads across the Gniloy Tikich River. Concentrated enemy attacks, however, prevented any further advance. In the difficult terrain east of

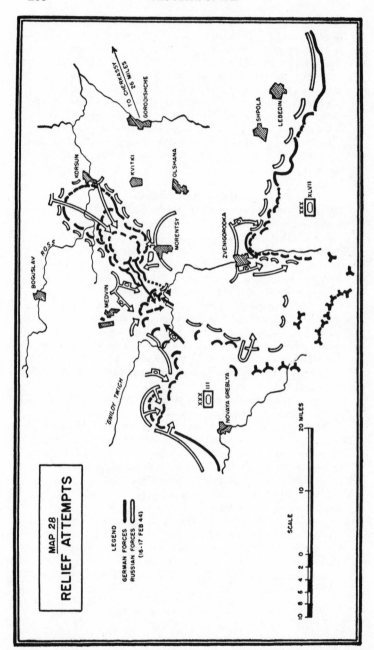

MAP 28
RELIEF ATTEMPTS

LEGEND
GERMAN FORCES
RUSSIAN FORCES
(16-17 FEB 44)

SCALE

10 8 6 4 2 0   10   20 MILES

TO CHERKASSY 26 MILES
GORODISHCHE
SHPOLA
LEBEDIN
KVITKI
OLSHANA
KORSUN
XXX XLVII
MORENTSY
ZVENIGOROOKA
BOGUSLAV
ROSS
MEDVIN
GNILOY TIKICH
XXX III
NOVAYA GREBLYA

the Gniloy Tikich, the German armored units were unable to make any progress, and this attack also came to a halt in the mud.

Army group now realized that it could no longer accomplish a reinforcement of the pocket. The encircling ring, therefore, had to be broken from the inside. The divisions of III Panzer Corps were ordered to engage and divert the Russian forces located in the area of Pochapintsy–Komarovka–Dzhurzhentsy, and to establish on the high ground northwest of Pochapintsy a forward rescue position that could be reached by the units breaking out of the pocket.

By 1105, on 15 February, the breakout order was transmitted by radio to General Stemmermann, the commander of the encircled German forces. It read, in part, 'Capabilities of III Panzer Corps reduced by weather and supply difficulties. Task Force Stemmermann must accomplish break-through on its own to Line Dzhurzhentsy–Hill 239 where it will link up with III Panzer Corps. The breakout force will be under the command of General Lieb [XLII Corps] and comprise all units still capable of attack.'

Further instructions, radioed on 16 February, emphasized the importance of surprise and proper co-ordination: 'During initial phase of operation tonight hold your fire so as to achieve complete surprise. Maintain centralized fire control over artillery and heavy weapons, so that in the event of stronger enemy resistance, especially at daybreak, they can be committed at point of main effort in short order. Air support will be available at dawn to protect your flanks.'

The Breakout

During the operation that was to follow, two separate phases could be clearly distinguished. At first everything went according to plan. In the proper sequence and under perfect control, the troops moved into position at night, despite the most difficult road and weather conditions. As they were compressed into a narrow area, unit after unit had to be channeled across the only existing bridge at Shenderovka which was under heavy enemy fire.

The bayonet assault started on schedule. The complete surprise of the enemy demonstrated that the attack had been properly timed. Without much action, and suffering but few casualties, the German breakout force penetrated the enemy lines and in a relatively short time reached the vicinity of Lisyanka. On the opposite front of the pocket the rear guards held fast and thus assured the success of the initial breakout.

The second phase, the evacuation of the remaining pocket force, rapidly deteriorated into a wild surge toward the west. Following closely behind the successful spearhead, altogether about 30,000 men broke through the Russian lines in front of the pocket. At daybreak, however, they ran into an unsuspected enemy front of antitank guns, tanks, and artillery, located on the line Dzhurzhentsy–Pochapintsy. Under massed enemy fire, enemy tank attacks, and infantry counterthrusts, the German force was split into numerous small groups, each attempting on its own to get through to the west wherever there might be a possibility. Their guns, tank destroyers, and heavy weapons, which up to now had been dragged along laboriously through snowdrifts and over broken terrain, had to be left behind and were destroyed after the last round of ammunition had been fired. Here too, as the last vehicles were blown up, the wounded taken along at the insistence of their comrades had to be left to their fate.

Meanwhile a new complication arose that was to have disastrous consequences. Subjected to heavy enemy fire, counterthrusts, and armored attacks, the great mass of German troops breaking out of the pocket had deviated from their original direction of attack. No longer did they advance according to plan toward the area northwest of Pochapintsy. Instead of approaching the forward rescue position established by III Panzer Corps, they passed by at a considerable distance farther south. Here, their advance to the west was blocked by the course of the Gniloy Tikich, the enemy holding the near bank of the river. There were no crossings, nor had III Panzer Corps established any bridgeheads, since a link-up in that area had not been foreseen.

Although greatly exhausted, the German troops were now forced to overcome the resistance of the Russian security detachments along the river and to swim across, leaving their last weapons behind. They suffered considerable losses as both banks of the river were under heavy enemy fire and not until they had placed this last obstacle behind them were they finally received by the forward elements of III Panzer Corps.

The German holding forces on the eastern sector of the pocket maintained contact with the enemy and successfully covered the breakout of the main body. This mission accomplished, they made their way westward according to plan and entered the lines of III Panzer Corps during the night of 17–18 February.

Contrary to expectations, the breakout had to be executed without air support. Unfavorable weather conditions during the entire operation made it impossible for the air force to play its part in the liberation of the encircled units.

Lessons

The developments mainly responsible for the encirclement near Cherkassy and its serious consequences might be summarized as follows:

1. Only the insistence of Army High Command to hold the Dnepr bend northwest of Kirovograd led to the isolation of two German corps in that area. Despite repeated requests, permission for a breakout was not obtained until too late. The enemy had grown too strong along the entire ring of encirclement, while the German pocket forces had been weakened to such an extent, through losses of personnel and equipment and shortages of supply, that they were forced to surrender their freedom of action and maneuver to the enemy.

2. The two German corps encircled by the enemy were the flank corps of two adjacent armies. Immediately after their encirclement, XLII Corps, heretofore part of First Panzer Army, was placed under the command of Eighth Army. While this assured unity of command inside the pocket, the same was not true of the relief operation in which forces under the command of two different armies were involved. The absence of a unified command on the army level made itself felt particularly as the need arose to co-ordinate the actions of the pocket force (Eighth Army) with those of III Panzer Corps (First Panzer Army).

3. The mission of III Panzer Corps on the day of the breakout was to divert and tie down those Russian units that blocked the path of the German troops emerging from the pocket. Because of terrain difficulties and shortage of fuel, the corps' forward elements failed to reach and occupy the commanding ground originally designated as forward rescue area. Thus the enemy was able to throw considerable weight against the German units breaking out. Also – as the breakout continued in an unexpected direction – the exercise of command in the relief force was not flexible enough to adjust to the changed situation and improvise a new forward rescue position along the Gniloy Tikich River. As a result, the pocket force remained virtually unassisted in its efforts at breaching the Russian lines and fighting its way out.

4. The Luftwaffe, as mentioned above, was prevented from taking any part in the operation; an effective means of support that had been counted on was thereby eliminated.

The two German corps succeeded, to be sure, in cracking the enemy ring and breaking out of the pocket; but they were so seriously weakened that they required a long period of rest and rehabilitation before they could again be committed on the Russian front Their absence had an immediate effect upon the defensive effort of Army Group South which was trying to counter heavy Russian attacks aimed at a break-through in the Uman area. Soon the entire southern sector was split wide open and the German Sixth and Eighth Armies were pushed across the Yuzhny Bug (Ukrainian Bug River) into Romania.

CHAPTER 35

Encirclement of a Panzer Army near Kamenets-Podolskiy

The Encirclement

In mid-February 1944 the front of the First Panzer Army extended across the western Ukraine along a general line north of Vinnitsa and Shepetovka, northeast of Ternopol. To the right, north of Uman, was the Eighth Army; to the left, the Second Army. After the two corps encircled west of Cherkassy had made their way out of the pocket (chapter 33), the front remained quiet until the beginning of March, while the Russians were reorganizing and regrouping their units. Then strong concentrations of Soviet tanks indicated that the enemy was getting ready to resume his attempts at forcing a decision.

The first large-scale Russian attacks, on 4 and 5 March, were directed primarily against the Shepetovka and Uman areas. Because of their great numerical superiority, the Russians succeeded in denting the overextended German lines in many places. While timely German counterattacks on the left flank eliminated the threat of a break-through aimed at Proskurov, the enemy was rapidly gaining ground in the Uman area and succeeded, by mid-March, in pushing across the Ukrainian Bug River. Having driven a deep wedge into the German front, the Russians were in a position to threaten the right flank of First Panzer Army. Since there were no German reserves available to close the gap, First Panzer Army was forced to withdraw its entire right wing and establish a new defense line facing east. Under the pressure of continued Russian attacks, planned withdrawals were also carried out on the central sector until the right flank of First Panzer Army was finally anchored on the northern bank of the Dnestr River east of Mogilev-Podolskiy.

On the left boundary of First Panzer Army, west of Proskurov, strong Russian armored units soon accomplished another break-through. On 22 March five armored corps followed by infantry poured south between the Zbruch and Seret Rivers, and two days later crossed the Dnestr in the direction of Chernovtsy. Since the enemy had also pushed across the river farther east, in the area of Yampol and Mogilev-Podolskiy, First Panzer Army was now contained in a large semicircle north of the Dnestr. Hitler's explicit orders prohibited any further withdrawal and eliminated the possibility of a more flexible

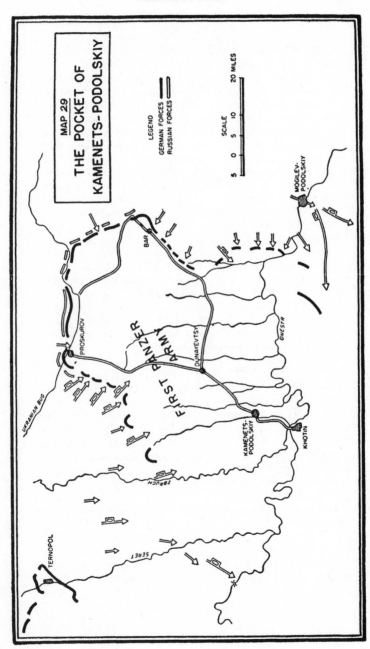

MAP 29

THE POCKET OF
KAMENETS-PODOLSKIY

LEGEND
GERMAN FORCES
RUSSIAN FORCES

SCALE

5   0   5   10   20 MILES

defense which might have established contact with other German forces to the east or the west. As could be expected, the two Russian forces, after crossing the Dnestr, linked up under the protection of the river line in the rear of First Panzer Army. By 25 March the encirclement was complete.

As in all similar situations, the first threat to make itself felt came when the last supply lines into the German salient were cut. Until 25 March First Panzer Army still had one supply route open, which led south across the Dnestr bridge at Knotin and was protected by a strong bridgehead on the southern bank of the river. Over this route all staffs and units that could be dispensed with were moved to the rear, and every nonessential user of supplies and equipment was taken out of the pocket before the ring was actually closed. As soon as it became evident that no more supplies could be brought up, stock was taken inside the pocket. While ammunition and rations were sufficient to last for about another two weeks, fuel reserves were found to be critically low. First Panzer Army therefore immediately requested supply by air and restricted the use of motor vehicles to a minimum.

All measures taken inside the pocket were made extremely difficult by unfavorable weather. At first snowstorms and snowdrifts hampered the air supply operation and obstructed movements on the ground. Then, practically overnight, the snow began to melt, and the roads quickly turned into bottomless morasses. The supply of motor fuel, which was flown in over a distance of 125 miles from the nearest German airfield, fell far short of requirements. Time and again vehicles had to be destroyed when they blocked the roads in long, immobilized columns. Finally, only combat vehicles, prime movers, and a few messenger vehicles were left intact.

Having completed the encirclement the Russians, as expected, decreased the intensity of their attacks. Only on the eastern sector enemy pressure remained strong; there was no more than moderate activity in the north; and from the west no attacks were launched against the defense perimeter of First Panzer Army. Apparently the continuous movements of German service units southward across the Dnestr had led the enemy to believe that the First Panzer Army was in full retreat toward the south. The Russians, in an effort that turned out to be a serious mistake, moved more and more units in the same direction on both sides of the pocket. Their lines of communication grew longer and longer, and they began to face difficulties of supply similar to those of the encircled German force.

In response to enemy pressure from the east and north, First Panzer Army deliberately shortened its front until it ran along a much smaller perimeter north of Kamenets-Podolskiy, assuring a greater concentration of the defending forces and a more efficient use of the limited ammunition supply. Local enemy penetrations were sealed off more easily and break-throughs could be prevented altogether. At the same time First Panzer Army deceived the enemy into believing that by day and by night large-scale evacuations across the river were taking place.

Even before it was completely cut off, First Panzer Army had requested authority to conduct a defense along mobile lines. When this request was turned down and the encirclement became a fact, a breakout remained the only possible course of action short of helplessly facing certain annihilation. Because of unfavorable weather conditions, the quantities of supplies that could be flown in were entirely insufficient to maintain the fighting power of the encircled troops. Relief of the pocket by fresh forces from the outside could not be expected. In this situation the enemy sent a terse demand for surrender, threatening that otherwise all soldiers of the encircled German army would be shot.

The reaction of First Panzer Army was to immediately make all necessary preparations to enable its total force of eight divisions to break out. Once more, in a systematic culling process, the divisions were relieved of all unfit personnel and superfluous equipment, while special arrangements were made with the Luftwaffe to assure that the transport planes bringing in supplies were used to evacuate casualties on their return flights.

The Breakout Plan

The question of the direction in which the breakout should be launched played an important part in all considerations. Was it more advisable to strike toward the west, along the Dnestr, or toward the south, across the Khotin bridgehead? An attack in the latter direction would involve the least difficulties, be opposed by the weakest enemy forces, and perhaps permit the withdrawal of the entire German force into Romania. In this case, however, there would be one less panzer army fighting the Russians, at least for some time. West of the pocket several successive river lines constituted natural obstacles in the path of an advance. There, too, the Germans had to expect the strongest concentration of enemy forces along the ring of encirclement. Breaking out in several directions at once was another possibility under consideration; this would have forced the enemy to split his strength in numerous local countermeasures and might have enabled some small German groups to make their way back to the nearest friendly lines with the least fighting.

The final decision was to break out to the west, in the direction involving the greatest difficulties, yet assuring a maximum of surprise. Simultaneously, on the outside, another German force was to attack from an area southwest of Ternopol (over 125 miles from the scene) in the direction of First Panzer Army.

Another highly important question was the formation to be adopted for the breakout. Desirable as it might have been to lead off with a strong concentration of armor, it was to be feared that these armored units, intent on making rapid progress, might outrun the infantry and thus break up the unity

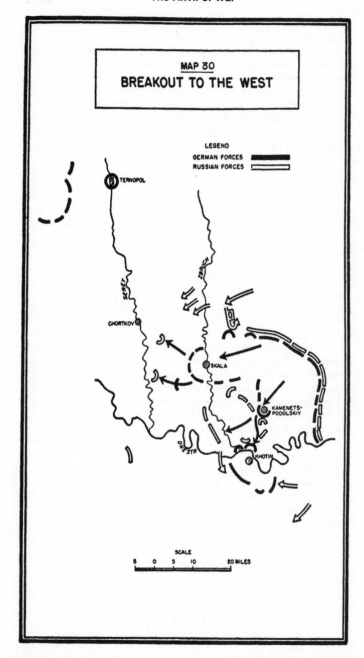

MAP 30
BREAKOUT TO THE WEST

LEGEND
GERMAN FORCES
RUSSIAN FORCES

of the command. The plan of attack, therefore, provided for a northern and a southern force, each consisting of two corps and specifically ordered to form an advance guard of tank-supported infantry and combat engineers, while the main body and the rear guard were to be composed of mobile units. This meant that the entire panzer army would be committed in two parallel formations attacking abreast, with units in column. Control over the operation, of course, could only be exercised from inside the pocket; evacuation of an operations staff via Khotin to the south, in order to direct the breakout from the outside, was out of the question.

The Pocket Moves West

On 27 March, having regrouped its forces according to plan and completed all preparations for the thrust across the Zbruch River, First Panzer Army launched its breakout toward the west. Simultaneously, the rear guards on the eastern and northern sectors of the pocket switched to delaying tactics.

In the zone of the northern attack force, the enemy along the Zbruch river was overrun with surprising speed, and three undamaged bridges fell into German hands. The advance of the southern attack force met greater resistance, and considerable difficulties arose as the enemy launched a counterthrust from the west across the Zbruch and was able to force his way into Kamenets-Podolskiy. The loss of this important road hub made it necessary to reroute all German movements in a wide detour around the city, an effort that required painstaking reconnaissance and careful traffic regulation. It was not long, however, until the enemy penetration was sealed off, and in this instance the Germans, themselves surrounded, were able to turn to encircle a smaller Russian force which was not dependent upon air supply and could no longer interfere with subsequent operations. As soon as several strong bridgeheads had been established across the Zbruch River, new spearheads were formed which attacked the Seret River line. Thus the panzer army maintained the initiative and kept moving by day and night.

Apparently the enemy was still uncertain about German intentions. Instead of combining all his forces from the eastern and northern sectors in an attempt to pursue and overtake the Germans pushing west, he persisted in attacking the pocket from the east and north, in some instances striking at positions already vacated by the German rear guards. His units southwest of the pocket actually continued to move farther south. Meanwhile, First Panzer Army kept up its westward advance; on 28 March the southern force was able to cut the road leading to Chortkov, severing enemy communication lines in that area; one day later German spearheads reached the Seret River, which they crossed during the following night.

The Russians then began to react. They recalled elements of their Fourth Tank Army from south of the Dnestr and, by 31 March, launched a strong

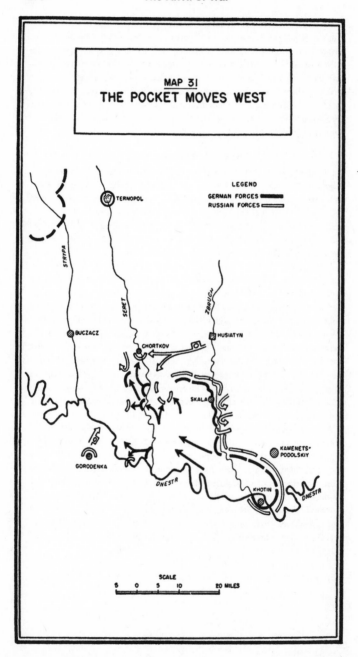

MAP 31
THE POCKET MOVES WEST

LEGEND
GERMAN FORCES
RUSSIAN FORCES

armored thrust toward the north from the area of Gorodenka. As a counter-measure, the southern attack force of First Panzer Army, deployed mainly between the Zbruch and Seret Rivers, assumed the defensive and was able to break up the Russian armored attack. Thereafter, since their supply lines had meanwhile been cut, these Russian units no longer constituted a menace to the German left flank.

A more serious threat existed in the north where Russian forces moving west could have overtaken and blocked the entire right wing of First Panzer Army. However, the enemy did not choose to do so, and the northern attack force continued to advance and was able to cross the Seret without major difficulty.

The Escape

The last week in March was marked by heavy snowstorms. A rapid thaw followed early in April, with the effect of seriously hampering all movements. Supply during this period continued to be the greatest problem. As the German force kept moving, the planes bringing in supplies had to use different airstrips every night. In the final phase of the operation supplies could only be dropped by air, a procedure that proved wholly inadequate to satisfy the requirements of an entire army. Despite the daily moves of the pocket force, the maintenance of adequate signal communications was assured at all times, primarily by the use of conventional and microwave radio sets.

Since the troops were constantly on the move, launching successive attacks toward the west, they never developed the feeling of being trapped in the slowly tightening grip of an encircling enemy force. Consequently, there were no signs of disintegration or panic, and the number of missing during the entire operation remained unusually low. By 5 April the leading elements of both the northern and the southern attack forces reached the Strypa River. On the following day, near Buczacz, they were able to link up with other German units coming from the west.

In two weeks of heavy fighting, but without suffering severe casualties, First Panzer Army had freed itself from enemy encirclement. Rear guard actions continued for a few days and then the Germans succeeded in establishing a new, continuous defense line running from the Dnestr to the town of Brody, which prevented any further advance of the enemy. Moreover, despite their considerable losses in matériel, elements of First Panzer Army were still able to launch an attack southeast across the Dnestr to break up an enemy force which had appeared in the Stanislav area. Enemy equipment captured and destroyed during the entire breakout operation amounted to 357 tanks, 42 assault guns, and 280 artillery pieces.

Evaluation

In its encirclement and breakout, First Panzer Army gained a number of experiences that may be applicable to many similar situations. Whereas in previous wars the double envelopment and encirclement of a unit was tantamount to its annihilation, this is no longer true today. The progressive motorization of ground forces, combined with the possibility of supply by air, tends to do away with this hitherto characteristic aspect of a pocket.

While it is true that the decision to break out from encirclement should not be needlessly delayed, it is equally important to realize that definite plans for the breakout should not be made too early, at a stage when the enemy is still moving and therefore capable of making rapid changes in his dispositions. Once the encirclement is completed, the enemy, since he is now operating along exterior lines, encounters difficulties of supply and communication and has lost much of his initial flexibility.

In an operation of this type surprise is the most important factor, particularly the surprise achieved by choosing an unexpected direction for the breakout. In the example described all movement prior to the encirclement of First Panzer Army had been from north to south. A breakout in the same direction was definitely expected by the enemy, and therefore this would have been the least favorable choice. The direction selected for the German thrust – practically perpendicular to the enemy's lines of advance – offered the best chance of success; the element of surprise actually proved of greater importance than considerations of enemy strength, terrain conditions, and the distance to the nearest German lines.

CHAPTER 36

Conclusions

The Significance of a Pocket

In modern warfare with its blitzkrieg tactics executed by motorized and mechanized forces, the encirclement by the enemy of large bodies of troops has become a frequent occurrence. It is, therefore, all the more important to be adequately prepared for this kind of fighting.

Combat in pockets, whether it be of long or short duration, has its own fundamental rules. Whatever circumstances may determine the length of the battle, it will always be advisable to seek an early decision. To make this possible, the commander of an encircled force must, on principle, be granted full freedom of action. He should be permitted, specifically, to use his own judgment regarding all measures and decisions incident to a breakout from the pocket. On many occasions in German experience, the futile attempt was made to evaluate a local situation and to conduct the operations of encircled troops by remote control from a far distant higher echelon, if not directly from Hitler's headquarters. Indecisiveness on the part of the pocket commander and measures which invariably came too late were the consequences of such limitations imposed by higher headquarters. Whenever a commander receives rigid instructions from a distance at which the capabilities of his encircled forces cannot be properly judged – and are usually overestimated – his willingness to accept responsibility will rapidly decline.

The notion that pockets must be held at all costs should never be applied as a general principle. Hitler's adherence to this mistaken concept during World War II resulted in the loss of so many German soldiers that the lesson learned from their sacrifice ought to be remembered for all time.

Special Operating Procedures

Experience has shown that only seasoned troops, in the best fighting condition and under the firm control of their commanders, are able to withstand the mental strain of combat in encirclement and are likely to retain the high degree of physical fitness needed under such circumstances. But even with troops that satisfy these requirements it is necessary to apply stern measures in order to prevent any slackening of control, which would inevitably result in lowering their morale. It is surprising how fast the bonds of discipline will disintegrate in an encirclement. Mobs of unarmed soldiers trying to proceed on their own, captured horses loaded down with superfluous equipment, and other similarly depressing sights were not uncommon in some of the larger German pockets in Russia. They had a contaminating effect and called for swift and drastic countermeasures.

The highest standards of discipline, more important in this than in any other situation, must be upheld by the officers and noncommissioned officers of an encircled force; it is their personal conduct that sets the example. Force of character, as in all critical situations, acquires the greatest significance; it sustains the will to fight and may, indeed, determine the outcome of the battle. More than ever the place of the commander, under such circumstances, is in the midst of his troops; their minds will register his every action with the sensitivity of a seismograph.

Particular attention in all matters of discipline must be paid to rear echelon units and the personnel of rear area installations that may be present in the pocket. Since these troops are usually the first to become unnerved, they must he held under strict control.

Another principle that has proved itself in the German experience is the delegation of authority (see diagram) by the pocket commander (A) to three subordinate command elements within the pocket; one (B) to maintain the defensive effort; another (C) to prepare and conduct the breakout; and a third (D) to be responsible for organization, traffic control, and the maintenance of discipline inside the pocket.

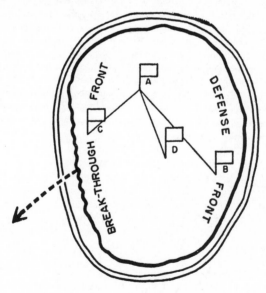

Communication and co-ordination with other friendly forces, particularly in the case of a relief thrust from the outside, will have to remain among the exclusive functions of the pocket commander. Presumably, he alone will have the necessary radio facilities at his disposal. It is, of course, an absolute requirement, for the delegation of authority described above, that all the forces inside the pocket be under one command. Since envelopment attacks are usually directed against tactical weak spots, such as army or corps boundaries, uniform command over the forces encircled by the enemy is not always assured at first. It must be established as soon as possible; otherwise, as demonstrated in chapter 33, considerable difficulties will be encountered in the defense of the pocket, as well as in the conduct of relief operations from the outside.

The tactical principles which, in an encirclement, apply to the various combat arms, may be summarized as follows:

1. Infantry

In the initial phase, during which the entire perimeter is to be held, *everything up front!* An encircled force can ill afford loss of terrain. Therefore, strong reserves must be held close by; the battle position must be a closely knit system of strong points with a well-co-ordinated fire plan for all infantry heavy weapons; and the outpost area must be kept under constant surveillance by reconnaissance and combat patrols, particularly during the night. If this cannot be accomplished because of inadequate forces, the perimeter should be shortened deliberately to the point where the defenses can be organized in accordance with the principles outlined above.

2. Artillery

In small- and medium-sized pockets the ordinarily undesirable bunching up of artillery units cannot be avoided. Here, however, it is of advantage in that it permits a rapid shift of fire, thus assuring direct support for large parts of the front without displacement to new positions. Also, centralized fire direction can be more easily established. A practice that proved particularly effective was the firing of a few batteries at a time, while the bulk of the artillery remained silent to avoid counterbattery fire. Massed artillery went into action only against large-scale enemy attacks.

3. Armor and Antitank Weapons

In the defense of pockets, tanks and assault guns have a dual mission. Contrary to the rules of armored combat under ordinary circumstances, they are scattered among the infantry and take part in the small-scale fighting along the perimeter. At the same time, they must be able to revert quickly to their original formation whenever they have to be used as mobile reserve against major enemy attacks. Similarly, the proper place for antitank weapons is with the front-line infantry. An antitank defense echeloned in depth, as is preferable in most other situations, must be ruled out for the same reasons that apply to the employment of the infantry.

The necessity for tight organization inside the pocket has already been emphasized. This applies particularly to traffic control which must be so enforced as to assure order and discipline, and to prevent panic. It may be necessary, for this purpose, to employ not only all available military police but also seasoned combat troops under the command of forceful and experienced officers.

All measures that must be taken inside a pocket will vary depending upon local circumstances; no two situations are alike. Therefore, set rules cannot be prescribed for fighting in pockets any more than for other types of military operations. Nevertheless, the fundamental principles outlined above seem to apply whenever troops are encircled by the enemy.

So long as the encirclement has not been completed – or before the enemy ring has been reinforced – an immediate break-through offers the best chance of success. Few tactical preparations will be necessary, if a command faced with encirclement can exploit the opportune moment by breaking out as soon as the enemy's intentions have been recognized. In most instances, however, all elements of the surrounded force will be locked in battle for several days, and the opportunity for such immediate action will pass before the situation in the pocket has become sufficiently clear. Then, especially in the case of larger pockets, a breakout can be launched only after the most careful preparations which must include some or all of the following considerations and measures.

The Breakout Decision

Unless the encircled forces have explicit orders to remain in place, or are so weak that they must rely on relief from the outside, the decision to break out must be made before the enemy has been able to forge a firm ring around the pocket. Only if this is done, and only if preparations are begun without delay, will all measures become part of one coherent plan, directed toward a single objective.

Such situations bring out the innate aggressiveness, flexibility, and initiative of a born leader. The need for quick decisions, however, must not be permitted to cause action without plan. The proper time and direction for the breakout, for instance, can only be determined after the following questions have been answered:

a. When – according to the tactical situation – is the earliest suitable moment for launching the attack?

b. Where is the enemy the weakest?

c. Which is the shortest way back to friendly lines?

d. What direction of attack would involve the least terrain difficulties?

e. What time of day and what weather conditions are most favorable for the attack?

f. Should one or several directions be selected for the breakout?

The answers to these questions will vary according to the situation, as can be seen from the preceding chapters. Actually, there may be situations in which – contrary to the principles advanced above – the direction for the breakout should not be fixed too early, at least not until the enemy's intentions can be clearly recognized (see chapter 34).

As a rule, unless the breakout is to be co-ordinated with the approach of a relief force from the outside, the units fighting their way out should follow the shortest route back to their own lines. In many instances the direction most favorable in terms of terrain and enemy resistance cannot be used if it does not permit a link-up with friendly forces in the shortest possible time. With troops in good fighting condition, the attack can be launched at night; if they are battle weary, the breakout must be made in the daytime, so as to obtain better control and co-ordination.

A breakout in several directions offers the least chance of success. It is attempted as a last resort, in order to obtain a greater dispersal of one's own forces, which might enable some small units to fight their way back to their own lines. Such an attempt is more or less an act of desperation – when relief from the outside cannot be expected, and the distance to the nearest friendly lines has become so great that it can no longer be bridged by the exhausted pocket force.

Special Logistical Preparations

A successful breakout is the result of sound planning and systematic preparation. It is also one of the most difficult combat maneuvers that a military force can be called upon to attempt. This fact must be taken into account in all preparatory measures. Prior to the breakout, for instance, the troops should be stripped of all unnecessary equipment, that is, of all equipment they might not need during the fighting of the next few days. This must be done without hesitation and without regard to their possible future requirements, should they have to be committed again *after* the breakout. The easier the lost equipment can be replaced afterwards, the less weight will be given to such considerations. German commanders in World War II were never allowed to forget that every weapon and vehicle was virtually irreplaceable – a typical sign of a 'poor man's war.' To some other nations, however, these limitations do not necessarily apply.

Until the pocket force is entirely surrounded by the enemy – but as soon as encirclement appears inevitable – the last open road must be utilized for the evacuation of casualties and of all nonessential staff sections, detachments, and service troops. If there is still time, excess weapons and equipment may be moved out over the same road. The commander should not fail, however, to make full use of this last opportunity to get rid of rear echelon troops; in an encirclement they are a greater burden than superfluous equipment, which can be destroyed if necessary.

Technical preparations in the pocket begin with what might be called the 'big clean-up.' All weapons that cannot be fully manned or adequately supplied with ammunition must be destroyed. The same is true of all heavy guns that might be a hindrance in view of expected terrain difficulties, as for instance all artillery pieces of more than 150-mm. caliber. As a rule, it is better to destroy one gun too many, than to drag along a single weapon that cannot be employed.

Similar principles apply to the destruction of motor vehicles. Exactly how many are to be destroyed will depend upon the availability of fuel and the requirements for the transportation of casualties and indispensable equipment; in any event, the majority of vehicles will have to be destroyed. Hardest hit by these radical measures are usually the supply services. Here, only a forceful officer in charge of destruction will be able to carry out his mission successfully.

Official papers are another victim of the general clean-up. Their destruction is a task that every soldier will undertake with fiendish pleasure. Files, administrative forms, voluminous war diaries, orders, regulations, and directives are consigned to the flames – the higher the classification, the greater must be the care taken to assure that they are completely destroyed. Only the most important papers, radio codes, and in some cases personal files, may be left intact, so long as there is hope that they might be saved.

Effective traffic regulation is a prerequisite for all tactical moves inside the pocket. If an adequate road net exists, separate routes must be designated for the movement of supply units and combat troops, and even for armor and infantry. The Germans found it expedient to co-ordinate all traffic in a pocket by preparing a regular timetable that had to be strictly observed.

However, the problem of traffic regulation inside a pocket is not confined to troop movements. The most carefully devised system of traffic control can be upset by streams of fleeing civilians who are likely to be stricken with panic when caught in a pocket. As a rule, therefore, it is imperative for the security of the encircled force to prohibit and prevent *any* movement of local inhabitants. Only in rare cases will it be possible to take along part of the civilian population during a breakout. Then, while the roads are kept clear, special paths must be assigned for the treks of civilians. Particularly in large pockets, the question whether able-bodied male inhabitants should be taken along or left behind deserves careful consideration; it can only be decided on the basis of local circumstances.

Extensive preparations will also be necessary if an encircled force is to be supplied by air; these preparations are described in detail in the Appendix.

Tactical Preparations

In an encirclement a deliberate effort must be made to increase the effective strength of the combat element at the expense of the service units. Selecting the proper personnel to be transferred from rear echelon to combat duty may be a slow process, but it is of the greatest importance at a time when active fighters are needed more than anything else. In such situations, the service units – having grown out of proportion to the combat element – are largely superfluous and actually impose a heavy burden on the command. At best, they constitute a manpower reserve which, after a thorough process of selection, will yield additional personnel for combat duty. One should not expect too much of this reserve – while it is composed of military personnel, it will include few combat soldiers. Assigning an excessive number of rear echelon troops to frontline duty will only swell the numerical strength of the combat element without, however, increasing its fighting power to the same degree. The procedure completely loses its usefulness when the men transferred from service units are no longer a reinforcement of, but a burden to, the combat element. Rear echelon troops whose services have become superfluous and who can no longer be evacuated, should be placed in a single unit and held under firm control.

Demolitions, which are to prevent rapid pursuit by the enemy or to slow his exploitation of recently abandoned terrain, are to be ordered and executed in time; condemned artillery ammunition makes a good explosive for this purpose. It is advisable, however, to confine such demolitions to a few important objects. Experience has shown that as a rule the troops have neither the time nor the inclination. On the other hand, the commander must take care to prevent senseless mass demolitions born of a spirit of destructiveness that is characteristic of encircled troops.

The success of a breakout will depend primarily upon the use of deception and the maintenance of secrecy. The fewer subordinate commanders informed about the actual breakout plan, the greater the chances that secrecy can be maintained. Especially telephone and radio communications must be carefully guarded. At the same time, radio offers the best means for deceiving the enemy. This may be done by transmitting dummy messages about one's own intentions, calls to imaginary relief units, reports that will confuse the enemy about the actual strength of the pocket force, misleading requisitions for supplies, and false information about drop zones and landing areas. All these rules are certain to reduce the number of casualties during the breakout.

Tactical feints and deceptive maneuvers must go hand in hand with the measures suggested above. By moving into different positions every night, launching attacks with limited objective from various points of the perimeter, and stubbornly holding on to unimportant terrain features, the encircled force must deliberately convey to the enemy a false picture of its situation and of its intentions. This purpose can also be served by having a sizable column composed of all available supply units move laterally across the sector from which the breakout will eventually be launched.

Effective deception can always be achieved by concentrating armor at a point other than that of the intended breakout. If these tanks proceed to execute a feint attack, the enemy, believing that he has located the main effort of the breakout force, will almost certainly divert the bulk of his forces to the threatened point. The attacking tanks are then shifted rapidly into the direction of the main break-through, and success will usually follow (see chapter 31). Such deceptive measures by tanks, depending of course upon the fuel situation, should be used both in the defense of the pocket perimeter and – as an ace in the hole – immediately before the breakout is launched. The desired result can often be achieved by having a single tank drive in circles at night to feign the assembly of a large armored unit. No matter what measures of deception are used, they will only serve their purpose if they enable the breakout force to take the enemy by surprise. In this respect the preparations for a breakout do not differ from preparations for any other type of attack. Here, as in any offensive action, secrecy, deception, and surprise are the basic elements of success.

The most important tactical preparations for the breakout – apart from diversionary attacks – are concerned with the gradual change of emphasis from the defense of the perimeter to the formation of a strong breakout force. As the situation permits, every soldier who can be spared from the purely defensive sectors must be transferred – possibly after a rest period – to the area selected for the breakout. This will weaken the defenses and, in some places, necessitate a shortening of the line which may involve considerable risks. Enemy penetrations are likely to occur, and such local crises, although they may have little or no effect upon the over-all situation, are usually over-estimated by the commanders on the spot. These difficulties, of course, are greatly reduced if the entire pocket keeps moving in the general direction of the breakout. The necessary shifting of forces is then more easily accomplished, and minor losses of terrain on the defensive front are no longer regarded as serious setbacks. The advantage of a moving pocket in terms of morale is obvious. No claustrophobia will develop because the troops are spared the feeling that they are making a last stand in a pocket from which there is no escape.

During the defense of a pocket, local crises are a daily occurrence. The pocket commander and his staff must be ready at any moment to take the necessary countermeasures against serious emergencies. Actually, each passing hour may bring new surprises and call for new decisions, and it is not always easy to distinguish between important and unimportant developments. The commander must keep in mind that his reserves are limited and should not be committed unless a major threat develops at a decisive point. It is a result of the unusual tension prevailing in a pocket that purely local emergencies are often exaggerated and may lead to urgent calls for assistance. Frequently, such local crises subside before long, and the situation can be restored without the use of reserves – provided the pocket commander does not permit himself to be needlessly alarmed.

At this point a few words might be added concerning the attitude that must be displayed by the pocket commander and his staff. In the midst of rapidly changing events the command element must be a tower of strength. The troops observe its every action with keen eyes. In this respect even the location of the command post is of particular importance. While it should be centrally located, its proximity to the momentary center of gravity is even more desirable. Never should the operations of an encircled force be conducted by remote control, from a headquarters on the outside. This proved to be an impossibility, both from a practical point of view and because of its disastrous effect upon the morale of the troops. By the same token, no member of the command group must be permitted to leave the pocket by air. Reassuring information, brief orders issued in clear language, and frequent visits by the commander and his staff to critical points along the perimeter will have an immediate beneficial influence upon the morale of the pocket force. At the same time, exaggerated optimism is definitely out of place. The troops want to know the truth and will eventually discover it for themselves. They are certain to lose confidence if they find out that their commanders have been tampering with the facts in an attempt to make the situation look brighter than it actually is. As a rule, the truth told without a show of nervousness cannot fail to have a reassuring effect and might even stir the troops to greater effort.

Arranged in their proper sequence, the tactical measures leading up to the breakout are the following:

a. Emphasis on defense; all weapons committed in support of the fighting along the perimeter.

b. Establishment of clear channels of command.

c. Stabilization of the defense.

d. Reinforcement of the combat element at the expense of the service units.

e. Evacuation of nonessential personnel; destruction of excess equipment.

f. Gradual change of emphasis from the defense to preparations for the breakout attack.

g. Formation of a breakout force.

h. Shortening of the defense perimeter; further strengthening of the sector selected for the breakout.

i. Deceptive maneuvers culminating in a diversionary attack.

j. Breakout.

Supply and Evacuation

The supply reserves carried in a pocket should be no more than what the force will presumably need until the day of the breakout. Sizable stores cannot be kept; they must either be given away or destroyed, regardless of quality or quantity. In such situations the Germans found it useful to prepare so-called individual supply packages which were composed of all kinds of items for certain units and could be distributed in advance to the points where they would be needed later on. Surplus rations can be issued to the troops for immediate consumption, but if this is done too generously it is likely to decrease their fighting power. The local population will always gratefully accept whatever the troops can spare.

If a pocket force is without adequate supplies and, particularly, if the required fuel and ammunition can only be brought in by air, the escape from encirclement must be accomplished as quickly as possible. Supply by air cannot satisfy all the requirements of an encircled force; it can only remedy some of the most important deficiencies. This fact was demonstrated during the operations described in the preceding chapters and confirmed by the personal experience of the author. It is not likely to change, even if absolute superiority in the air is assured and an adequate number of planes can be assigned to the operation.

One of the most important logistical problems is that of evacuating casualties. Whether or not the wounded are taken along has a profound effect upon the morale of the encircled troops. Any measure from which they might derive the slightest indication that wounded personnel is to be left behind will immediately reduce their fighting spirit, especially if they are facing an enemy like the Russians. In such situations the commanders are under the strongest moral obligation to take the wounded along and must bend every effort to make this possible. German experience has shown that minor casualties can endure transportation over considerable distances on horse-drawn vehicles padded with straw, even in very cold weather and during snowstorms. On such movements the wounded were accompanied by medical officers who administered every possible aid during the frequent halts. The German troops encircled near Kamenets-Podolskiy (chapter 34) regarded their convoy of casualties as their sacred trust and fought all the more stubbornly to protect their wounded comrades. Consequently, it was possible to evacuate nearly all casualties during that operation. In the pocket near Cherkassy (chapter 33) the situation was less favorable. There, because of the most severe weather conditions and a confused tactical situation, the wounded had to be left behind in the care of doctors and other medical personnel.

Every opportunity should be used to evacuate casualties by air. They must have priority on transport planes returning from a pocket, and this priority must be assured, if necessary, by force of arms. The desperate struggle for space aboard transport planes in the pocket of Stalingrad should serve as a warning for situations of this kind.

Relief Operations

The difficulties encountered by an encircled force may be considerably reduced if strong relief forces are available in the vicinity of the pocket. Even inadequate attempts at relief from the outside are better than none at all. The basis for real success, however, is the employment of experienced troops in the best fighting condition who are not likely to bog down at the half-way mark. The need for relief from the outside depends, of course, on the tactical situation and the physical condition of the encircled force; it is greatest when the troops inside the pocket are battle worn and show signs of weakening; it may appear less urgent in other situations. But wherever friendly troops are surrounded by the enemy, assistance from the outside is desirable and should be provided without delay.

Such relief operations must be planned with the same care that is used in preparing every action of the encircled force. This applies to the selection of the route of advance, the choice of the proper moment for the attack, and the timely allocation of fuel and ammunition. A relief thrust cannot be launched on the spur of the moment, and undue haste will surely result in failure. Tactical preparations must follow the same principles as those for any other type of attack. The necessary strength of the relief force must be determined on the basis of the enemy situation and the distance to the objective. In most cases armor and adequate artillery support will be indispensable. All relief forces must be under one command, even if they consist of units that were originally parts of two separate armies (see chapter 33).

Preparatory measures in the fields of supply and administration will greatly exceed those that might be taken for an ordinary attack, since the relief force must try to anticipate the needs of the troops breaking out of the pocket. All kinds of supplies, especially stimulants, must be held ready in sufficient quantities; rescue and rehabilitation areas must be prepared; and facilities must be provided that will improve the physical condition and the morale of the pocket force. Among these are troop quarters (heated shelter in winter), bathing facilities, clothing, and arrangements for mail service. These measures play an important part in getting the pocket force back into shape and ready for renewed commitment. Proper care for the wounded must be assured by assembling all available medical personnel and preparing shelter for the pocket casualties. Information as to the number of wounded inside the pocket must be obtained by radio.

The decision as to the time and place for launching the relief attack depends on specific arrangements with the pocket force. Unless a safe wire communication exists, such arrangements can only be made by radio, in which case great care must be taken to maintain secrecy. The distance to the pocket may be so great as to require the use of special types of radio equipment. In such situations the Germans used their so-called *Dezimetergeraet*, a microwave radio set operating on frequencies between 500 and 600 megacycles.

If at all possible, the relief attack must be launched on a broad front. A single thrust confined to a narrow frontage has little chance of success and is justified only if insufficient forces are available (see chapter 31). The relief force, in this case, will have its long flanks dangerously exposed and will hardly be able to reach its objective. If such an emergency method must be used, the operation should be carried out at night.

The conduct of the relief operation must be marked by a high degree of flexibility. Frequently a prearranged plan must be discarded or modified because of unexpected enemy action, particularly if such action is directed against the troops attempting to escape from the pocket. The joint effort of the two converging elements must be geared to the needs of the encircled units who are always fighting under less favorable circumstances than the relief force. The latter must be able to react with swift and effective countermeasures to unforeseen changes in the situation.

The battle west of Cherkassy (chapter 33) clearly demonstrated what difficulties can be encountered in a relief operation. There, all efforts were frustrated by a combination of unfortunate circumstances. The sudden start of the muddy season had rendered the terrain virtually impassable. Relief forces approaching from the south were whittled down in numerous local engagements before they could be assembled for the main attack. Complicated channels of command and diverging directions of attack further added to the confusion. Certainly, flexibility was lacking in the conduct of the relief operation from the west. The breakout, to be sure, did not proceed entirely according to plan, as the majority of the troops emerging from the pocket missed their direction. Even then they followed a line of advance only a few miles south from the one that had been agreed upon. Because of this minor change, the relief force proved unable to link up with the pocket forces at the point where they had actually pierced the ring of encirclement.

The Breakout

Once the pocket force has begun its break-through in the direction of friendly lines, it must apply the same tactical principles and will be subject to the same contingencies as in any other type of attack. A particular difficulty lies in coordinating this effort with that of the relief force, for the purpose of accomplishing a junction of the two converging spearheads as soon as possible. German experiences vary as to what would be the most desirable attack formation for a breakout. Since the answer to this question depends largely on the local situation, no definite rules can be offered. In any event it is advisable to adopt a mixed formation composed of motorized and nonmotorized units supported by tanks and all weapons suitable for the attack. Armored units must be held with close rein so as to prevent them from outrunning the infantry. They should only be permitted to advance by bounds, with some of the armor held back. This is a necessary precaution to prevent deep thrusts by individual armored units that can be of no advantage to the progress of the main force.

Specific orders must be issued both for the timely integration of all remaining elements to be withdrawn from the defensive sectors and for the conduct of rear guard action to cover the breakout attack.

A major crisis during the breakout will arise as soon as the original plan, for some reason, can no longer be followed and improvisation must take its place. As a rule this will be the result of some unforeseen enemy action. With troops that are severely overtaxed by heavy fighting in the pocket such crises may easily lead to panic. The call 'every man for himself' is the signal for general disorder marked by useless attempts of individual soldiers to make their way back to friendly lines. This can only be prevented by firm leadership and strict control, and by taking advance measures that will anticipate such emergencies, as for instance by keeping a mobile reserve, composed of armor and antitank weapons, that can be employed with a high degree of flexibility. Even a few tanks committed at the right moment can serve as a very effective means to overcome a local crisis.

The capabilities of the troops must be carefully weighed and are the basis for the timing of the entire operation. If the troops are battle weary and if the breakout is expected to involve long and heavy fighting, the operation must be conducted in several phases to provide rest between periods of movement or combat. For reasons of security, especially in the case of small pockets, all movements should be carried out during the night. Control of the troops is greatly facilitated if the fighting can be confined to the daytime.

If a breakout must be executed without simultaneous relief from the outside, a new position should be selected in which the liberated pocket force might be able to rally and to face the pursuing enemy; in most instances that will be no more than a line designated on the map where the troops are to be reorganized after their successful escape from encirclement.

Summary

The lessons learned by the Germans during World War II on the relative value of pockets left behind the enemy lines might be summarized as follows:

a. As a method of defensive combat designed to tie down substantial enemy forces, the deliberate stand of an encircled force rarely achieves the desired result.

b. The deliberate creation of a pocket and the insistence on its continued defense can only be justified if the surrounded force consists of experienced and well-disciplined troops who are able to cope with the unusual difficulties involved in this kind of fighting. Otherwise the price will be excessive since the encircled troops are usually lost and even those who manage to escape are certain to remain unfit for combat for a long time.

c. Whenever friendly forces are cut off and surrounded by the enemy, steps must be taken without delay to assure their liberation. The senior commander of the encircled units must be *immediately* authorized to force a breakout. It is even better to issue a standing order at the beginning of hostilities that would make it mandatory for the commander of an encircled force to break out as soon as possible. Only then can there be any hope of saving the surrounded troops without suffering excessive losses. The German High Command during World War II greatly overestimated the defensive value of such pockets. Orders for a breakout from encirclement were issued either much too late or not at all. This turned out to be a grave tactical error which could not fail to have a disastrous effect upon the entire conduct of operations on the Russian front.

Air Support of Encircled Forces

General Principles

The air support available to an encircled force will usually determine the feasibility of a breakout and the manner in which it must be executed. As a rule, it will depend on the availability of air cover whether marches and combat actions should take place in the daytime or during the hours of darkness when so many additional risks and difficulties are involved. Since a breakout on a large scale will necessarily include actions that can only be carried out in the daytime, such as frontal attacks over difficult terrain or assaults against well-defended enemy positions, a strong concentration of air power, at least during these phases, is indispensable for the success of the entire operation. In an extensive theater of war, where the air force has to accomplish many diversified missions against widely separated targets, there is always the danger of a dissipation of air strength. It will therefore be the responsibility of the top-level air force command to create in time the tactical and technical prerequisites for temporary mass employment of air power at points of main effort. This is accomplished by establishing and maintaining adequate ground installations in all crucial areas so that the rapid diversion of adjacent air force units (at least for one day's operations) will not present serious difficulties.

How many air force units are required to support an encircled force must be determined on the basis of known enemy strength, the size and vulnerability of the pocket, and its distance from the nearest friendly lines. How much air support can be provided will depend essentially upon the capacity of the airfields, the supply situation, and the intensity of combat on other sectors. The air strength actually needed in such situations can hardly be overestimated. It has to make up for the critical deficiencies that always aggravate the situation in a pocket (lack of artillery ammunition, heavy losses of weapons and tanks, etc.), and to bolster the morale of the encircled troops during their difficult struggle. In addition, since the immediate vicinity of a pocket is usually the scene of large enemy concentrations, the supporting air units will find numerous opportunities to weaken the forces of the enemy. Here, even more than in most other situations, an adequate reserve of air strength should be available, specifically for the following reasons:

a. The defense of a pocket often takes an unexpected turn and may require the rapid commitment of additional air support that can only be provided if ample reserves are available for instant use.

b. The possibility of heavy aircraft losses must be taken into account, particularly as a result of enemy bombing attacks on friendly airfields.

c. The most serious crisis in a breakout may suddenly arise at a late stage of the operation. This will automatically increase the need for immediate air protection, and without adequate reserves such additional air support will not be available at the decisive moment.

d. Entire air force units may suddenly be grounded because of unfavorable weather and terrain conditions such as dense fog or deeply mired airstrips.

Long-range weather forecasts covering a wide area should be made available to the command of the ground forces. Such data can be of the greatest importance in selecting the most favorable time for a breakout, especially if they include an accurate forecast of bad weather periods during which the enemy air force will be unable to operate. Even local and temporary weather conditions can have a direct bearing on tactical decisions. It is conceivable that an encircled force might take advantage of temporary weather disturbances over enemy air bases, which may have the effect of grounding the bulk of the enemy's local air support, while more favorable weather conditions exist behind friendly lines, permitting one's own air units to carry out their missions.

The command over all air force units in an area where ground troops are encircled by the enemy must be in the hands of one air force commander, who should also have tactical control over air formations from adjacent sectors whenever they are committed in support of the encircled force. In addition, all antiaircraft units in the area must be under his command. [It should be remembered that in the German organization most antiaircraft units were part of the Luftwaffe.] In the case of an encirclement on a large scale with adequate airstrips and supply facilities existing inside the pocket, it is advisable to appoint a special air force commander for the pocket area, who should be located in the immediate vicinity of the pocket command post. This air force officer should receive his orders from the air force commander responsible for the entire area.

Preparatory Measures

All preparations for air support must be carried out as inconspicuously as possible. Great care must be taken to conceal the intentions of the pocket force and, specifically, to avoid offering any clues as to the time and place of the impending attack. Air supply operations should be initiated at the earliest possible moment, to assure that the ammunition and fuel requirements of the troops for the days of the breakout can be adequately covered. With few exceptions supply by air is indispensable for the success of a pocket force attempting to break through the enemy ring of encirclement. Yet, under the most favorable circumstances supply by air remains an extremely uneconomical measure. Therefore, when encirclement appears inevitable, every possible effort should be made *in advance* to build up an adequate supply reserve, at least of heavy and bulky items; even after the encirclement has become a fact, this might still be done by a strongly armed supply convoy forcing its way into the pocket.

If a force is compelled by specific orders to submit to encirclement by the enemy, it should seek to make its stand in an area that contains at least one usable airfield. Type and condition of the terrain may render it extremely difficult to accomplish the construction of new airstrips with the limited manpower available. At least one and if possible two or more airfields for the use of supply planes – preferably with cargo gliders in tow – should be in operation as soon as possible. In this instance the ground troops must provide the necessary manpower for grading operations. In some situations it may be imperative to accomplish a widening of the pocket by local attacks, in order to capture a suitable airfield or to place an existing field beyond the range of enemy artillery.

For night operations, which as a rule cannot be avoided, each airfield must have a radio beacon, a light beacon, and an adequate supply of signal flares. All airfields inside a pocket must be under the command of forceful officers supported by experienced personnel, a sizable number of technicians, and an adequate labor force for the unloading, stacking, and rapid distribution of supplies.

In pockets where suitable airfields do not exist from the outset and cannot be constructed, supply by air is limited to the use of cargo gliders. Although the volume of supplies, in this case, will be considerably smaller, the facilities on the ground, except for the length of airstrips, will have to be virtually the same as described above.

Dropping supplies in aerial delivery containers is an extremely wasteful procedure. Losses from drifting or from breakage upon impact range up to 60 per cent; they may be as high as 90 percent if the containers are dropped into the rubble of a destroyed town. Yet, in the case of very small pockets, this may be the only possibility for supplying the surrounded force by air. In that event, the dropping point must be fixed by specific arrangements with the encircled troops since the enemy will make every effort to mislead the approaching planes and cause them to drop their loads over enemy-held territory.

Air Reconnaissance

Air reconnaissance units must provide the pocket commander promptly with the essential information on which he is to base his decisions as to time and place of the breakout and his specific plans for the conduct of the entire operation. The missions to be accomplished by air reconnaissance include the following:

a. Gathering information about enemy dispositions, so as to determine in what area around the pocket the enemy is weakest and where a break-through would have the best chance of success.

b. Furnishing specific information about enemy units located in the prospective break-through area, and indicating targets for counterbattery and air attacks.

c. Detecting enemy reserves and preparations on the flanks of the prospective zone of attack and opposite the rear of the pocket.

d. Providing aerial photographs and photo maps of the prospective break-through area, showing traffic arteries, bridges, and major terrain obstacles, and determining whether or not the terrain is suitable for armored combat.

e. Spotting airstrips (by using aerial photography), which might exist in the path of the planned attack, that could be used for supply by air during the breakout.

Fighter Aviation

If the encircled ground troops are in the possession of adequate facilities and supplies, a considerable advantage can be gained by having part of the fighter force operate from airfields inside the pocket or at least use these fields as advance airstrips for daylight operations. The greater the distance of the pocket area from the main air bases, the greater will be the importance of such measures for the maintenance of the pocket.

As the enemy can be expected to commit strong air units in his major attempt to annihilate the encircled troops – especially if he recognizes their preparations for a breakout – friendly fighter forces eventually have the opportunity of attacking enemy air formations that are confined to a small area, and of shooting down a relatively large number of enemy aircraft.

Close Support of Ground Actions

The employment of fighter-bombers (*Schlachtflieger*) has particular significance in the defense of a pocket where, as a rule, there is a shortage of artillery ammunition and an increased need for concealment and for saving the strength of the encircled troops. Close tactical air support is especially needed during the regrouping of the pocket force just before the breakout. At such time, close-support aviation may have to assume the role and perform the missions of the artillery. To avoid a dissipation of strength, the effort of fighter-bombers must be concentrated on a few target areas of major importance. At the same time, great care must be taken against revealing the intentions of the encircled ground troops. The strength and conduct of fighter-bomber units committed immediately before the breakout, for instance, should be largely the same as on preceding days. The targets selected should not permit any conclusions as to the actual direction of the impending attack. If it is necessary to neutralize certain areas in the path of the breakout, this must be done either sufficiently in advance or as soon as the attack on the ground has begun. In addition to providing direct support for the attacking breakout force, fighter-bombers are also employed to prevent the enemy from bringing up reserves and from regrouping his forces for the purpose of blocking the break-through attempt.

As a rule – chiefly for reasons of supply – close-support aircraft must operate from bases outside the pocket. Bombs and other appropriate ammunition that may be available at airstrips within the encirclement should be saved for a maximum air effort on the day of the breakout. Since positions along the perimeter are usually within close range of the enemy and difficult to identify from the air, the greatest caution must be used in the briefing of air crews operating over the area. This applies particularly when long-range aircraft from adjacent combat sectors are employed, a procedure which could otherwise lead to serious losses among friendly ground troops. Such aircraft should first be transferred to airfields close to the area of commitment where the crews can be properly briefed and quickly apprised of local changes in the situation.

Employment of Antiaircraft Units

Conspicuous changes in the disposition of antiaircraft units before the breakout may provide the enemy with definite clues as to the intentions of the encircled force. Antiaircraft guns and other tell-tale antiaircraft equipment should therefore be left in their positions (or replaced by dummy installations) until the very day of the breakout. Antiaircraft supply and service elements must be regrouped at an earlier stage, but without attracting undue attention. Similarly, the antiaircraft protection for the ground troops during their assembly before the breakout must be so arranged as to produce the least possible change in the existing pattern of antiaircraft positions. At the same time, an ostentatious concentration of antiaircraft units or dummy positions in an area unrelated to the main effort might conceivably be used as a means to deceive the enemy.

If ammunition reserves are available, which must be left behind, or if the breakout force is without adequate artillery support, it may be advisable to employ some antiaircraft units in direct support of the attack on the ground. These units should be moved during the night before the breakout to double-purpose positions from which they can participate in the initial phase of the operation by delivering direct fire on important ground targets in addition to providing antiaircraft protection.

The general regrouping of antiaircraft units before the breakout should take place as late as possible and with a view to protecting leading ground elements, flank units, artillery positions, and critical points such as bridge and defiles. At this stage it is usually impossible to avoid stripping the remaining ground units and installations of their antiaircraft defenses. Success in carrying out these measures depends in most cases on the degree of mobility retained by the antiaircraft units.

In all these preparations it is essential to keep in mind that the main objectives in the employment of antiaircraft units are protection against low-level enemy air raids and against all air attacks that cannot be warded off by friendly fighter forces. Particularly when the protection offered by fighter aviation is inadequate, the greatest care must be used in co-ordinating the efforts of antiaircraft and fighter units.

For the breakout phase specific plans should be made to regulate the forward displacement of antiaircraft units and their priority of movement during the advance, provided it is at all possible to anticipate the various moves that might become necessary.

Evacuation by Air

Detailed arrangements must be made by the air force to use supply aircraft returning from the pocket for the evacuation of wounded, of surplus personnel and equipment, and to assist the ground command in carrying out other evacuation measures (to include, in some cases, the removal of industrial equipment). The Army, on the other hand, is responsible for providing adequate medical facilities at the air bases to which the wounded are evacuated. Since casualties must be expected to occur at a high rate during certain phases of the operation, it will be necessary to take care of large numbers of wounded in the shortest possible time.

Air Support During the Breakout

In view of the great difficulties normally encountered during a breakout, the ground troops need protection against persistent attack from the air, as well as continuous tactical air support. Both are indispensable for the success of the entire operation. This is particularly true for the most critical phases of the breakout which occur, first, during the initial attack; second, when the enemy commits his reserves against the flanks and rear of the pocket force; and, finally, when he attempts to overtake and block the troops withdrawing from the pocket. During these phases the air force commander must concentrate all available air units and exert steadily mounting pressure at the critical points. In the intervals between these main efforts he has the missions of preventing interruptions in the advance on the ground, and of keeping his flying units in the highest possible state of readiness. It is, of course, impossible to devise a standing operating procedure for air support during a breakout, since no two situations are alike. Nevertheless, the following basic principles should be kept in mind.

During the initial phase all available air units should be committed in direct support of the leading ground elements. Air attacks on ground targets, beginning with a strong opening blow and continued in successive waves, must be closely co-ordinated with the fire plan of the artillery. The targets of fighter-bombers comprise objectives that cannot be observed from the ground (enemy artillery positions, assembly areas, tactical reserves); also enemy positions offering particularly strong resistance, enemy movements approaching the combat area, and hostile elements threatening the flanks of the advancing spearheads. Standby reserves of fighter-bombers, circling some distance away or, better still, at considerable altitude above the combat area, must be employed to eliminate any reviving enemy resistance and to reduce newly identified enemy strong points. Their presence in the air will greatly strengthen the morale of the attacking ground troops. Experience shows, moreover, that as these planes appear over the battlefield, enemy batteries will cease firing, to avoid being identified from the air. At the same time, low-flying aircraft will often draw fire from hitherto unidentified enemy positions which are thereby exposed to artillery action. Another practicable measure may be the placing of small smoke screens to blind enemy artillery observation.

To avoid hitting friendly ground troops, bombers should operate in the depth of the zone of advance against enemy artillery positions, assembly areas, and similar objectives. They might also be employed to lay large smoke screens, specifically to eliminate enemy observation from high ground off the flanks or from dominating terrain ahead of the advancing troops. Important objectives in the area of penetration should be reduced before the breakout by thorough bombing attacks, so as to lighten the task of the ground troops during the initial phase of the operation. This cannot be done, however, if such attacks are likely to reveal the plans of the breakout force. Nor does this rule apply to enemy command posts; these must be attacked at the most opportune moment, immediately after the breakout, when the resulting confusion among the enemy offers the greatest advantage to the attacking force.

The regrouping of enemy units, which, according to German experiences in Russia, might take place between six and ten hours after a breakout has begun, must be recognized and reported by friendly reconnaissance aviation as quickly as possible. From that time on, the enemy should be kept under constant air observation.

In breakout operations of long duration the available fighter forces are usually unable to provide effective air cover at all times. In that event, their efforts must be concentrated on supporting those phases of the breakout which, in terms of terrain and enemy resistance, are expected to involve the greatest difficulties and the highest degree of exposure to enemy air attack. Between these periods of maximum air effort – which must be used to full advantage by the ground troops – it will often be necessary to restrict the employment of fighter aircraft, chiefly because of logistical limitations such as insufficient ammunition and fuel supply. Nevertheless, an adequate fighter reserve must always be ready for immediate take-off in order to defend the advancing ground troops against unexpectedly strong enemy air attacks. The more obscure the enemy air situation, the greater must be the strength of the fighter force held in reserve.

The air support for a relief force that is advancing in the direction of a pocket must, as a rule, be kept to a minimum, in order to assign the strongest possible air cover to the troops that are emerging from enemy encirclement. The forces approaching from the main front line are usually in a much better position to compensate for this deficiency by increased use of artillery and antiaircraft weapons. In such situations, the supporting fire from friendly aircraft must be carefully regulated to avoid inflicting casualties among the advancing ground troops, especially just before the link-up of the two converging forces. Even after the junction has been effected, the former pocket force might require special air protection, at least while its reorganization and rehabilitation are being accomplished.